PELICAN BOOKS

A530

THE PSYCHOLOGY OF PERCEPTION

M. D. VERNON

M. D. VERNON

THE PSYCHOLOGY OF PERCEPTION

*

With 37 text figures

PENGUIN BOOKS

BALTIMORE · MARYLAND

Penguin Books Ltd, Harmondsworth, Middlesex
u.s.a.: Penguin Books Inc., 3300 Clipper Mill Road, Baltimore 11, Md
australia: Penguin Books Pty Ltd, 762 Whitehorse Road,
Mitcham, Victoria

—

First published 1962

—

Copyright © M. D. Vernon, 1962

—

Made and printed in Great Britain
by C. Nicholls & Company Ltd
Set in Monotype Baskerville

CONTENTS

EDITORIAL FOREWORD

As the author of this book remarks, 'to the man in the street' it may seem idle to discuss the manner in which he perceives the world around him. It requires study to see the problems with which the psychologist is concerned when he sets out to explain why we see things as we do. This 'man in the street' has been encouraged in his doubts about the need for explanation of the facts of perception by some sophisticated philosophers. These philosophers take the line that the only facts of perception which call for explanation are the abnormal facts such as illusions. They say that we can properly ask for an explanation of the fact that two lines which are in fact equal appear to differ in length, but we do not need to ask for an explanation of the fact that two lines that are equal appear to be equal. So too they say, we can properly ask why snow which is white looks yellow, but we cannot properly ask why snow which is white looks white. They say that when two lines that *are* equal appear to be equal it is a sufficient 'explanation', if this is to be called 'explanation', to say simply, because they are equal. So too, *mutatis mutandis*, with the white snow.

The difference between the psychologist on the one hand and the man in the street and these philosophers on the other arises perhaps from the failure of the latter to do justice to the fact that there are many different *kinds* of explanation. There *is* the kind of explanation of the fact that grass looks green – which may satisfy the philosophers and the man in the street – which is simply that grass looks green because it *is* green. There *is* the sort of explanation which appears to satisfy some chemists and some botanists which takes the form of saying that grass is green and looks green because it contains chlorophyll. There is another kind of explanation which satisfies physiologically-minded psychologists which is given in terms of rather complicated 'theories of colour vision'. Perhaps also some notice should be taken of the kind of explanation which satisfies children and devout old ladies who would say that grass is green and looks green because God arranges things so because green is a restful colour.

There are however both philosophers and psychologists who in giving explanations have in mind a guiding principle not unlike the well-known principle of salesmanship: *The customer is always right*. The principle is that if anyone is puzzled and asks 'Why?' the answer must satisfy the person who asks the question. Sometimes giving the answer may be a sort of therapeutic procedure showing that if the facts are understood the question does not arise (e.g. the question why it is that we perceive things the right way up when the retinal image is inverted). Psychologists are interested in therapy, but not so much in this kind of philosophical therapy. The psychologist who studies percepts attempts to formulate as clearly as he can reasonable questions which can be answered by scientific procedures. He tries to show the man in the street that there are such questions and to tell him what, so far as present knowledge goes, the most reasonable answers are.

This is precisely the purpose of this book. No one is better qualified than its author to state the scientific problems of perception and critically to appraise the alternative solutions proposed. For the student of psychology this book is quite certainly the most comprehensive test. But this book is not just a textbook for students of psychology. It has been written with insight into the needs of parents and teachers who have the best of reasons for interesting themselves in the development of perception in young children. Its treatment of problems of perception is sufficiently broad to contain a judicial appraisal of the value and limitations of visual aids in education. It assesses the evidence for subliminal perception – a problem of such public concern that some politicians advocate legislation to protect the public in a free society against subliminal advertisements. If 'the man in the street' takes up this book with the preconception that there is little or nothing to explain regarding human perception, it is a safe bet that before he puts it down he will have changed (and improved) his mind.

C. A. MACE.

ACKNOWLEDGEMENTS

ACKNOWLEDGEMENT for permission to reproduce figures is made to the following:

The American Psychological Association, for Figs. 1 and 37, reproduced from the *Journal of Experimental Psychology*, Vol. 15, p. 80, by Carmichael, L., Hogan, H. P., and Walter, A. A.; and Vol. 32, pp. 336 and 7, by Schafer, R. and Murphy, G. The American Journal of Psychology, for Figs. 4 and 9, from the *American Journal of Psychology*, Vol. 44, p. 476, by Perkins, F. T.; and Vol. 52, p. 40, by Orbison, W. D. Archives de Psychologie, for Figs. 5 and 22, from *Archives de Psychologie*, Vol. 30, p. 212, by Osterrieth, P. A.; and Vol. 34, p. 205, by Piaget, J. and Stettler-Von Albertini, B. Springer Verlag, for Figs. 8 and 21a, from *Psychologisches Forschung*, Vol. 8, p. 300 by Gottschaldt, K.; and Vol. 4, pp. 263 and 7, by Rupp, H.; and Fig. 16, from *Zeitschrift für Klinisches Medicin*, Vol. 23, pp. 139 and 140, by Goldscheider, A. and Müller, E. Dr M. Johansen and Ejnar Munksgaard for Figs. 10, 11, and 12, from *Nordisk Psykologi's Monograph Series*, No. 5, pp. 7, 8, and 9, by Johansen, M. Mrs R. F. Street and Teachers' College, Columbia University, for Fig. 13, from *A Gestalt Completion Test*, p. 41, by Street, R. F. The Cambridge University Press, for Figs. 14 and 15, from *Remembering*, pp. 19 and 20, by Bartlett, F. C.; the Cambridge University Press and the British Journal of Psychology, for Figs. 18, 25, and 26a, from the *British Journal of Psychology*, Vol. 12, pp. 229 and 234, by Granit, A. R.; and Vol. 36, pp. 152 and 3, by Vernon, M. D. Dr Lauretta Bender and the American Orthopsychiatric Association, for Fig. 21b, from *A Visual Motor Gestalt Test and its Clinical Use*, pp. 4 and 132, by Bender, L. Dr. L. E. Lehtinen, and Grune and Stratton, for Figs. 23 and 24, from *Psychopathology and Education of the Brain-Injured Child*, pp. 32, 44, and 45, by Strauss, A. and Lehtinen, L. E. The Journal Press, for Fig. 29, from the *Journal of Psychology*,

Vol. 39, p. 233, by Semmes, J. *et. al.* and for Fig. 36, from the *Journal of Social Psychology*, Vol. 21, pp. 258 and 9, by Luchins, A. S. Professor G. Johansson, for Fig. 30, from his *Configurations in Event Perception*, p. 78. The National Academy of Sciences, National Research Council, for Fig. 31, from *Form Discrimination as Related to Military Problems* (ed. by Wulfeck, J. W. and Taylor, J. H.), p. 146, by Henneman, R. The North-Holland Publishing Co., for Fig. 32, from *Acta Psychologica*, Vol. 11, p. 347, by Smith, G. J. W. and Henriksson, M.

WHAT DO WE PERCEIVE?

To the man in the street it may appear idle to discuss the manner in which he perceives the world around him. He is so familiar with this 'real world' and the objects it contains that it would not occur to him that there is any need to speculate as to how it is that the world appears as it does. The objects are out 'there' in space; they appear in their familiar aspects and therefore he knows what they are, what they do, and what he can do with them. Their identity is well known to him, and he does not expect them to change from moment to moment unless he can perceive something causing them to change – a wind to blow them away, a fire to burn them up. Moreover, even when they are hidden from view, he will expect them, or at least most of them, to be there when he again looks at them. Some of course may move away and disappear. But these fall into a particular category of movable objects. He would be greatly surprised if the buildings and the landscape changed while he was looking in another direction. Indeed, he *is* often surprised and even shocked if he returns after a few days to find that the houses which he knew have been pulled down for rebuilding. This change in the apparently stable features of his world may give him an uncomfortable feeling of mutability and insecurity.

Knowledge of the identity of objects and features in the environment is obviously valuable to us. Not only does the apparent stability and permanence of most of them create a feeling of security; it also enables us to react to them rapidly and appropriately. We learn by experience what are the uses of houses, shops, and other buildings. We also learn how to react to moving objects. There are appropriate forms of action with regard to vehicles, to animals of various kinds, to people. Once having learnt the most effective form of action – what we can do about these objects and what we can do with them – we can proceed without further thought to act in the same way whenever we encounter them. Again, if they do not behave in the expected way we are surprised and perhaps annoyed. But even then there are certain limitations on their activities which also come within our expectations. The train may fail to stop for us, the car travel much faster than we expected and we must hurry to avoid it; but neither is likely to soar up into the sky, nor vanish in smoke. So also with people: their appearance and their behaviour varies only to a limited extent. It is only in dreams that 'your attorney . . . from Devon is a bit undersized and you don't feel surprised when he tells you he's only eleven'!

But how is it that we know what objects are, that we assume they will retain their identity unchanged, and that we expect them to behave in a characteristic way? Presumably the usual answer to the first question would be that we can see them with our eyes, and that they have always looked like that. But in fact the eyes play only a part in the identification of objects, in the perception of their appearance, their position in space, and so on, although of course it is an essential part. When we look at the world around us, those parts towards which our gaze is directed reflect light to the eyes which comes to them from the sun or from some source of artificial illumination. This light varies in wave-length, and the wave-length of the reflected light varies also, producing the variations in colour of the objects. The brightness of these objects also varies with the brightness of the light falling on them and the reflecting power of their surfaces. The light which reaches the eyes is focused by the lens on to the retina, the light-sensitive surface at the back of the eyeball. The cells of the retina react by initiating nerve impulses in the nerves of the eye, and these are conveyed by the optic nerve to an area at the back of the brain called the occipital area of the cortex.

We tend to think that a picture of the external world falls on the retina and is conveyed to the brain, and that this picture is similar to the picture formed on the film of a camera. But what in fact reaches the brain is a pattern of nerve impulses, the frequency of which corresponds more or less to the brightness of the light reaching the eye. And the particular point on the brain surface stimulated corresponds to the point excited in the retina, which in turn is related to the particular point in space from which the light comes. We know also that differences of wave-length in the light striking the eye are perceived as differences of colour, although the exact mechanisms by means of which this takes place are at present obscure. If therefore we could be directly conscious of the visual pattern created in the brain, we might see a flat pattern of light, shade, and colour. But it would be more like an 'abstract' picture, or a variegated piece of textile material, than the view of the world around us of which we are normally aware.* There would be nothing to tell us that this visual pattern represented solid objects with well-known identities, distributed about us in space. Therefore between the projection of this visual pattern on the brain, and our full consciousness of the world of objects, a series of elaborate mental processes takes place

---

*In fact, the Impressionist painters apparently set out to represent nature in patches of light, shade, and colour as these appeared to them, irrespective of the objects which these patches formed. E. H. Gombrich, in *Art and Illusion* (Phaidon Press, London, 1960), has pointed out that these painters never were, or could be, completely successful in divorcing light and colour from their sources, the perceived objects.

which converts the visual pattern into the perception of the world as we know it. Some of these processes occur spontaneously. Thus the child from early infancy has some awareness of the shapes and colours of things round him. But he knows little or nothing of their identity; nor has he any idea of what we conceive to be the nature of the physical environment and the objects it contains. This knowledge must be acquired, in a manner which will be described in the next chapter.

There is another point of importance. The visual pattern that impinges on the brain is not static; it continually moves and flickers. The light and shade and colour of the pattern alter as the light reaching the eyes changes in colour and brightness – as the sun rises and sets, or is covered by cloud. The patches of light and shade and colour shift their position whenever we move about; they flow backwards and forwards across the field of view as we look to and fro or move our heads. Again, if we were directly conscious of this pattern, we should see something like shimmering lights reflected from moving water. Yet the essential feature of the world as we perceive it is its constancy and stability. Thus the impression of the continuing identity of objects, the unalterability of their appearance, their steady and motionless position in space, is something which arises within the brain itself. We have to learn that when a visual impression passes across the moving eyes, it is the eyes or the body which are moving in relation to the environment and the objects in it, whereas these objects are motionless in space. We also learn that even the shape of a perceived object may vary when we see it in different positions in space; thus a dinner plate is circular when viewed directly from above, but elliptical when seen tilted or sideways – but it is still the same plate. Again, a pillar-box which appears scarlet in ordinary daylight may look purple in blueish artificial light. But we do not think that the pillar-box has changed; the alteration of colour is attributed to the change in colour of the illumination.

We shall consider later in more detail how it is that these changes in the visual pattern do not destroy our awareness of the identity of the objects, nor even greatly affect their appearance as we normally perceive them. But enough has been said to suggest that the perception of the world around us is by no means the simple affair that we may suppose; and that its appearance is not given us merely by the physical properties of the light falling on the eyes and the resulting physiological processes in the eyes and the optic nerves.

CHAPTER 2

HOW THE CHILD LEARNS TO PERCEIVE
THE WORLD AROUND HIM

I · THE INFANT

By the time the child is born, the physiological structure of his eyes and optic nerves is fairly well developed. The physiological processes which are set up when light falls on the eyes are much the same in the newly-born child as in the adult. Yet what the child makes of the visual pattern which reaches the brain is a very different affair. He can see a sudden light shining into his eyes, and react to it by starting and blinking. Sometimes it seems as if his attention is caught; he looks steadily outwards, and for a time his restless bodily movements are quieted. Immediately after birth he may use one eye only, but in a few weeks he looks with both eyes; and by the end of the second month he can direct them accurately on to an object dangled in front of him. If the object is moved to and fro, he follows it with his eyes, at first in an un-coordinated manner, but soon with increasingly accurate fixation. Thus it seems that early in life he begins to see something, and especially something bright or moving. Such things stand out in space and are distinguished from their background. But to him they are just something that happens to him. Again, if something touches his skin – if he hits his hand against it – that is just something which happens to him, perhaps in a painful way, in which case he immediately withdraws from it. When his mother's nipple or her breast touches his lips, he sucks; and the milk flows pleasantly into his mouth and fills his empty stomach.

These are all things that happen to him, pleasant or

unpleasant, but he does not know anything more about them. He makes little distinction between lights and sounds which come from a distance; touch, heat, cold, and pain which affect the surface of his skin; taste which comes from the mouth; and fullness, emptiness, and stomach pains which come from inside the body. The philosopher William James once said that the infant was conscious only of a 'big, booming, buzzing confusion'. Perhaps one might call it more properly a random set of lights, noises, touches, tastes, and so on, without any connexion or any known cause. However, it seems probable that within the first two months of his life the infant begins to realize that certain of these events recur regularly, and in particular that some of them frequently occur together, at the same time and in the same place or direction. The warm touch of the nipple and the breast, the taste of the milk, the relief of his empty stomach, are pleasantly associated together at frequent and regular intervals. Indeed, it has been shown that first of all the touch of the breast, and later the movements of handling and nursing his body, become signals to the infant by means of which he anticipates feeding, though not with any clear consciousness of this. Whereas at first he begins to suck only when the nipple touches his lips, after a time he sucks when he sees the nipple moving towards him, and even when he is taken up to be fed. At a later stage, he shows that he sees something of his mother's face, and hears the sound of her voice. He smiles at these indications of the pleasurable experiences of handling and feeding. It cannot be supposed that during the first few months he is aware of his mother as a person; rather, she represents to him a combination of patterns of touch, sight, sound, and taste, which patterns he begins to recognize and associate together because they recur regularly in conjunction with the pleasurable experience of feeding. Even for the bottle-fed baby, sight, sound, and handling by the person who feeds him become linked to the feeding experience.

However, although we may suppose that the infant begins to recognize recurring visual patterns in this kind of way, there is direct evidence of other instances of the realization that certain patterns of sensation 'belong together'. Thus Gesell in America and Piaget in Switzerland[1] observed that infants at about three months look at objects from which sounds are coming – human beings and their voices, for instance – and appear to realize that they belong together. During the fifth month, the infant flings out his hands towards an object dangling in front of him, and if it touches one of his hands, the hand may close on it. Presently, he deliberately reaches out and grasps it, and if he can, pulls it towards him and puts it in his mouth. These actions indicate that the baby is beginning to realize that if he sees something, he can also reach out and touch it; that he can move it about and try to taste it. He is learning that certain visual and touch impressions may belong together; and that by his own actions he can investigate how this happens – how something with a particular visual appearance will feel when he touches, handles, and mouths it. This is the real beginning of all the experimentation and observation which children carry out to find what the world, and the objects in it, are like.

However, this realization takes place in a number of successive stages. First the infant begins to understand what shape is. The shape that he sees visually corresponds to the shape that he can feel with his hands. Moreover, these perceived shapes are the same whenever they are encountered. Again, most objects have solid shapes; they can be touched on all sides, but they resist touch, and the baby cannot put his hands *through* them. Thus he learns about the qualities of objects which are near to him and which he can handle for himself. But it is not until about the end of the first year that he begins to realize that objects have an identity and a permanent existence; and that this identity remains the same although they are shifted about in space, or hidden altogether from view. Indeed, before this time he may be quite surprised if one of his toys is covered over, and then reappears when it is uncovered. If he is playing with a toy which falls from his hand, he may not try to reach for it, because it seems to have gone altogether. Again, he may cry for his bottle as long as he sees it, but cease to do so as soon as it disappears. But after a time he learns to look for something which has been hidden. If a thing is hidden in one place and he finds it there, and then later hidden in another, he may go back to the first place to look for it; the reappearance of the object is associated with his movements in finding it, rather than with the actual position of the object.

The infant also has to learn that the same object may look different when it is seen from different aspects and at different distances; and that there is a large number of different visual patterns which belong to the same object. Thus until about the ninth month, if the baby's bottle is given him with the nipple turned away from him he makes no attempt to grasp it as he would if the nipple were turned towards him. Its appearance in the former position is so different from that in the latter and more familiar position that he does not recognize it as his bottle. However, as he turns his toys over and over in his hands, he sees how the shape of the part facing him changes. He finds that each object possesses a series of shapes corresponding invariably to its different positions in space. Thus he learns the way in which any given object can vary its appearance according to the aspect from which it is viewed; and just how these aspects appear in different spatial positions of the object. While he is little, he may actually have to turn the object round before he can recognize it; but at about the end of the first year, he has learnt to recognize what it is when he sees one aspect only.

In the same way, the infant learns about the distances of objects from him. At first, he reaches only for comparatively near objects, and if they are more than about a foot away he seems to ignore their existence, because they are outside his reach. However, people bring things towards him and take them away; or he is carried about, and as he moves things come towards or recede from him. As he follows these objects with his eyes, he learns to recognize them at greater and greater distances; though for a long while he may be able to recognize only the objects which he has touched at some time or other. He does not estimate their distances at all accurately, and reaches out for things which are beyond his grasp. But when in his second year he is able to move about himself, he rapidly extends his field of exploration, and becomes familiar with more and more things at greater and greater distances. However, as we shall see later, it may be many years before he really understands the nature of far-distant objects which he cannot reach at all.

One of the difficulties of recognizing objects at a distance is that the actual size of the pattern of light they project on to the retina is much smaller than when they are close. We are familiar with the manner in which objects photographed at different distances appear to vary greatly in size; near objects look too large and far objects too small. The impressions of these objects produced on the retina vary in the same way, but we have learnt to compensate for the variations in our perceptions, in a manner which will be described in Chapter 4. But the baby has to learn that a toy which at a distance looks very small is the same as one which near to looks quite big. However, he is able to learn this by seeing things gradually receding or coming closer, and appearing to change size as they do so. And before the end of his first year, he shows that he realizes that there has been no change of identity in an object which has changed its distance. But again this applies only to fairly near objects, and not to things which are a great way off – the sun and moon, or even far-distant buildings.

A further difficulty for the young child is that he tends to perceive situations as a whole. Objects are seen as part of the settings in which they most frequently occur, and the qualities which characterize their identity cannot be differentiated from other non-essential qualities, including their spatial surroundings. Thus a familiar person may not be recognized if he appears in new and unfamiliar clothes; or he may seem different if he is encountered in a different place. Piaget[2] noted that his daughter, aged just over a year, saw her father in the garden and smiled at him. Her mother asked her: 'Where is papa?' She looked up towards the window of his study where she was accustomed to see him sitting at work. It was not that there were two different 'papas', so much as that 'papa' appeared unusual and different in unusual surroundings. Again, at a year and a half, she played happily with her sister downstairs; but then climbed upstairs to the bedroom, where the sister had just spent a week in bed, and was surprised to find her no longer there.[3] Another child, the son of M. M. Lewis, said the word 'mama' when he saw not only his mother but also a variety of helpful and smiling adults, and even a poster depicting a smiling woman; but he refused to use it for his mother's reflection in a mirror.[4]

It is clear, therefore, that children, at least until their second year, are not able to abstract the essential qualities which characterize the identities of objects. Neither are they able to generalize these qualities, and classify together things which are similar in nature but not identical. Thus Lewis's son learnt at about nine months to look or reach for a small white ball when someone asked him: 'Where's ballie?' But he did not respond in the same way to a larger coloured ball until he was over a year old.[5]

However, during the latter part of the first year onwards, the child does begin to learn for himself about the essential qualities of objects, by experimenting with them as far as he is able. He learns not only what they look and feel like and what they can do, but also what he can do with them. We noted that he found that solid objects were things which could be handled, and were also resistant to touch; and that he explored their shapes by touching and looking at them simultaneously. So also he strikes things to see if they will move; and shakes them to find if they rattle. If an object is slippery and slides through his fingers, he may deliberately repeat the sliding movement in order to study the quality of slipperiness. He pushes things to find if they will roll. He drops them and tries to pick them up; notices how they fall and where they go. He observes how water splashes; how some things float on it and others sink. He is most interested in hollow objects, opens boxes, and examines them carefully inside; and tries to fit hollow shapes together. In these ways he finds out, in terms of his own actions, what are the essential qualities that characterize classes of solid object.

He also begins to realize that many things do not remain motionless and passive. They are interesting to him as much for their own activities as for what he can do to them. He tends to class together all moving things; and indeed for many years he may fail to differentiate between animate and inanimate moving objects. However, certain types of animate objects are especially important. Human beings make up a great part of his world, and for them he has a special class of reactions, the social responses of smiling and crying, babbling, talking, questioning, and so on. As early as two to three months, he smiles in response to social situations, and appears to perceive people as different from things. During the first year he learns to distinguish between familiar persons with whom he tries to make every form of social contact, and unfamiliar people with whom he may be timid and shy.

Children are also greatly attracted by animals, and probably in the first instance they differentiate them chiefly in terms of their different movements: animals which run rapidly along the ground, those which move more slowly and heavily, those which jump up, and those which fly in the air. One child of about a year, known to the author, used to watch with fascination the seagulls circling and swooping above him as he lay in his pram. Other animal actions are also noted – scratching and biting for instance, and the relation of these to friendliness and dangerousness. Animals also make characteristic noises, and the child may then identify them in terms of these. This is not surprising, since infants begin to notice and be interested in sounds at a very early age, and learn to recognize the characteristic sounds made by people and objects around them.

2 · THE TALKING CHILD

The process of learning to classify objects in accordance with their qualities of appearance, behaviour, and use is greatly facilitated by the development of speech and language. The infant accompanies his actions with babbling sounds which for some while are to him an intrinsic part of the action. But also he uses these babbling sounds as a form of social reaction to the sounds which he hears made by people around him. He imitates their speech-sounds more and more accurately, and is of course greatly encouraged in this by the pleasure expressed by adults when he does so. Again, when he reaches for food or a toy, his mother makes a particular sound which is its name. The child associates the name with the object, just as he associates with it its appearance and behaviour. The name becomes a part of his experience of that object. When he in turn learns to utter a sound which is sufficiently similar to its name, he finds that people will give him the object. Thus naming becomes a useful method of obtaining what he wants. He finds that everything has a name, and so he tries to name everything he notices. When an unfamiliar object appears, he may give it a name, or a verbal description, belonging to something similar. And so in turn he finds that some names belong to classes of objects with similar characteristics of appearance and behaviour.

But as we have seen the child does not always observe the essential qualities of the objects he perceives; and he may then classify them incorrectly, by means of superficial or irrelevant characteristics, and give them the wrong name. Numerous examples have been reported as to the manner in which children class together, under a single name or verbal description, objects to which we should give different names. In the first place, a word originally learnt as the name of a single object may be applied to a variety of objects of similar appearance and shape, as in the case of the child who learnt the word 'moo-i' for the moon, and subsequently used it for various round objects and even for circles drawn on paper.[6] Another child used the name 'wow-wow' first for a dog, but later for a squeaking doll, a fur collar with buttons on it, and even for the buttons on a coat.[7] A single word may be used for a variety of animals. Thus a child learnt the word 'tee' for cat (kitty).[8] Subsequently he used it for dogs, cows, sheep, and horses. Then he learnt the name 'goggie' for his toy dog, but for some time 'tee' was retained for the live dog. About the same time he acquired the name 'hosh' for a horse, and then applied it on seeing a large St Bernard dog.

Often the same word is employed for objects to which the child reacts in similar ways. Thus one child used the word 'hot' for everything he was forbidden to touch because touching it would cause pain. A little German girl used the name '*puppi*' firstly for her doll, but also for other toys with which she played in the same way.[9] The characteristics of function may also be important in classifying and naming. A French child, having acquired the word '*ato*' for 'hammer' ('*marteau*'), applied it to various objects used as tools, including a button-hook, a comb, and a saucepan. An Italian child used the word '*aqua*' for glass, a drinking glass, and what was drunk from it.

Of course it must not be supposed that the child does not perceive the difference between these different objects. What he is trying to do is to classify similar objects together by giving them a single name. Thus live domestic animals were classified together as 'tee', whereas the lifeless toy dog was not included. The St Bernard dog looked more like a horse than a dog, therefore it was called 'hosh'. The adult, on the other hand, has learnt to give a common name to all varieties of dog, although their appearance and behaviour varies greatly. It is only gradually that the child acquires the ability to classify objects by their appearance and behaviour in the same manner as adults do. He hears the names which adults use; he finds that he can make himself understood if he uses these correctly; and the encouragement and approval given him when he does this stimulate him to continue trying. However, it may be some while before it is done with ease and readiness. Thus although children aged one to two years could be taught to give the names 'chair', 'ball', 'animal', 'flower' to specific examples of these objects, they did not seem to understand that the names could also be used for other differently shaped or coloured chairs, balls, etc. And if they learnt the name of one of these objects when it was in a particular setting, they might fail to produce the name when the object was in a different setting.

Although in time the child learns to use mainly the

characteristics of appearance and behaviour in classifying and naming, there is, as we have seen, a tendency among younger children to employ other methods of classification. One example of these is the classification in terms of the functions of objects, as with the toys called '*puppi*' and the tools called '*ato*'. But another method peculiar to children is the classification in terms of the child's own desires and feelings – as in the use of the word 'hot'. Though adults may employ these methods privately, their habitual use of language prevents them from doing so openly in speech. But in his very early years the child is particularly influenced by the interplay of feeling between himself and the people around him. Thus, as we saw, in early infancy he perceives and responds readily to a smiling face; and indeed the smiling expression is more important to him than the actual familiarity of the facial lineaments. He soon learns to recognize the emotions of people around him, and reacts promptly to his perceptions of fear and anger in adults. Throughout life we attach great importance to the various forms of social behaviour; we perceive them rapidly, and react by behaviour appropriate to what we have perceived. In doing this, we classify types of expression and behaviour in terms of what is characteristic of particular types of people – for instance, Englishmen or foreigners, upper or lower social classes; and so on.

The importance attached by children to emotional characteristics is illustrated by the fact that they have been found to attribute such characteristics to inanimate objects, meaningless drawings, etc. Thus one child of three and a half years said that the number 5 looked 'mean' and the number 4 looked 'soft'; while another child said that the figure

looked 'cruel'.[10] A child known to the author was so

terrified by the 'evil' appearance of a twisted tree-stump on one of his picture bricks that the brick had to be hidden. Again, feelings and actions may be attributed to inanimate objects, as when a child called a broken biscuit 'poor biscuit', or said, when he caught his stocking on a chair: 'The chair grabbed hold of my stocking.'

This attribution to objects of emotional characteristics may also affect their classification. It was reported that children, asked to group sets of meaningless drawings, called one set 'prickly' and another set 'mean'. Thus these emotional characteristics seem in some cases to look to the child more striking than do the shape characteristics which appear more obvious to us. At the same time, the importance of this feature of children's perceptions should not be exaggerated. It seems possible that children are normally most concerned to find out how things work and what they can do with them. It is only in situations where this is impossible that they tend to liken their activities to those of human beings. This may occur with the heavenly bodies, the sun, moon, and stars, which the child can neither understand nor experiment with. And it may also occur when the child is set what appears to him rather a meaningless task, such as grouping shapes.

Thus the most important and fundamental type of classification is probably that which is made in terms of the behaviour which the child finds by experience is appropriate in response to his perceptions. Though it is true that the child is immensely interested in his environment, and wants to find out all he can about it and understand it well, nevertheless the function of perception is primarily to enable him to react effectively. In the first place, he must learn to perceive and classify food objects as distinct from other objects; and also the food he likes and that which he dislikes. Although at first he may put everything he can grasp into his mouth to find whether or not it is palatable, before long he learns to distinguish by vision alone most of the kinds of food that usually come his way.

Again, it is most important that he should recognize the kinds of object that are likely to be dangerous – things which move rapidly towards him, things which are sharp or rough, things which are hot. Although from birth the child reacts reflexly by withdrawing from painful stimulation of the skin, it is clearly desirable that he should be able to identify visually objects which may fall into one of these classes, in order that he may be able to take the necessary evasive action before they actually touch him. This he learns to do fairly rapidly in the case of moving and falling objects, but more slowly, and probably with a good deal of adult assistance and instruction, with other classes of dangerous object. And of a similar nature are the classes of situation in which he himself may run into danger – for instance, places from which he may fall, or in which traffic may run over him. Again he learns to classify these as situations to which he must react in the appropriate way.

Then also there are the innumerable social situations which we considered above. These are classified in terms not only of the appearance and behaviour of other people, but also in terms of the sort of behaviour which it is appropriate for the child to show. Authoritarian, friendly, and un-friendly adults; children who may be approached and those who are best avoided; these the child tends to group together in his mind, because it is desirable for him to behave towards them in a particular way. So also when he grows up, he learns that there are customary ways of behaving to bosses, policemen, doctors, shop assistants, etc.; to persons to whom one can give orders, and to those from whom one can seek help. These people, as often as not, are perceived and thought of not as individuals, but as a class of people behaving in a particular way. And unless one behaves appropriately to them, one may suffer frustration, shame, or punishment.

At first sight it may appear that this lengthy discussion of the child's capacities for classification and naming is somewhat irrelevant to the development of his perceptions. But this is not in fact the case. We saw that in the first instance the child might learn to identify individually some of the more important things in his immediate environment – his mother, his family, his bottle, his toys, and so on. But in order to do this satisfactorily, he had to abstract those qualities of the objects which were essential to their identification, and learn to recognize them even when they varied somewhat, for instance, in different spatial positions. Thus before he can perceive and identify these objects, the child must be able to classify the different shapes and sizes which a single object may appear to have when it is seen in different surroundings, from different aspects, and at different distances. Very soon also the number of new and unfamiliar objects which the child encounters, even in his somewhat restricted environment, becomes bewilderingly great. He may not be able to handle and examine each one of them in detail and find out what it does and what he can do with it. But if he can perceive and remember sufficient of its essential qualities to be able to compare it with other similar objects he has perceived previously, then he can class it as being the same type of object. And he can predict that it is likely to behave in the manner characteristic of that type of object, and that he should react to it in a particular and appropriate way. When he sees at a distance something quite new and unfamiliar, he is not obliged to recollect severally all the objects of similar appearance which he has previously perceived. All he needs to do is to classify it into the most appropriate category; and then he has at least some notion of what it is. If it fits readily into some familiar class of objects, then he can identify it easily and quickly. If not, he may need to examine it more carefully and think about its qualities before he knows exactly what it is. But there are of course certain situations, such as those which are potentially dangerous, in which he has to make a quick judgement, and there is no further opportunity for further examination. Then he must make a rapid assessment, guess what type of object it is most likely to be, and react appropriately. If he finds that his guess was incorrect and that his actions are inappropriate, he may if he is able revise his assessment subsequently. But again in cases of danger this may not be possible. Finally, there are objects and situations which it is impossible to perceive satisfactorily because they cannot be seen clearly, or they are so strange and unfamiliar that there is no category of objects into which they can be fitted. In such cases, perception is ambiguous, and reaction may be slow and uncertain. We shall discuss some of these cases in detail in Chapter 3.

CHAPTER 3

THE PERCEPTION OF OBJECTS
BY ADULTS

IT might be argued that the process of perceiving in older children and adults is so rapid and accurate as to be quite dissimilar from that of little children; and in particular that there would be no time for all the processes of classification described in the last chapter to take place before objects are fully identified. However, perception is never instantaneous. If we show people an object for a very short time, perhaps one tenth of a second or less, they may not be able to identify it. They may guess the kind of thing it is, but they may be mistaken. It is possible to halt or retard the perceptual process in various ways, and thus to study its gradual development. A series of very short exposures may be made. Or the object may be shown in very dim light (we shall discuss such effects more fully in the next chapter). Or something may be presented at the edge of the field of vision, so that the observer can see it only out of the corner of his eye. If it is then brought in by steps towards the centre of the field, again the process of perception will develop gradually. The observer may then be able to report what happens.

A large number of experiments has been carried out in these various ways, to investigate the perceptual processes of adults. It has been found that people are first of all conscious that there is 'something there', something standing out from and different from the general background of the field of view.[1] Next this 'something' begins to assume a shape; first the outline is perceived, then the main interior features, their colour and brightness. And then begins the process of classification and identification. The observer may say: 'It looks like such-and-such a type of thing'; or 'I got the impression it might be an object of a certain kind.' Then he may say: 'Yes, it *is* so-and-so'; or 'I made a mistake, it is really something quite different.' If what he is looking at is not a familiar and easily recognizable object, but rather a complicated and unfamiliar thing, perhaps a picture, he may say: 'I think it is a picture of such-and-such, but I must look at it for longer to be quite sure.' Then he may need up to two or three seconds of central vision in a good light before he can make up his mind. But almost invariably he will want to go on examining the object or the picture until he is quite sure what it is and what it means to him; and he will end by naming it or describing it in words. He may be able to utilize information coming to him from senses other than the visual. In recognizing people, the sound of their voices is often as important as the sight of their faces. In identifying objects, they may be touched and weighed in the hand. If they are food objects, they may be smelt and tasted. Thus the observer may continue examining the object and piecing together the various sensory impressions until he has made up his mind what it is.

In everyday-life situations where objects can be clearly seen there will be corroboration between a variety of different types of information as to the nature of the objects. Shape, colour, texture, spatial position, movement or absence of movement, will all be congruent, and will fit what the observer expects to encounter in such situations. Sometimes it is said that in these cases there is a 'redundancy' of information, all of which leads to the same conclusions as to the identity of the objects. In such cases, perception is rapid and accurate, and the observer will be able to react promptly in the appropriate manner without further thought, and then dismiss the situation from mind. Indeed, the whole procedure may occur without conscious awareness, as in many of the situations in which we act automatically. Here the process of classification according to the pattern of appropriate behaviour takes place without any thought on our part, because through frequent experience it has become habitual, automatic, and effective. Thus in crossing a road on which there is traffic, we may note the oncoming vehicles, their speed of approach, how far they have to go to reach us, and how wide the road is. Our previous perceptual experiences of the time taken to reach us by objects moving at various speeds, and the time we take to cross the road at various speeds, have become related together so intimately that they lead automatically to the appropriate form of behaviour – walking at a leisurely pace or running hurriedly across – without our having to think out what we should do. Even less conscious are the perceptions and responses made, for instance, in riding a bicycle. We perceive visually whether the bicycle is upright in relation to the road, and this is assisted by various internal senses of position; and we react automatically by throwing the body to one side or another, so that it and the bicycle continue to balance. In fact, in all the innumerable skilled activities we perform in the ordinary course of our lives, perception of the external environment leads automatically to the appropriate form of behaviour without the necessity of deliberating about what we are perceiving, what it is called, and what we should do about it.

But to revert to the cases in which it is difficult to perceive what is there – because it is not clearly lit, or is far away, or exceedingly complex; or because it is so novel that the individual does not know what to make of it. He may then carry out a search of his memories of similar situations which have occurred previously, and try to match the objects or events now before him against anything of a similar nature which he has encountered before. In doing this, he may use both imagery and language. Let us first consider the use of imagery.

It often happens that when we perceive something rather vividly, or when we perceive it so frequently as to become thoroughly familiar with it, we form a *mental image* of it. In the case of things perceived visually, this image is like a picture in the mind. Immediately after the original perception, the image may be so clear, vivid, and detailed, that we are able to examine it 'in the mind's eye', and recall from it details of the original which we did not perceive at the time. However, this 'primary memory image', as it is sometimes called, fades rapidly and becomes much vaguer and less detailed. Nevertheless, images of striking events may be retained for long periods of time. The author still retains a memory image of the eclipse of the sun which she witnessed in the 1920s. But many of the images used in perceiving and remembering are of classes of objects rather than of any one specific object. Moreover, they need not be visual. We have auditory images of familiar voices and tunes; smell images of scents, and even of places characterized by particular scents; taste images of foods. We also have tactile imagery relating to the touch sensations produced by different kinds of surface – rough, smooth, shiny, velvety, and so on; and kinaesthetic, or movement, imagery of the movements we make with our bodies in skilled activities such as cycling, skating, dancing, and so on. When we are thinking about particular objects and events and trying to remember them, we may employ this imagery to aid our recollections. And when we are confronted with a new and unfamiliar object, we may try to match what it looks like, or feels like to the touch, with imagery of objects perceived in the past. We may smell or taste a new fruit, to judge whether or not the smell and taste are the same as the images we retain of fruits smelt and tasted in the past. Just as any one object may arouse a complex of different sensory impressions, so these may be compared with a complex of imagery associated with similar objects. Thus in trying to identify the fruit, for instance, visual and touch imagery will normally be used as well as taste and smell. If we try to identify an object by touch alone, the touch sensations normally give rise to corresponding visual imagery of the shape of the object; and thus its shape can be recognized. A great deal of visual and auditory imagery is also used in the reading of words – in a manner which we shall consider more fully in Chapter 7.

Sometimes imagery is utilized not so much for purposes of recollection and indentification, but for its own sake, because it helps to make the whole experience more vivid and more enjoyable. Thus the perception of pictures may be accompanied by dwelling on their form and colour in conjunction with imagery of other similar pictures. The appreciation of language, and particularly of poetry when read silently, incorporates imagery of the sounds of the words. Again, a variety of feelings and emotions may enter into the perceptual experience, for instance, in evaluating and appreciating what is perceived, and in deciding whether it is pleasant, useful, well constructed, unpleasant, or harmful. Such feelings may not, as a rule, affect classification and identification, as they may with children – at least they will not normally do so in the case of inanimate objects. But they may have a considerable influence on the perception of people, as we shall discuss in connexion with so-called 'social perception' (see Chapter 11). And in any act of perception, they may cause us to take particular notice of the experience and to dwell on it in thought. In some cases it seems as if these feelings were closely associated with imagery. Thus a Frenchman, returning to France at the end of the last war, described what he felt as he recognized from his imagery the 'smell of

France'. It is also possible of course to experience feelings of this kind in conjunction with imagery when the latter occurs in recollection only, and without relation to immediate perception.

At the same time as he makes use of imagery to help him to identify objects, an observer also commonly employs language. If he cannot identify the objects easily, he may think about his experience in words. He also uses naming to recall to mind objects of the same class as the present one. Finally, he may clinch the present perceptual experience by giving a name to the object before him. And once he has named it, he seems to be satisfied with the experience; to think that he has identified it adequately even if in fact there are many aspects of it which he has overlooked. Indeed, there is evidence to show that the naming of an object, even in rather a loose and superficial manner, may affect the way in which it is perceived at the moment and recollected in future. Experiments have been carried out in which ambiguous drawings were presented to people for brief periods of time, and at the same moment the drawings were named. Subsequently the drawings were reproduced, and it appeared that the reproductions resembled the kind of figure that was commonly associated with the name more closely than they resembled the original figure. In one experiment[2] the series of shapes shown in Fig. 1 were presented, each being named as it was shown. One group of observers was given one set of names, and another a second set of names, for the same shapes. Subsequently all observers had to reproduce the shapes they had been shown. It was found that characteristic modifications were made in the reproductions, as shown in Fig. 1, making them more like the named objects than were the original drawings. A later experiment[3] showed that this effect was even more pronounced when the observers did not know at the time they perceived the drawings that they

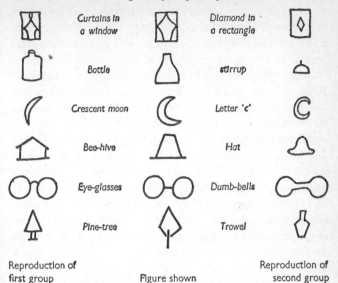

1. Effect of naming on reproduction of shapes

would subsequently have to reproduce them. Thus it appears that we have certain conventional ideas about the shapes of objects when they are drawn on paper which are closely related to the names of these objects. And when we perceive such drawings, we classify them according to their names and the ideas associated with them, and perceive and remember them in those terms.

There are certain cases in which the ability to name and identify objects is impaired. Thus an injury to the left-hand side of the rear part of the brain, the occipital area of the cortex, may produce a defect called 'visual agnosia', in which the patient is still able to perceive the shapes of objects and even to recognize them as familiar.[4] Sometimes also he can use them in familiar activities. But he cannot give them a

37

name, nor does he appear to be quite certain what they are if he pauses to think about it. Extensive deficiencies in the ability to perceive and identify objects visually have also been reported in patients almost blind since birth from cataract who have recovered their sight after operation.[5] They may remain for a time excessively confused as to the nature and identity of the objects they see, and may have to handle them before they know what they are.

When a normally sighted person finds it difficult to identify the objects or events he perceives, he usually takes some steps to relieve himself of his doubt and uncertainty. No one likes such states, which are liable to cause anxiety and disquiet. The observer may, if he is able, dismiss the whole affair from his mind, and this may occur without much actual awareness. The perceptual process may stop short of reaching full consciousness, and the observer ignore or fail to perceive consciously things which are too unclear and too unfamiliar for him to identify adequately. Thus from childhood upwards people habitually overlook things which they do not understand, provided that these are not forced upon their attention. A particularly good illustration exists of the reactions which may occur in an ambiguous situation in which what was presented was contrary to expectation. An experiment was undertaken in which observers were shown, for a very short time, playing cards in which the colours of the suits were transposed – hearts and diamonds were black, clubs and spades red.[6] In some cases the incongruity was recognized, but in others it was ignored, and the observer reported either the shape in its habitual colour, or the colour with its habitual shape. In other cases there was a compromise, the observer perceiving purplish spades or greyish hearts. Occasionally perception broke down altogether, and the observer was not sure even if what he saw was a playing card.

Thus when an incongruous or an unexpected experience

cannot be overlooked, the tendency is to guess what in the circumstances it is most likely to be. In guessing, we are guided by our past experience of previous similar situations, and by what we expect to see in the present. It must be remembered that in ordinary everyday life, events do not often occur singly and in complete isolation from other aspects of the situation. Objects appear in relevant and appropriate surroundings, so that we do not expect to see an oak tree in the middle of the desert, or houses sticking up out of the sea. Events follow each other in a continuous sequence in time; thus we can often predict what is likely to happen next from what has just happened in the immediate past. A car is likely to proceed in the same direction and at approximately the same speed along the road; and an object which begins to fall will continue to fall vertically but with increasing rapidity. We have already considered the manner in which we classify events, situations, and activities of particular kinds together. By utilizing these classifications in combination with what we perceive to be associated in time and space with a particular event, we can make a reasonable guess as to how that event will develop. We rely on things behaving reasonably, sensibly, and meaningfully; which is to say that if we have sufficient knowledge and understanding of that kind of situation, we can predict more or less correctly what will happen; and, more important still, we know what is the most effective way of reacting to it. If our prediction proves incorrect, we may, as we noted, dismiss the experience from consciousness. If this is impossible, then we must look and think again; and reaction will be correspondingly delayed.

CHAPTER 4

THE PERCEPTION
OF SHAPE BY ADULTS

I · PERCEPTION OF CONTOUR, 'FIGURE', AND 'GROUND'

WE noted that the first stage in the development of perception consisted in the perception of the form or shape of the object before us. It is obvious that we cannot fully identify any object in either visual or touch perception unless we first perceive certain essential aspects of its shape, since it is by means of their shapes that objects are characterized and differentiated from one another. But it is a matter of some difficulty to determine just what features of shape are essential to this process, since clearly not all the minute details of shape are taken into account. However, the most important feature seems to be the general outline or *contour* of the object. Since the child begins to learn how to identify objects by handling them and running his fingers round their edges, it is natural that this pattern of touch should become associated with the contour of the object perceived visually. And in point of fact whenever we look at objects, they seem to be clearly outlined and demarcated from their background; although of course with a solid object the particular contour exhibited to us at any one moment varies with its position in space. The visual shape of a square-topped table is square only when we look at it from above. Nevertheless it seems that the child in infancy learns which visual shape corresponds to the shape which he perceives by touch; and he can as it were refer back to this preferred visual shape even when he sees the object from a different aspect.

We shall discuss more fully below how this takes place.

Experiment has shown that the perception of contour depends mainly upon a sharp gradient in brightness between the surface of the object and its background. It might be supposed that colour differences were also important. But in fact if two surfaces are juxtaposed which differ in colour but not in brightness, it is difficult to differentiate between them; one seems to shade off into the other.[1] This effect is one which sometimes worries amateur painters in water colour. The objects they depict do not stand out from their surroundings because there is insufficient difference of brightness between them. The painter is sometimes forced to outline his objects in pencil, thus introducing a sharp gradient of brightness between the black outline and the surfaces on either side of it. Indeed, it has been shown experimentally that it is not necessary to use a black contour line; a white contour line between two surfaces will delimit them effectively.[2] Of course, in normal circumstances objects are commonly at different distances from the observer; and his perception of their distances and solid depth assists him in seeing that they stand out from one another and from the background. However, the perception of actual difference of distance is not necessary to the experience. Even on a flat surface, one part may appear to stand out from the remainder. The two parts must differ in brightness; and commonly the part which seems to stand out will be the smaller, and will be surrounded by the other part. But the experience of standing out will be stronger if the first part has some meaning or interest for the observer, especially if it seems to represent a real object of some kind. In drawings consisting of patterns of black lines, any line which surrounds an area, and which is recognized as representing an object, is quickly picked out by the observer; and it then seems to him to stand out from the background in an obvious manner.

This type of phenomenon has been called the '*figure-ground*' experience, and it is one which is fundamental in perception from very early childhood.[3] No field of view which is differentiated in any way – which is not simply a continuous and homogeneous mass or fog – is perceived all at one dead level. Some part of it will always tend to become 'figural', and to be differentiated from the rest of the field which forms the 'ground' to this 'figure'. The 'figure' then stands out, and is readily perceived and attended to, and its appearance and details are noted; it may also seem brighter and more strongly coloured. But the 'ground' tends to fall back and not to be perceived with any clarity; its details are not noticed and it is quickly forgotten. Although prominent and interesting objects, central in the field of view, or anything particularly striking and vivid, more readily become 'figural' than others, there is no hard-and-fast rule as to what is perceived as 'figure'. Nor need it always be the same object or part of the field. By a switch of attention to different parts of the field of view, or by sweeping his eyes to and fro across it, an observer may see a succession of objects as 'figural', each one in turn. Or sometimes if he fixes his gaze closely on one part of the field, there may be an alternation between the 'figure' and the 'ground'. Anyone who stares hard at the drawing shown in Fig. 2a may see as 'figural' first of all the cross with the horizontal and vertical arms; but after a time it may fade into the background, and the cross with diagonal arms will become 'figural'. If, however, one set of arms is made to contrast strongly in colour or brightness with the page on which it is set, as in Fig. 2b, the alternation is less likely to occur, and the black cross will tend permanently to be the 'figure'. Again, if a drawing is presented the two parts of which are equally meaningful, as in Fig. 3, there may be an alternation of 'figure' and 'ground' between them.

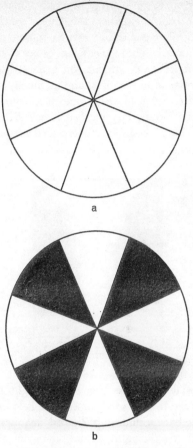

2. Alternating 'figure' and 'ground'

This 'figure-ground' experience is apparently fundamental in perception. It occurs at an early stage in a slowly
developing perception, when the shape of the objects in
the field begins to emerge in consciousness. It is probably

essential to the development of perception in infants, at the stage when certain events begin to emerge from the general 'booming, buzzing confusion' of their consciousness. Before the mother's face can be seen as a face or her voice heard as a voice, they must stand out from the general background of light and noise, and be noticed and attended to as 'figures' in themselves. 'Figural' experiences of course need not necessarily be visual; any pattern of sound, touch, taste, smell, etc., which is consciously perceived as such, must first become 'figural'. When people blind from birth from cata-

3. Alternating 'figures'

ract are operated upon and recover their sight, their earliest experiences are that certain parts of the field of view stand out from the background in a 'figural' manner, characteristically differing in brightness and taking on contours. This occurs before these people are able to identify the parts of the field as objects.

The emergence of the 'figure' from the 'ground' is not an instantaneous process, although in ordinary daylight vision it takes place too rapidly for the observer to be conscious that it is happening. In very dim light, however, he may be aware that a vague formless 'something' is arising in his field of view before he can perceive its shape; and after that, that some aspects of shape emerge before he can identify the shape as a whole, and perceive it in detail. This gradual process can also be interrupted by presenting a large bright field almost immediately after the presentation of a rather dimmer shape such as a circle, a square, etc.[4] If the interval of time is too short, the shape is not perceived at all. If it is rather longer, of the order of 0·03–0·10 seconds, a break in the complete homogeneity of the bright field is observed, followed by the appearance of some part of the shape, a side or an angle.

If the field of view is completely homogeneous, and no part of it is in any way different from the remainder, then the 'figure-ground' experience is impossible. The observer can perceive nothing but a vague mist or fog of light or colour, which has no definite position in space. He sees no kind of surface, hard to the touch, but looks right into it and through it. This experience can be demonstrated by making an observer look into a uniformly illuminated hemisphere, so that he sees nothing else; or even to look through a small hole in a dark screen at a uniformly illuminated surface. What he then sees has been called 'film colour', differing in the manner described from the more normal experience of 'surface colour' perceived in surfaces which are not completely homogeneous in appearance. It has been reported that in certain cases of injury to the brain, as the patient recovers, colour vision may be restored first as 'film colour' before any differentiated shapes can be perceived.[5] It is only later, as shape and form perception come back to him, that he again perceives 'surface colour'.

Distinction between 'figure' and 'ground' is also of fundamental importance in the perception of more complex visual material where it may consist not so much of an immediate and spontaneous perceptual process, but of the selection of certain parts of the field which together constitute a meaningful figure, in contrast to other irrelevant parts of the field. We shall consider this process more fully below.

2 · PHYSICAL AND PHYSIOLOGICAL FACTORS IN SHAPE PERCEPTION

The perception of shape depends upon certain physical conditions and upon certain properties of the eyes of the observer. In some circumstances, there may be a transitory and uncertain 'figure-ground' experience, but shape will be perceived only very vaguely, and the observer will not be sure what he sees. The important factors are the intensity of the light illuminating the field of view, and the brightness differences of the objects and surfaces in the field. We all know that if the illumination of the field is sufficiently reduced, the objects in it become invisible. There is a certain physical intensity of light at which objects are just visible but only just. This point is called the *absolute threshold of vision*, and in certain conditions its intensity is relatively constant and uniform for different people, though it is lower towards the margin of the field of vision than at the centre. So also a certain degree of change in the intensity of light is necessary for the perception of change; or a certain difference between the brightnesses of two surfaces. This change constitutes the *differential threshold of vision*, and in general the change in intensity is proportional to the absolute brightness of the illumination. The brighter a surface, the more its brightness must be increased or decreased before any change can be perceived. Again, to distinguish between different parts of a surface, the difference in brightness between these must be greater, the greater the general brightness of the surface.

These thresholds of vision depend on certain changes taking place within the retina which are known as *dark adaptation.* The retina is much more sensitive to very dim lights when it is dark adapted. If one goes from ordinary daylight into an almost dark room, at first one can see nothing. But after a time objects loom into view. We are familiar with this experience in going into a cinema; whereas when we enter we can scarcely find our seats, after a time we can see round us comparatively clearly. This is because the sensitive cells of the retina have become adapted and the threshold has been lowered; they now react to the dim light coming to them and send information through the optic nerves to the brain, whereas at first they did not do so. The process of adaptation appears to be related to chemical changes in substances in the retinal cells, but it is not known precisely how. Adaptation takes place gradually and may continue for as long as an hour in very dim light. But the brighter the light to which the eye was previously exposed, the slower will be the process of adaptation.

However, dark-adapted vision does not have the same clarity as ordinary daylight vision. If we go out on a star-light night, we may be able in time to see sufficiently well to stumble about. But we do not see objects at all clearly or in any detail; neither do they appear normally coloured. They may be seen merely as different shades of grey; or occasionally they may take on a greenish or bluish shade. The reason for this is that there are two types of sensitive cell in the retina. The first type, called *cones*, is situated mainly in the centre of the retina. The cones enable us in normal daylight to see details of shape and colour, but they do not adapt to more than a small extent to dim illumination. The other type of cell, called *rods*, is situated outside the centre of the retina. The rods do adapt gradually to dim light, but do not convey any impression of colour. They respond maximally to blue light, and not at all to red light. Moreover, since the nerve supply of the outer parts of the retina is sparser than that of the central parts, details of shape and position of objects are less accurately perceived in rod vision than in cone vision. Thus although rod vision is very sensitive to the difference between dim light and complete darkness, it cannot enable us to identify objects very easily. But if we know beforehand what objects are likely to be there, we can often guess the identity of the vague shapes we can see. Also, they can be seen better if we look at them slightly 'off centre', so that their images fall on the rods situated outside the central area of the retina; whereas the central area, containing only cones which do not respond in very dim light, is almost blind.

When we go from a very dimly lit room into bright daylight, at first we feel dazzled. This is because the retina requires a few seconds to become adapted to the daylight, and to react in its normal daylight fashion. We may also be dazzled by glare, for instance, by the headlights of a car shining in the dark. The retina adapts to the brightness of the headlights, and is then insensitive to the dimmer light coming from other parts of the field of view. Thus it is difficult if not impossible to see pedestrians, and even cyclists whose lamps are much dimmer than the car headlights.

In full daylight, it is not always possible to perceive all the details of shape if they are very small or far away. The ability to discriminate detail is called *visual acuity*; it is usually measured by the smallest separation between two black lines which can be perceived at a given distance. Thus it depends primarily on the size of the image of an object or part of an object falling on the retina. But it is also affected by the shape of the object. The separation of two lines placed end to end (the so-called 'vernier acuity') can be perceived more readily than the separation of two lines placed side by side. Very important also are the brightness of the field, and the brightness contrast between the object and its background. Acuity increases with increase in intensity of illumination.

Again, we saw that the perception of contour depended on the difference between the brightness of an object and of its surroundings, the differential threshold. The greater the difference in brightness, the steeper the brightness gradient and the easier the perception of the object even if it is very small. This means that details in the shape of an object are most readily perceived in strong light, when the object is dark or black on a light or white background; or conversely light on a dark background. For various reasons, the former condition is preferable; and that is why black print on a white page is more legible than any other colour combination of ink and paper.

Acuity also varies in different parts of the retina, for the reason noted above, that the nerve supply is greatest in the centre and decreases farther out into the periphery. In consequence, if in daylight we vaguely perceive some object at the margin of the field of view which we wish to examine in more detail, we then turn our eyes in the direction of the object so that its image falls on the centre of the retina. However, sensitivity at the margin is relatively greater for moving than for stationary objects. Thus any movement may 'catch the eye' and stimulate us to turn and view it in central vision.

Different people vary both in their capacity for dark adaptation and in their visual acuity. In an individual who is short-sighted, long-sighted, or astigmatic, the lens of the eye does not refract the light falling on it correctly and does not focus it to form a sharp image on the retina. Naturally this impairs visual acuity, often to such an extent that the individual cannot see clearly without corrective lenses in spectacles. Dark adaptation may sometimes be affected also. Both acuity and dark adaptation tend to decrease with increasing age; and the latter is sometimes impaired by a lack of vitamin A in the diet, since the substance in the rods which reacts to light is formed from a derivative of vitamin A.

Even in young and healthy observers there are appreciable variations in sensitivity, that is to say, in the absolute threshold of dark-adapted vision. Closely related to these are differences in visual acuity for small objects in dim light. In both cases, some observers appear to require a greater intensity of illumination for vision than do others. The perceiving of more complex objects in dim light may also be limited by the sensitivity of vision, though not all observers with high sensitivity necessarily perceive these with great accuracy and detail. Such perception is also a function of the psychological factors to be discussed in section 3.

3 · PSYCHOLOGICAL FACTORS AFFECTING ACCURACY OF SHAPE PERCEPTION

We must now consider more fully the characteristics of shape perception. Naturally, the simpler the actual shape which is viewed, the more likely it is to be perceived accurately. Thus if we are shown geometrical shapes such as circles, squares, rectangles, and triangles, we perceive them readily because they are both simple and familiar. We can see them in relatively dim light, or when they are shown for very short periods of time. In some experiments it has been found that circles and squares are the most readily perceived, because their shapes are the simplest and most regular of all. Indeed, when other shapes are shown in very dim light, there is sometimes a tendency for them to appear circular before their actual shapes can be fully discriminated. But other experiments have shown that the first shapes to be accurately perceived are triangles, because their angularity is quickly apparent. We can measure the degree of accuracy with which any given shape is perceived by requiring the observer to match it against a series of shapes varying from it by different amounts. We find that there is a general tendency to perceive any shape with the maximum degree of simplicity, regularity, and symmetry. Thus if an observer is shown a shape which is almost circular but slightly elliptical, or one which is an almost square rectangle, he will probably think that the shape is actually a circle or a square. If he is shown a shape which is slightly asymmetrical, he will overlook the lack of symmetry, as is shown in the reproductions of asymmetrical shapes shown in Fig. 4.[6]

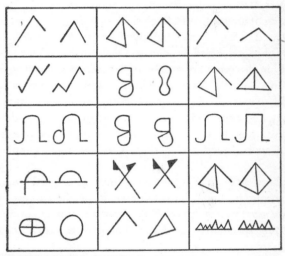

4. Reproductions of shapes showing tendency towards symmetry and regularity. In each compartment is shown an original figure and its reproduction

To this tendency to perceive shapes not exactly as they are but in somewhat modified form, great importance was attached by a German school of psychologists known as the *Gestalt* psychologists, whose work became widely known in the period between the wars. The word *Gestalt* means 'form'. These psychologists, Wertheimer, Köhler, and Koffka, emphasized the fact that normally our percepts always possess some kind of form or arrangement. Completely formless fields look like a mist or fog, with no definite localization in space. The forms or 'configurations' which we perceive are of course in part determined by the objective physical shapes of the objects, etc., in the field of view. But also we have a tendency to modify the formal qualities of what we perceive, particularly when this consists of so-called 'meaningless' shapes, that is to say, figures drawn on paper which do not represent anything else. Such shapes tend to be perceived in as 'good' a form as possible; that is to say, to be striking and easy to perceive and remember. Qualities making for 'goodness' in this sense are simplicity, regularity, symmetry, continuity, and certain others which need not concern us here. Thus shapes which in themselves exhibit these qualities are easily and accurately perceived; and shapes which do not possess them tend to become modified and to be perceived with more 'goodness' – that is to say, more simplicity, regularity, etc. – than they actually possess. Köhler in particular went on to hypothesize certain physiological processes in the brain which he considered to be the cause of this tendency towards 'goodness'. However, this hypothesis is entirely speculative, and it is not necessary to discuss it here.[7]

The perceptual tendencies studies by the *Gestalt* psychologists may be explained somewhat differently by saying that we do not in general attempt to perceive accurately every detail of the physical structure of the shapes and objects viewed. Indeed, it seems probable that the visual mechanisms of the eyes and the brain are incapable of providing us with sufficient information to do so, at least without prolonged search. But quite apart from the physiological limitations on vision, we are as a rule concerned to perceive only as much as will enable us to identify what we see, that is to say, to allocate it to a particular class of objects or shapes, with which we are familiar. As we shall see in Chapter 10, this depends to a considerable extent upon the probability of appearance of a particular type of object. Again, in the tasks of differentiating, describing, reproducing, or classifying shapes, the observer tends to perceive only as much detail as he thinks necessary to perform the particular task, and ignores the rest. Indeed, as we shall see, he may stop short of this, and then his perceptions will be incorrect. However, if shapes are regular and symmetrical, they are comparatively easy to perceive because only parts of them need be seen; the remainder is 'redundant', sufficiently similar to be inferred from what has been perceived. But with more complex shapes more detail must be observed if they are to be perceived effectively. In general, greater intensity of illumination and more time are required to perceive more complex shapes.[8]

There are of course many ways of increasing complexity, but as a rule this implies more detail and more variety of detail. Silhouette shapes have been found to appear increasingly complex if the changes in direction of the contour are increased in number and variety.[9] Outline shapes may be made more complex by increasing the amount of interior detail, in which case simplification may occur in perception, along *Gestalt* lines. Thus a complex form such as that shown in Fig. 5 may be perceived as a rectangle with diagonals across it, a triangle added to one end, various appendages adhering to it, and other details inside it.[10] Another form of simplification may be through continuity. A shape with a broken, discontinuous, or dotted outline may be perceived as a whole continuous figure. For instance, the dotted figures in Fig. 6 are generally perceived as a triangle and a square. The observer does not trouble to perceive and remember the

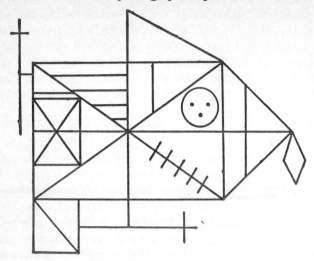

5. Complex figure with interior detail

exact pieces of the outline, but only its shape as a whole.

But there are further difficulties in perceiving complex forms accurately in detail resulting from the inability to perceive the parts of the shape independently of the whole. Many of the so-called 'visual illusions' make their effect because the observer's perception is influenced by the inclusion of their parts in the whole pattern. Thus in Fig. 7a, the upper horizontal line tends to look shorter than the

6. Discontinuous figures

lower, because it is difficult if not impossible to estimate the lengths of the two lines independently of the arrow heads which form part of the same figure. In Fig. 7b, the horizontal lines are actually straight and parallel, but because they are combined with the oblique lines, they look curved. In some

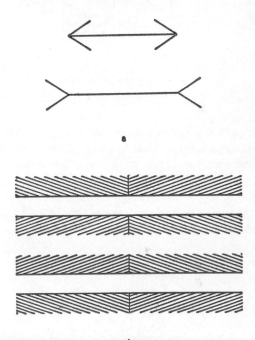

a

b

7. Visual illusions

cases, a smaller figure may become swallowed up in a larger whole. In an experiment, simple figures like that in Fig. 8a were presented a number of times, and followed by complex figures, such as Fig. 8b, each of which contained within it one of the simple figures.[11] The observers rarely if ever noticed spontaneously the simple figures in the complex ones; and they had difficulty in doing so even when told to look for

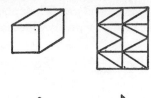

a   b

8. Simple figure and complex
figure containing it

them. Finally, Fig. 9 shows that a shape may be altered even by the background on which it is superimposed.[12] The two horizontal lines are in fact straight and parallel although they appear curved.

Naturally the accuracy and the amount of detail with which shapes can be perceived depends on the length of time available for viewing them. A period of about half a second

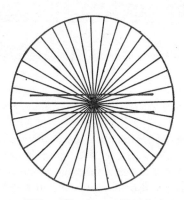

9. Effect of background on figure

is necessary for visual acuity to reach its maximum. Experiments have been carried out to determine the amount which can be perceived in shorter intervals of time. A special instrument, the tachistoscope, is used for these experiments, which exposes figures in a window or on a screen for a constant interval of time of a fraction of a second. Usually the observer is given a 'fixation point' on which to fix his eyes, and at which the figure will appear. Even with a time interval as short as a hundredth of a second he can usually perceive something of what is shown. He may also in this instant of time be able to form a 'primary memory image' which he can continue to examine for a second or two after the figure has disappeared, thus obtaining more information as to what was shown. After some practice in directing his attention and making observations of this kind, an observer can perceive considerably more than at first.

The length of time taken to perceive a simple shape is related to its size and brightness. The threshold intensity of illumination at which shapes are perceptible has been found to decrease up to an exposure time of about one and a half seconds, after which it became comparatively constant.[13] This value differed little as between different simple shapes. But contrast also is important; if the outlines are blurred, or if they are projected on to a grey or mottled background, a much longer period of time may be required to perceive them.[14] Another factor which affects the perceptibility of a shape is its orientation; if a shape is turned round through 90° it becomes harder to perceive and recognize.[15] But this effect seems to depend upon the change of orientation in relation to the background rather than in relation to the position of the head, because if the head is slanted to one side, the shape is still quite difficult to perceive.

In normal circumstances we are more often confronted by a large number of shapes or objects than by single ones.

Numerous tachistoscopic experiments have been carried out to determine the number of things which can be seen at a single glance, the simplest experiments using black dots scattered over a white field. In about one fifth of a second, an unpractised observer can perceive the number of dots correctly when there are not more than five or six of these; a practised observer, as many as eight. Dots in the centre of the field of view are more likely to be perceived than those at the margin. If the dots are regularly arranged, they are usually perceived as a pattern rather than as isolated dots. Even irregular arrangements can be perceived, discriminated, and remembered as patterns, though less easily than can regular ones.[16]

If a number of different shapes is presented, and the observer has to perceive what these shapes are, his task becomes more difficult, and he can perceive only a few of them in a limited time. It was found that with an exposure of three seconds, observers could pick out a 'critical' shape with fair accuracy from among up to thirty other shapes. But when the number was increased to between sixty and a hundred, then exposures of six to twelve seconds were required.[17]

In our ordinary everyday life we seldom have to perceive shapes of this kind rapidly; but the ability to do so is sometimes important in various technical operations. Sometimes also it is necessary to perceive the appearance of solid objects with which we are unfamiliar. Comparatively little experiment has been devoted to this type of perception, though it seems reasonable to suppose that they also may be perceived as more simple, more regular, and more symmetrical than they actually are.

However, some interesting studies have been made of the perception of complex unfamiliar solids of the kind shown in Figs. 10, 11, and 12.[18] Seen from the aspect shown in Fig. 10,

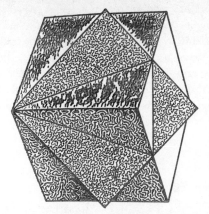

10. Complex solid: first view

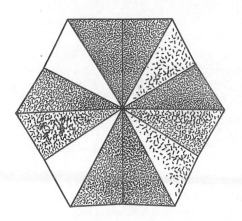

11. Complex solid: second view

this solid appeared like a cube with irregular projections forming a square. But if it was viewed from in front, instead of from the side, as in Fig. 11, it looked like a star or rosette.

And in an intermediate position (Fig. 12), it appeared different again. When observers were shown this object in these three different positions, and were not told that they were being shown one and the same object, they did not realize this, and thought that they had seen three different objects. Only when the solid had been presented a number of times in these positions did they realize what had happened. This seems to show that it is only when we see an object in a

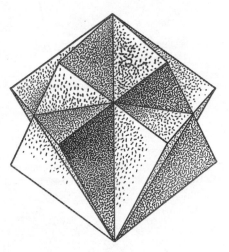

12. Complex solid: third view

continuous succession of different aspects that we gain some idea of its shape as a whole. With familiar objects we go through this process in childhood; but with unfamiliar ones, we have to learn by experience. Nevertheless, people may have some idea of the shape of that part of an object which they cannot see at the moment. When observers were shown the object from the position in Fig. 10, and asked to guess what was the shape of the part hidden from view, they often perceived the square as a cube facing them and penetrating right through the other cube seen from its edge.[19] Thus people may have images in their minds of the shapes of objects which may or may not correspond with their actual shapes. In another experiment, observers were shown a solid which was hemispherical on the side facing them but flat behind.[20] They tended to think that the object was spherical on the hidden side also, even when they were allowed to feel the flat surface with their fingers.

4 · PERCEPTION OF 'MEANINGFUL' SHAPES

Returning to the perception of plane shapes, we must now consider the kind of modification which may arise when these appear to have some special 'meaning', for instance, to represent real objects. We often overlook the fact that in perceiving such drawings, we follow the conventions which are current in our society as to how solid objects should be represented when they are reproduced on plane surfaces. Outline drawings are in fact entirely unlike the objects they represent; they are not even very like photographs of these objects. But the artist learns that if he draws certain types of lines on paper, they will convey to the observer the appearance of certain solid objects which have become associated with them through the conventions of drawing. In caricatures, the unlikeness of the drawings to the people depicted has been grossly exaggerated, usually in such a way as to suggest certain characteristics of the personalities of these people, or what the caricaturist thinks and feels about them. Because we have learnt the convention, we have little difficulty in recognizing the people who have been caricatured. Yet we sometimes scoff at the conventions of earlier societies – for instance, in Egyptian paintings or in medieval pictures such as those of the Bayeux tapestry – because these appear to us bizarre and unrealistic representations. In fact, they are no more so than the elongated ladies of our fashion pictures!

Observations have been made on certain primitive peoples which show that they differ in their ability to interpret European representational drawings.[21] One West African tribe, the Yoruba, was found to understand pictures fairly easily, because they were accustomed to use 'realistic' drawings and paintings themselves, in their decorative designs. But another tribe, the Nupe, whose designs were formal and ornamental, found it considerably harder to grasp the meanings of pictures. Again, African Negro children living in French Guinea had unusual difficulty in putting together the pieces of puzzles which depicted a manikin and a face.

Normally Europeans have little difficulty in combining together the pieces of representational shapes which have been separated, as in Fig. 13.[22] Particularly if it is given a name, or if the observer is merely told what kind of object it represents – for instance, an animal – then he may quite suddenly perceive it as a picture, and have little difficulty in recognizing it on subsequent occasions.

In other cases, highly simplified drawings may be perceived as representing real objects even when the observer has not been instructed to perceive them in this way. And if he is asked to draw them from memory, he may make his drawings look more like the conventional idea of the named object than was the drawing originally presented. We saw that in the experiment described on page 36, drawings named by the experimenter were reproduced in such a manner as to resemble the named object. But the observer may provide a name for himself, and make similar modifications. Thus an observer shown the shape in Fig. 14 called it a 'pick-axe' and represented it with curved prongs; another

13. Incomplete figure

14. Named figure

observer called it a 'turf-cutter' and showed it with a rounded blade.[23] Several called it an 'anchor', and exaggerated the size of the ring at the top. Again, the shape shown in Fig. 15a was called a 'picture frame' by some people and reproduced as in Fig. 15b and c. But it was correctly reproduced by the observer who described it as 'two carpenter's squares placed together'.

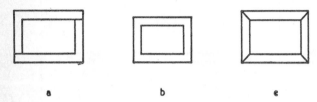

a   b   c

15. Named figure and two reproductions

Not only are people ready to perceive outline drawings as representing real objects; they also perceive them more easily than figures which have no 'meaning' of this kind but are seen merely as shapes. In general, we find that perception takes place more rapidly, when only a short interval of time is available for perception, in so far as the material perceived has some 'meaning' beyond its mere shape. It seems that with figures which can be taken to represent real objects the observer perceives something in the shape which suggests this object to him, and does not trouble to notice all the details of the shape, as he must do in perceiving 'meaningless' shapes (except in so far as he assumes them to be simple, symmetrical, etc.). Furthermore, an observer can perceive a large and complex picture in a time which would be quite inadequate for the perception of a complex collection of meaningless shapes. This effect of 'meaning' is exemplified also in the perception of letters and words. Letters can be perceived more quickly than can the shapes making up the letters if the latter are jumbled together (see Fig. 16).[24] Again, letters forming words are perceived more rapidly than the same letters jumbled. Although presumably in the short time

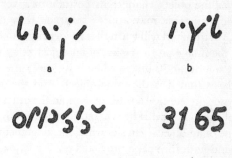

16. Effect of meaning
a. jumbled parts of letters   b. letters
c. jumbled parts of digits   d. digits

available some kind of shape must be perceived in both cases, the full perception of what is presented develops more rapidly when it is assisted by the inference of a familiar meaning. This process is sometimes called 'coding'. When the original sensory impulses reach the brain, they are coded more quickly into the familiar categories of pictures, letters, or words than into the relatively unfamiliar codes of shape as such.

5 · EFFECT OF SURROUNDINGS ON SHAPE PERCEPTION

We must now consider certain cases in which judgements of shape are affected by their relation to their surroundings. Here we see again that people are unable to make exact judgements of shape because they cannot isolate the objects they are judging from their setting in the surrounding field of view. We noted in Chapter 2 that the child learns quite early in life that the perceived shape of a particular object may change as the object changes its position in space. Thus a square-topped table may appear trapezoidal or diamond-shaped, yet the child will learn that its identity is unchanged. So also the image on the retina of an object at a distance is much smaller than its image when it is closer; but again the child learns that it is the same object. And the adult will actually see, in one case a tilted square, in the other a distant object of constant size. If he is asked to make a judgement of the shape of an object seen sideways, his judgement will not correspond with the shape projected on the retina, but will to a greater or less extent resemble the shape of the object if viewed from directly in front of it. Thus if he is asked to estimate the shape of a circular plate tilted at an angle, the estimated shape will be more circular than the ellipse which is projected on to the retina. This compromise judgement is shown in Fig. 17a.[25] It can be demonstrated either by asking

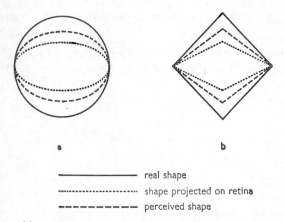

a   b

——————— real shape
···················· shape projected on retina
– – – – – – – perceived shape

17. Figures showing the effect of shape constancy

the observer to draw what he thinks to be the shape of the tilted object; or by requiring him to match it against one of a series of ellipses looked at directly without any tilt. The same effect occurs with square or rectangular surfaces (see Fig. 17b). It appears that because the observer can perceive that he is looking at a surface tilted towards him, he compromises between the shape of the image projected on the retina, and the shape the object would have if it were viewed directly from in front, which of course is also the shape which would be felt by touch.

So also if an observer is asked to judge the size of an object at a considerable distance away from him, his judgement will not normally conform to the size of the image projected on his retina, but to the size of the object he would see if it were at the distance at which such an object is usually viewed. Indeed, he may be able to estimate the 'real' sizes of objects when they are quite a long distance away, up to about a quarter of a mile. It is only at greater distances that objects begin gradually to look smaller;[26] though of course when they are really far distant they may appear tiny. Seen from the side of a mountain, men and cars in the valley below look like flies and beetles, and it is only by a process of reasoning that we can identify what they are. But over comparatively short distances, and as long as we can perceive what their distance is, we do not notice any change in size of objects. And if we are asked to estimate their size, our estimates will be approximately equal to the 'real' measured sizes of these objects. These effects are sometimes called the phenomena of *shape* and *size constancy*, because the shapes and sizes of objects appear to remain relatively constant whatever their position in space, within certain limits.

The amateur artist soon becomes aware of these effects when he tries to make accurate perspective drawings of slanted or distant objects. He finds that he makes the slanted objects too wide in the direction of slant, and the distant objects too large, to fit into his picture properly. If he is to make a correct perspective drawing, he will usually have to hold a pencil close up in front of one eye and measure off the dimensions of these objects in relation to their surroundings. This is of course tantamount to measuring the dimensions of the image projected on the retina. If he does not do this, if he merely goes by what the objects look like at a quick glance, his drawing will look out of perspective, like a child's drawing – or like some types of modern painting! The objects will probably be too large to fit into the space available for them. However, when his skill has been increased by practice, he may learn to make the necessary corrections without actual measurement. For instance, he may compare the sizes of the objects in his picture with the sizes of the spaces between them; and if he estimates these size relationships correctly, he can reproduce the objects in proportion to the retinal images they cast on the eye.

If the surroundings of an object are concealed from the observer, so that he cannot see whether or not it is tilted in space, nor what its distance is, then he is forced to rely on the projected image, and his judgement will be made in accordance with this alone. Thus if he looks at a tilted circle placed against a black background with one eye through a tube which cuts out all view of the surroundings, he may perceive an ellipse of the dimensions shown in Fig. 17a; though if the surface is rough or patterned in some way, he may be able to see from the gradual change in its surface texture from back to front that it is tilted, and perceive it more or less as a tilted circle. If he is shown a tilted circle for a short period of time only, about one tenth of a second, he will not have time to see how it is related to its surroundings, and will tend to perceive it as an ellipse and not as a tilted circle.[27] Again, if the observer views an object at a distance, with all view of the surroundings eliminated, it will appear as small as the projected image. If the view of the surroundings is not clear, but is not cut out altogether, then an intermediate judgement is made. Thus it seems that normally we relate the size of any object to the sizes of all the other objects in the total surroundings at that distance; and the size is perceived in relation to the size scale of objects at that distance. We perceive these surroundings as extended all round us in space, and fit each object into this total pattern, at its appropriate position. But for surroundings at great distances, the nature of the pattern becomes unclear, and hence we may no longer be able to perceive the relationship; then judgement of size becomes difficult if not impossible. But we still attempt to make such judgements, as can be seen by comparing a direct view of distant mountains with a photograph of them. In the latter, which shows the mountains in their perspective or 'retinal image' size, the mountains appear smaller than in direct view.

In some cases in which it is impossible to see the position of an object and how far away it is, the observer may fall back on his knowledge of the usual size of such an object, in judging both its size and distance. Thus if he is shown a half-sized playing card at the same actual distance as a normal-sized one, in conditions in which no information as to its actual distance is available, he tends to see the half-sized playing card as having a normal size, but as being situated twice as far away as the normal-sized playing card.[28] However, the effect of known size on estimation of distance and perceived size is much greater with objects of characteristic and invariable size such as playing cards and it may operate even when the distance of these objects can be clearly perceived. With objects of variable or relatively unfamiliar size, the effect is much less, or altogether absent.[29]

In experiments on the matching of the shapes of tilted

objects and the size of distant objects, it has been found that the type of match made may vary with the observer's procedure in performing his task.[30] Some people may make an immediate snap judgement, and in this case size and shape constancy are high, and matches tend to approximate to the real shapes and sizes of the objects. Such observers judge mainly in the light of their knowledge as to what the objects are, and what their shapes and sizes may be when they are seen from a short distance and from directly in front. Other people may deliberate over their judgements, and reflect that what they perceive is something different from the real shape and size. Their shape and size constancy is lower, and their judgements tend to approach the shape and size of the retinal projection, though not to be identical with it. The former type of judgement is more commonly made unless special instructions are given. But by varying the instructions, it is usually possible to obtain judgements of either real or projected size or shape; the degree of constancy will then vary accordingly.

CHAPTER 5

THE PERCEPTION OF COLOUR

WE all recognize colour as a characteristic and identifiable quality of the appearance of objects. Indeed, certain objects may be differentiated from one another largely by means of colour, for instance, an orange, an apple, and a tomato. The physical basis of colour is constituted by the wave-length of the light reflected from objects to the eye; and there is a continuous succession of colours, known as the colour spectrum, from red to orange, yellow, green, blue, and violet, which corresponds to successive wavelengths of decreasing magnitude. Yet as we shall see, although we can discriminate with great accuracy between colours of slightly different wave-lengths, the perception and identification of colour in objects depends on other factors than the wave-length of the light actually reflected from an object.

There seems to be some disagreement as to whether colour is perceived at the earliest stage of perceptual development. Certainly it is not differentiated as soon as the 'figure' emerges from the 'ground'. In adults, the identification of objects has become to some extent independent of colour perception, as can be seen from the readiness with which we can identify uncoloured photographs. But reaction to colour appears to begin at a comparatively primitive stage in perception. Colour appeals strongly to children, as we shall discuss in Chapter 6. Patients blind from birth who had been operated on for cataract perceived colours more readily than even quite simple forms.

Colour perception is often associated with feelings of pleasure or displeasure. Most people have preferences for certain colours rather than for others. Indeed, the order of preference seems fairly constant among Western peoples. It is as follows: blue, red, green, purple, orange, and yellow.[1] Intermediate colours are usually felt to be less pleasant than pure colours. But there are considerable individual variations; in particular, some people seem to prefer bright colours, others softer and less saturated ones. Again, particular colours may give rise to particular emotional reactions:[2] red to excitement or anger, blue to calm pleasure, black and grey to sadness or depression. But it is rather doubtful to what extent these emotional reactions are spontaneous, or whether they are symbolically associated through cultural traditions. However, people with highly emotional or neurotic dispositions seem to give characteristic reactions to colour. In the Rorschach Ink-blot test of personality, in which people are asked to name anything which the blots suggest to them by way of association, formless responses to the coloured parts of the blots such as 'sunsets', 'blood', 'sea', etc., are said to indicate a high degree of emotionality.[3] And some neurotic individuals experience what is called 'colour shock', and are unable to respond, or are very slow to respond, to the coloured blots.

It is interesting to note that although people can discriminate between shades of colour with a high degree of sensitivity, they do not normally identify and remember individual colours with as great a degree of accuracy and certainty as they identify and remember shapes. It is fairly easy to identify simple colours, for instance, the red of a pillar-box or the yellow of a sunflower. But intermediate colours, which shade into one another, are far more difficult. This is particularly apparent with the large range of blues and greens. It has been found that different people show different degrees of skill in remembering even the simple colours, red, yellow, green, and blue. Green is the hardest to remember accurately. But skill in remembering can be improved by practice.

One of the obstacles to remembering colours, especially the intermediate shades, is the paucity of generally accepted colour names, and only eight of these seem to be in common use: red, pink, orange, yellow, green, blue, purple, and brown. Yet the number of discriminable shades runs into many thousands. Other colours are given descriptive titles such as sky-blue, sea-green, and so on. But these seldom correspond accurately with any particular wave-length of light. Textile manufacturers and dress designers invent innumerable names such as cerise, maroon, ecru, taupe, etc., for particular shades of colour, but it often seems that there is little consistency in the way in which these are applied. Also colour dyes vary from time to time, and hence the shade corresponding to any particular name. However, colour charts have been prepared, known as the Munsell and Ostwald charts, in which standardized coloured surfaces are arranged systematically in groups, and from which colours can be identified.[4] Again, American textile industries issue annually cards carrying samples of coloured textiles each with a definite name which is standardized for that year. But of course these are not generally familiar, and people have no opportunity of learning and remembering the new names for specific colours.

A good deal of discussion has been devoted to the question as to whether certain primitive peoples do not perceive colours as we perceive them, since their languages do not include the colour names included in ours. In some cases the name used by such peoples may be that of an object which it characterizes. Thus the word for green is often the same as, or derived from, the name for grass or other vegetation. Fijians use the same word for blue and green, but there seems to be another term for green used only in connexion with foliage. Also they tend to stress the dark quality of certain colours, and both dark blue and dark red may be called by the same name, 'dark'. Possibly this association between darkness and shades of blue and red may account for the Greek epithet of the 'wine-dark sea'. Again, other primitive peoples may regard bright and dark blue as totally different colours and name them accordingly. However, a lack of nomenclature does not seem to indicate inability to differentiate colours. When a group of Fijians were shown sets of differently coloured cards, they unhesitatingly gave them different names.

In some cases, the nomenclature of primitive peoples may be more elaborate than our own. Thus Eskimoes have three different names for snow, corresponding to the different types or conditions of snow. It is reported that the Kaffir language has more than twenty-six terms to designate the different colour markings of cattle. It seems probable that naming corresponds to utility. Primitive peoples can discriminate and name those colours which are significant to them, but they may not trouble to do so for colours in which they have no particular interest. Red and yellow pigments are easily prepared and are extensively used by primitive peoples for decorative purposes. Thus it is often found that the nomenclature for reds and yellows is clearer and less ambiguous than that for greens and blues, which are less often used in this manner. The former are also much more common in the colours of animals, which again have great significance for these people.

These theories as to the development of colour naming are highly speculative. But it does seem that the exact hues of colour which possess simple and commonly accepted names are remembered and recognized more easily than those of other colours. In an experiment with European adults, the eight colours with well-known names listed above were presented together with sixteen other colours; and the observers were asked to recognize them subsequently from among a set of 120 different colours.[5] They recognized the eight colours more quickly and with greater consistency than the other sixteen; and they also reported that they attempted to remember the colours by naming them. But some Zuni Indians, who carried out the same task, frequently confused orange and yellow when they tried to recognize them; these Indians use the same name for these two colours.

In addition to the influence of naming on the perception of colours, there are other factors which may make it difficult to perceive colours accurately and consistently. Colours vary in brightness and saturation (degree of admixture of white and coloured light), and these qualities affect judgements of colour. The appearance of a colour also varies according as to whether it is seen as 'surface' or 'film' colour, as we noted on page 45. Again, we can look through a film of colour to something beyond it and perceive another colour through it; this phenomenon is called 'transparency'. A partially transparent coloured fluid in a bottle has a voluminous appearance and the colour seems to be distributed through-out the fluid; it may be called 'volume colour'. Again, if we look at a coloured lamp, we see 'luminous colour'.[6]

Surface colour may vary in appearance with the type of surface, according to whether it is dull, rough, or shiny in texture. Light is reflected in a different manner by shiny surfaces, or by dull, or matt surfaces, and this affects the appearance of the colour. There is also a difference between the appearance of colours in diffuse and in concentrated lighting, which is important particularly in colour photography. Again, colours may seem to spread into one another, especially if the areas of colour are very small. Thus the 'pointilliste' painters, such as Seurat, were able to obtain striking effects by juxtaposing small 'points' of different colours. There are also certain characteristic 'contrast' effects which occur between differently coloured surfaces. We do not as a rule perceive the colour of an object or surface in isolation; our perception is affected by the colour of the surrounding surfaces. But before we proceed to discuss these effects, it is necessary to consider briefly how colour is perceived by the retina and the brain.

Although we do not know exactly how the cells of the retina and their nerve fibres respond to different wavelengths of light falling on them, they appear to function as if there were at least three different types of mechanism responding maximally to the red, green, and blue regions of the spectrum. These are called the 'primary colours'. Sometimes it is supposed that a yellow mechanism exists also; but in fact yellow can be produced by a mixture of spectral red and green, whereas none of the three primary colours can be made by mixing other colours. By varying the wavelengths of the stimulating light, and hence the degree of stimulation of the three primary mechanisms, any other colour in the spectrum can be produced; and so also can white and grey. In general, a mixture of two colours close together on the spectrum produces an intermediate hue; for instance, red and yellow mixed give orange. But if two colours far apart on the spectrum are mixed, such as red and blue-green, or yellow and blue, then the result is not a mixed colour, but a neutral grey. Any pair of colours which together produce a neutral grey are said to be 'complementary' to each other.

Now when we view coloured surfaces in close juxtaposition with each other, or one surface immediately after another, we perceive that the colour of one seems to affect the colour of the other in such a way as to enhance the *contrast* between them. In particular, one of a pair of complementary colours tends to give rise to the other. Thus a surface adjacent to a red surface will be tinged with blue-green, and vice versa; a surface adjacent to a blue surface appears yellowish, and vice versa. This effect can be seen most clearly if a grey surface is surrounded by a strongly coloured background; the grey surface appears tinted with the complementary colour. Again, if we look steadily for a period of time at a red surface, and immediately afterwards at a grey surface, the latter will appear to be tinged with blue-green; and the same effect appears with blue and yellow. These effects, known as *simultaneous* and *successive contrast*, are the result of a process of adaptation which takes place in the retinal colour mechanisms. Strong prolonged stimulation of any one of these has the effect of decreasing sensitivity to that colour, and hence the corresponding colour perception; but sensitivity to the complementary colour is enhanced. Thus from the mixed wave-lengths reflected from a grey surface (exposed simultaneously in adjacent areas, or successively in the same area), those of the complementary colour are perceived. There are, however, certain cases, for instance of stimulation by very bright coloured lights, in which the mechanisms continue responding themselves after stimulation has ceased. Thus if we look steadily at a bright red light in an otherwise dark room, and then switch off the light, we may perceive alternating patches of red and blue-green in front of the eyes. These are known as *positive* and *negative after-images*. But if we look at coloured surfaces, which are much less bright, negative after-images are almost always seen and positive after-images are rare.

This is a greatly over-simplified account of a complex set of phenomena. But we can see that surfaces of variegated contrasting colours may enhance one another, and make each other look more vivid. Such effects are not as striking, however, as those which occur when the general illumination is coloured – when, for instance, we view coloured surfaces in a yellowish or bluish artificial light. It might be supposed that we should perceive the colour of such surfaces as a mixture of the colour of the surface and the colour of the illumination; that is to say, a blue surface in a green light would look greenish-blue, and so on. If the illumination is of a pure colour, green, for instance, with no admixture of white light, bright surfaces of the same colour, green, will appear a stronger green; but dimmer objects may appear in the complementary colour.[7] Surfaces of other colours will tend to appear grey. However, the conditions determining these effects are very complex. More often the illumination is a mixture of coloured and white light. There then appears a compromise between the colour which the surface possesses in white light and the colour reflected by the surface to the eye in coloured light. Thus blue surfaces in a green light will be slightly greenish, but less green than the colour of the light which the surface actually reflects. We are quite well aware that some modification of surface colours occurs in coloured illumination, and thus in matching textiles we try to avoid this modification by studying the textiles in white light. But we do not realize that if we judged only by the quality of the light reflected to the eye we should see a much greater modification of colour. This phenomenon is called '*colour constancy*', and it resembles the phenomena of shape and size constancy which we discussed earlier. It seems that we learn by experience to distinguish the colour of the illumination, as judged by the general colour of the surroundings, from the colour inherent in the surface; and are able to compensate to some extent for the former in our judgements of the latter. This is especially likely to happen if the surface colour belongs to some particular well-known object – for instance, the red of a pillar-box or the green of grass.

If we look at a surface in coloured illumination with one eye through a narrow tube which cuts off all view of the surroundings, we cannot see how the illumination colours these surroundings, nor how it affects the colour of the surface. No compensation is possible, and we perceive simply the combination of the colours of the illumination and of the surface which comes to the eye.

We can also normally differentiate between the colour of a surface and the colour of a transparent film placed in front of it. This can be demonstrated in an experiment in which a coloured disc, of blue, for instance, with one sector cut out of it, is rotated rapidly in front of a surface of another colour, say yellow.[8] The observer will see the rotating disc as a blue film in front of the yellow surface. But this will happen only if he can see clearly that there are two surfaces at different distances from him. If he looks through a tube or through a narrow aperture in a screen which allows him to see only the rotating disc and that part of the yellow surface which lies immediately behind it, he will be unable to distinguish the blue film from the yellow surface, and will perceive a single neutral-grey surface.

Similar effects of contrast with surroundings occur also in the perception of the brightness of neutral – black, grey, and white – surfaces. As the result of retinal adaptation, a piece of grey paper placed on a white background looks darker than a similiar piece of paper placed on a black background. Other factors are involved when a grey surface is placed in shadow. As a rule, its appearance is not as dark as might be expected from the brightness of the light actually reflected to the eye, provided that the observer can see that there is a shadow cast on the surface. Again, as with the coloured light, he is able to differentiate between the part of the brightness which is due to the reflecting qualities of the surface, and that which is due to the illumination, or the shadow, in which it is situated. Hence the phenomenon of '*brightness constancy*'. But if the observer looks at the surface with one eye through a tube which cuts off his view of the surroundings, and hence the distribution of the general illumination, he will be unable to differentiate in this way, and will perceive simply the brightness of all the light which reaches his eye, combining the light from the surface and from the general illumination. There are other circumstances, it is true, which may make it impossible to perceive that the shadow is a shadow, and hence to prevent discrimination. Thus if the shadow is surrounded by a white contour line, it appears like a simple dark patch on the surface rather than a shadow.

Phenomena of this kind do not depend simply on the functions of the retina, but involve also processes which go on in the brain. There are, however, certain other modifications of colour vision which appear to be due to retinal function alone. In the first place, as we mentioned on page 47, only the cones of the retina give colour responses. Thus in very dim light, no colour is perceived. Moreover, the rods are insensitive to red light, the cones to blue light. This effect is apparent only when very small areas of the retina are stimulated, and not in ordinary vision, when large areas of mixed rods and cones are stimulated. In daylight vision, yellow appears the brightest of the colours; in dark adapted vision, blue. If the intensity of the light falling on the eye is gradually decreased, yellows become relatively dimmer and blues relatively brighter. This may have the effect of making coloured surfaces appear to shift from yellowish to bluish.

Finally, as is well known, there are certain people whose colour vision is defective in some way. In fact, there are many different types of defective colour vision, and only in a few cases can those with defective colour vision be said to be '*colour blind*'. In some individuals it seems that the retina is lacking in cones, and that they have to depend mainly or entirely on rod vision. Not only can they see no colour, but they are commonly what is called 'photophobic', that is to say, dazzled by strong light; and their visual acuity is poor, since form discrimination is lower in rod than in cone vision.

The most common type of colour defect is that in which either red or green are not perceived in the normal manner. Sometimes red is not seen at all; red objects appear greyish, and reddish objects brown or yellow. In other cases, perception of green is defective, and green objects are seen as yellow. Sometimes both types of colour vision are affected, and there is inability to distinguish between red and green. Or red and green vision may merely be weak, so that these colours appear pale and unsaturated, or yellowish in hue. One may be normal and the other defective. Thus if an observer is asked to match a mixture of red and green against yellow, he will introduce too much red or too much green into his mixture. In rare cases, blue and yellow vision are defective, and may appear as unsaturated or greyish. It seems that in these cases there is some deficiency in the retinal mechanisms responsible for colour vision but we do not know what the defect may be.

About seven and a half per cent of the male population of this country suffer from some form of defective colour vision; defective green vision is the most common form. Colour defects are rare in women. It appears that defective colour vision is a sex-linked hereditary characteristic, which occurs predominantly in males, but is transmitted by females. Thus the sons of a woman whose father had defective colour vision are liable to have some colour defect, though not necessarily of the same type as that of their grandfather. Occasionally the woman will show some colour defect of a minor character, particularly if not only her father but also her mother's father had defective colour vision.

These defects of colour vision are of considerable practical importance in a number of occupations – not only the more obvious ones such as painting, dress-designing, and the matching of textiles and dyes, but also those which necessitate a rapid and accurate response to coloured signals. Thus entrants to the Navy and Air Force are given tests of colour vision, because it would be dangerous if this were so defective as to prevent them from discriminating between red and green signal lights. It might be supposed that an individual would be well aware of the defects of his colour vision, and would automatically avoid such occupations, but this is not always the case. Colour defectives often do not realize that their colour vision differs from the normal. They manage to discriminate and recognize colours up to a point through clues afforded by brightness differences, spatial position, and so on; for instance, with traffic lights the red is always above the yellow and the green below. They name what they see as shades of brown and yellow with the names given by normal people to red and green. Often they resist the implication that there is anything wrong with their colour vision, and it is impossible to demonstrate this without the use of specially designed tests. These include tests of matching – for instance of a mixture of red and green against yellow, such as we noted above. But perhaps the best-known test of colour vision is one called the 'Ishihara' test.[9] Sets of differently coloured dots are arranged in such a way that numbers are formed from sequences of reddish or greenish dots, and these contrast with the background of dots of other colours. A person with normal colour vision can read the numbers, but someone with defective colour vision cannot differentiate the red or the green dots from the background.

There also appear to be certain people whose colour vision has suffered from the effects of injury to the brain; but these defects are quite different from those of the colour blind individual.[10] In the first case, extensive injury to the occipital cortex, the rear part of the brain, may destroy colour vision altogether. As the patient begins to recover from the injury, colour vision may reappear by stages. Before it is completely restored, he may be able to perceive some colour, but it will appear as 'film' colour and not as surface colour. The colour cannot be definitely localized as belonging to the surfaces of objects, but seems to be soft and hazy and to lie over them like a film. The colour does not seem to be an inherent property of the objects, and it is difficult for the patient to name or remember colours of objects. Such cases are uncommon, however, and we do not know a great deal about the nature of their defects.

There is one curious peculiarity of colour vision which seems to originate at an early age in some people and to persist into later life. This phenomenon is known as '*synaesthesia*'. It appears that stimuli of different sensory modes, vision, hearing, etc., are somehow linked together, so that in 'coloured hearing', for instance, auditory stimuli are perceived in conjunction with images of colours so vivid that they almost resemble percepts. The theory is that in young children there is little differentiation of primary sensations from one another, and that visual, auditory, and other modes of sensation which occur at the same time become so closely linked that in later life perception of one type of stimulus is liable to arouse imagery of the others. Now it is true that little children do not perceive and differentiate the separate sensory qualities of objects which are meaningful to them and which they perceive as wholes. Therefore in later life percepts or images related to such objects and situations might in fact arouse a mass of sensory imagery associated with them in the past. This does in fact happen, especially perhaps in the case of smell; a particular odour may recall vividly imagery of past experiences. But this is not what is meant by synaesthesia. Here the link seems in many cases to be between sounds with no particular personal associations, for instance, the notes of the scale, and a corresponding series of colours. The experiences of one individual were that imagery of brown and orange arose in response to hearing low tones, imagery of blue with medium tones, and imagery of green with high tones.[11] Sir Isaac Newton is said to have associated red with the note C, orange with D, yellow with E, green with F, blue with G, and violet with B.[12] The musician Scriabin experienced colours, not in association with specific notes, but with particular musical keys. The keys from C to F sharp were connected with the colours passing through the spectrum from red to purple.[13]

Different studies of University students found that twenty to forty per cent claimed to 'see' colours while listening to music, while many others 'associated' colours with music.[14] It is doubtful to what extent such associations have any basis in actual perception or imagery. They are frequently acquired from literary sources, in phrases such as the 'scarlet trumpet'. Indeed, the use of such analogies is frequent even in common parlance, as when we talk of 'warm' and 'cold' colours, 'loud', 'hard', or 'soft' colours, 'bright' or 'dark' 'tone colour' in music. Often high-pitched notes may be felt to match bright colours, low notes dark or dull colours. Emotional reactions to colour and sound frequently enter into these associations also.

These are not, however, examples of genuine synaesthesia, in which the associated imagery arises immediately and quite spontaneously, and does not appear to be the result of previous experience. A general characteristic is the rigid linkage between specific series of notes or of musical keys, and specific colour images. However, as in the cases of analogies, other sensory qualities may be associated with colours, such as tastes, odours, and touch sensations. Some individuals experience a variety of these. Sometimes also colour schemes are associated with numbers, days of the week, months of the year, voices, and so on; but it is more doubtful if these are genuinely synaesthetic and not learnt associations. One particularly curious case was reported of a man who had been blind since the age of eleven, but who since early childhood had experienced colours in connexion with touches and sounds, which experiences continued after he became blind.[15] These colours appeared to be an integral part of his perceptions of many patterns of sound and touch, such that they were an essential aspect of their meaning, which was not fully apprehended until the appropriate colour imagery had developed.

That there may be some linkage between visual, auditory, and tactile sensation has also been shown in numerous experiments in which it appeared that stimulation by one of these could lower the absolute threshold of the others. Such findings suggest that our perception of these sensory qualities may be linked in some way and not completely discreet even when they are not associated together as the qualities of particular objects. Curiously enough these experiments do not appear to have been performed with colours.

CHAPTER 6

THE DEVELOPMENT OF SHAPE
AND COLOUR PERCEPTION IN CHILDREN

I · PERCEPTION OF SHAPE

WE have seen that the perception of shape and colour by adults depends partly on the functions of the eye and partly on those of the brain. Some at least of the latter have been acquired through learning and experience. Moreover, a young child may not only lack the necessary experience to perceive some types of form, but may also not possess a sufficiently mature intelligence to enable him to do so. It is usually impossible to differentiate between the effects of maturation and of experience in the development of shape and colour perception. But it is possible to trace some of their lines of development, and to indicate how the child's perceptions differ from those of the adult.

We have already noted that a young child seems to lack the ability to perceive some shapes accurately and in detail. However, infants as young as six months were found to be able to discriminate between solid blocks with circular, square, and triangular faces.[1] These were presented in pairs, one immovable, the other, coated with a sweet substance, which the child could take up, handle, and put in his mouth to taste. The younger children were slow at first to learn which was the sweet-tasting shape; some made as many as a hundred attempts before they chose correctly. But after this they were much quicker in learning to discriminate the other shapes, though naturally those which were most alike, for instance, the circular and oval, were the most difficult. Once the children had learnt these discriminations, they could make them regardless of the size and position of the shapes. The children were also able to discriminate between flat cut-out shapes which they could touch and handle. They could even learn to discriminate between shapes drawn on flat surfaces. In one experiment, two-year-old children were shown two boxes, one empty with a plain lid, the other, containing a piece of chocolate, with a triangle on the lid.[2] The children soon learnt to reach for the latter. They could do the same thing if there was a square or a circle on the lid of the empty box; or if the triangle on the box with the chocolate was changed in size or turned upside down. Triangles of different shapes could also be discriminated from each other, provided that the difference was fairly marked. Recognition of a cross was quickly learnt in the same way. When these shapes were placed on differently shaped forms as backgrounds, they were still responded to immediately, showing that the children had no difficulty in differentiating the 'figure' from the 'ground', and perceiving the former as the essential feature of the experience.[3]

However, that a child of six to twelve months needs prolonged experience to learn to choose between one shape and another shows that his immediate perception of shape is extremely limited. Moreover, he may be learning to discriminate between shapes rather than to perceive a single shape as such. For if the movable block described above was placed among several others, then the child found it harder to choose the correct one, especially if some of the blocks were very much alike. His memories of the exact appearance of the correct shape were therefore not at all clear. The ability to match one from a number of shapes, such as a diamond, triangle, trapezoid, and irregular quadrilaterals appears to develop at about four years of age. In the Terman-Merrill test of intelligence, the average child of four years is found to be able to match eight out of ten of such shapes.[4]

But it is probable that the child learns more easily the shapes of familiar objects which are useful or interesting to him. By the end of the first year he recognizes their characteristics with sufficient clarity to be able to identify these objects, even in different spatial positions. But there is little doubt that such shapes are perceived at an earlier age than are the essential characteristics of geometrical shapes, particularly when the latter are drawn on a flat surface. The child has little natural interest in such shapes, and indeed may often tend to see them as representing real objects: the circle as a ball, the triangle as the roof of a house, and so on. Even older children show a strong tendency to see shapes as suggesting real objects; and if they are asked to reproduce them, they make their reproductions more like the objects named than were the originals. Thus children of nine to eleven years, shown the shape in Fig. 18a, gave it the following names: (1) 'a boot with a strip'; (2) 'a duck on the water'; (3) 'a water-cock'; (4) 'a bird'. Fig. 18b was

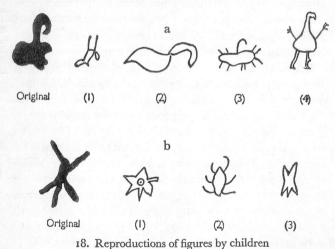

18. Reproductions of figures by children

called: (1) 'a star'; (2) 'a fly'.⁵ But it was also reproduced by one child in a more symmetrical version of the original (3), indicating the tendency towards symmetry and regularity which also appears in adults. However, children are seldom much interested in shapes of this kind, and rarely take much trouble to reproduce them accurately.

Certain characteristics of shape as such do seem to be perceived at a fairly early age. Of these, angularity as contrasted with smoothness or flatness seems to be one of the most important, probably because in handling shapes sharp corners stick out and are easily perceived by touch. So also an adult touching a shape he cannot see notices most readily angularity and sharp corners. A little later, shapes with straight edges and angles are distinguished by the child from those with continuous curved edges. But this may be preceded by the distinction between open and closed figures, while there is still a tendency to confuse simple closed figures such as a circle and a square. Figures with holes in them, or one figure surrounding another, are recognized quite early.⁶

The lack of recognition of the essentials even of simple shapes is shown in the drawings of little children. After they have passed the scribbling stage, and have begun to be able to copy shapes, they tend to reproduce all closed shapes in a roughly circular form, whether these are circles, triangles, or squares (see Fig. 19).⁷ They can, however, show quite clearly if one shape encloses another. But sometimes they will indicate the corners of a square or triangle by two strokes protruding from their circles. At the next stage, curved and straight line shapes are differentiated, but not triangles from squares. The sloping sides of the triangle seem to cause some difficulty. This is even more noticeable in reproductions of diamonds, where the child even up to the age of five or six may find it hard to slope his lines properly and

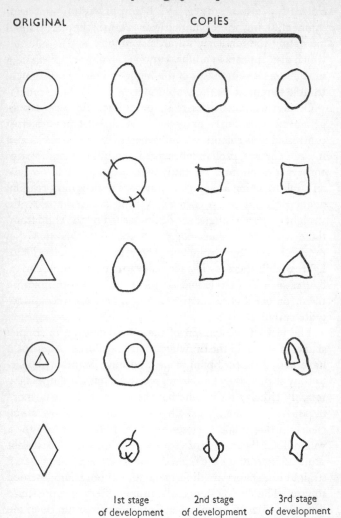

ORIGINAL

COPIES

1st stage
of development

2nd stage
of development

3rd stage
of development

19. Copies of simple geometrical shapes by children

make them meet; sometimes the lines show abrupt alterations of slope, which look rather like ears, at the lateral
corners!

The perception of more complex shapes, containing
interior detail, develops more slowly. The perception of
children under six or seven years is said to be 'syncretic' –
meaning that they perceive 'wholes' rather than details.
They may be able to discriminate between two shapes
presented simultaneously which differ only in detail. But if
they are required to copy shapes, they often fail to see the
relation of interior detail to the outline or to the whole
pattern. With a shape such as that shown in Fig. 20, the two
interior crosses are not correctly related till about seven years

20. Shape with interior detail which was copied incorrectly

of age.[8] If children are shown figures in which there is a
clear and obvious over-all structure, then this will be perceived and the detail overlooked. Thus shapes copied by
modelling are made simpler, more regular, and more
symmetrical than are the originals.[9] If the figure is not strong
and clear in outline, then they may tend to perceive only a
mass of unrelated detail. Thus young children could not
continue correctly figures such as those shown in Fig. 21a.[10]
Figures such as that in Fig. 21b tended to become fragmented
in reproduction.[11] And with a complicated diagram such as
that shown in Fig. 5 (page 54), the general structure of the
enclosing rectangle with the other details filled into it was
not reproduced correctly until about eleven years of age.

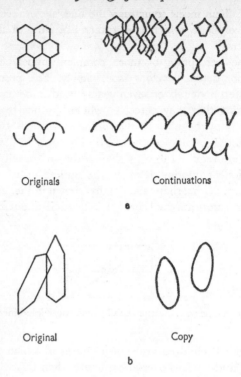

Originals   Continuations

a

Original   Copy

b

21. Shapes copied incorrectly

Before that, separate details were copied juxtaposed together irregularly.[12]

It appears, then, that below a certain age children are not able to analyse shapes correctly, giving due weight to the general structure and relating detail to it. The lack of ability to isolate the parts of a figure from the whole and perceive them as such, which appears in perceiving visual illusions, such as those shown in Fig. 7 (page 55), is more noticeable in children than in adults. Thus, for instance, in the illusion shown in Fig. 7a, children over-estimate the line with the protruding arrow-heads to a greater degree than do adults.[13] Again, if they are shown overlapping shapes, such as those in Fig. 22, and asked to trace out the separate shapes with the finger, they may find difficulty in doing this before five to six years of age.[14] Even more difficult are embedded shapes such as that in Fig. 8b (page 56); even at eight years of age children make more mistakes than do adults in identifying the simple in the complex figure.*[15]

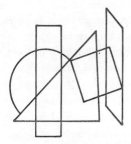

22. Overlapping figures

Piaget has recently described extensive studies of the perception of visual illusions by children of various ages, and of their eye movements during perception.[16] With the younger children, there was a general tendency towards '*centration*' of regard upon one part of the visual field, with disregard of the remainder. Only when they had reached a certain age were the children able to explore the whole field systematically, comparing one part of it with another and thus perceiving accurately the inter-relationship of the parts.

*It should be noted that the figures used in this experiment were on the whole simpler than that in Fig. 8; and that the child was shown the simple and the complex figure together and asked to trace out the former in the latter.

Another characteristic of the perception of young children which has aroused much interest is their apparent lack of attention to the *orientation* or spatial position of shapes. It seems natural that as the child learns to recognize and identify objects whatever their position in space, he should cease to notice what position they are in, and that they should look the same to him when they are upside down as when they are right side up. He may then extend this lack of discrimination to shapes on flat surfaces, as was seen in the case of children who could recognize a triangle when it was inverted. Thus it is not surprising to find that children may be able to recognize pictures in a book as easily when the book is upside down, though for adults this is often difficult if not impossible. The child may not see anything odd in holding the book upside down. But the consequence of this may be that the child is unable to distinguish a shape which is inverted even when it is important for him to do so, as in distinguishing the letters 'n' and 'u'. Again, he makes no particular distinction between left and right, and hence tends to confuse shapes, and especially letters such as 'b' and 'd', which differ only in their spatial orientation. In fact, children of five may be unable to see the difference between a shape and its mirror image even if this is pointed out to them.

This tendency to ignore spatial orientation may again indicate the child's inability to analyse what he perceives, to separate out certain aspects and to give them due weight when, as in reading letters, they are important. He seems to show a certain rigidity and stereotyping in his perceptual processes, so that if he has once perceived anything in a particular way, he cannot perceive it from a different point of view. Piaget has explained this as an instance of the fact that it is only as he grows older that the child is able to use his intelligence actively in reasoning about what he sees. Before that, he tends to accept things passively, as they come to him, attending only to those aspects which are important and interesting to him at the moment. Or his attention may become 'centrated' on a particular feature of what is shown him, and he may fail to examine other parts of it. Again, it seems probable that children are less able than are adults to guess what a shape is if it is complex or incompletely shown. The children require more and clearer information to see things correctly and in detail.

There are certain cases in which the perceptions of children are noticeably confused and inaccurate – namely, in children with brain injuries, for instance those who suffer from cerebral palsy.[17] These children seem unable to perceive and attend to the essential characteristics of shapes and patterns. They are unusually easily distracted by irrelevant details, and may even be unable to distinguish between 'figure' and 'ground'. But if they have perceived a certain figure or part of a figure, they may stick to it rigidly, and be unable to see it in any other way. With complex shapes and patterns, their perceptions may be fragmentary; they pick out a few details and do not notice the whole structure. This tendency of course appears sometimes in young normal children, but it is much more noticeable in the brain-injured. Thus they may have particular difficulty in perceiving simple solid shapes by touch alone, because this necessitates combining together the tactile impressions obtained by touching successive parts of the solid.

The disability of the brain-injured children was shown up particularly clearly in an experiment in which they and normal children of various ages were required to copy a pattern of marbles by arranging another set of marbles in a frame. The brain-injured children started and stopped anywhere in the pattern, or made disconnected bits of it isolated from one another (see Fig. 23). Mental defectives and young normal children, on the other hand, placed the marbles in an orderly sequence along the outline of the pattern, showing that they had grasped its essential outline shape. Older and more intelligent children analysed out the essential constituents of the pattern and constructed these in an orderly fashion.

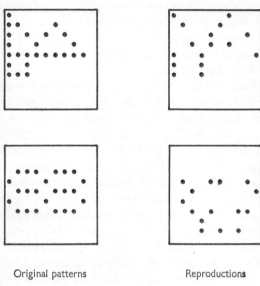

Original patterns   Reproductions

23. Marble-board patterns

The inability of brain-injured children to distinguish the 'figure' from the 'ground' was shown by the fact that if the marble pattern had a structured background, they were extremely distracted by this. Again, they found it difficult to perceive shapes obscured by lines, as in Fig. 24, if these were exposed for only a short period of time. They were also very likely to be distracted by the unimportant details of complex figures. And the greater the severity of the impairment to the brain, the greater their difficulty in detecting simple figures embedded in complex ones, such as those of Fig. 8 (see page 56).[18]

24. Obscured figures

It seems therefore that these children do not only lack the ability to analyse their experiences, but also their brains are incapable of co-ordinating and integrating perceived experiences. It is as if a mosaic of isolated pieces were perceived, without relation to one another, which cannot be put together to form a whole, either in a pattern of shape or a picture of coordinated meaning.

We have already noted that there are certain important characteristics of the perception of shapes in relation to their background known as shape and size constancy. It was pointed out that children learnt very early in life to recognize and identify objects whatever their spatial position and distance, at least over comparatively short distances. Moreover, it has been shown that children of six months can distinguish between a rattle close to them and a rattle three times the size presented at three times the distance.[19] The retinal images of these would be of the same size, but the real sizes quite different, and the infant can perceive this. However, we cannot assume from this that if young children are required to match relative sizes of near and more distant objects, they will do this in the same way as do adults. Over comparatively short distances, children appear to see objects as slightly smaller when they are further away than when they are nearer.[20] But at greater distances, of thirty feet and over, children may match a near object with a distant object of much greater size, showing that the latter appears much smaller than its real size.[21] It has been claimed that such judgements occur only when one object is immediately behind the other, a condition stressing the comparison of retinal images rather than real sizes. It is also possible that perceiving the real size of objects may be harder for children than for adults when they cannot easily perceive the relationships of these to their surroundings. Thus children of six were found to be able to estimate fairly accurately the sizes of familiar objects in natural surroundings.[22] But in experiments in which the surroundings were partly concealed, children of this age perceived objects as appreciably smaller than their real sizes.[23] This effect is even greater at far distances. The story is told of a child who thought that the village he could see on the other side of the Lake of Geneva consisted of toy houses, because they looked so small.

Again, it has been found that when children are asked to judge the perspective or projected sizes of objects, at seven to eight years they may perform this task more accurately than do adults.[24] Perhaps therefore we must conclude that children gradually acquire general schemes of the relationship of sizes of objects to their surroundings at varying distances. These develop comparatively early for near objects, but later for distant objects; and the children are less adept than are adults in utilizing this knowledge for making exact assessments of size in experimental situations.

2 · PERCEPTION OF COLOUR

It seems doubtful whether young children perceive and discriminate colour as such, just as they fail to perceive and discriminate shape as such. Of course little children are attracted by bright saturated primary colours, and prefer them to sombre or pastel colours.[25] Indeed, it seems possible that the primitive response to colour is one of emotional excitement, and that it is not until the child is older that he thinks about colours and observes them at all accurately. However, that he does differentiate them to some extent was shown in an experiment in which a spot of coloured light was moved to and fro on a background of a different colour – for instance, red on green, yellow on green, etc.[26] Even children as young as fifteen days followed the moving spot with their eyes, showing that the two colours were differentiated. Another experiment showed that infants of about three months gazed longer at a piece of coloured paper than at an equally bright piece of grey paper.[27] From six to fourteen months of age they showed increasingly strong tendencies to reach for a coloured disc than for a grey one. Red was the favourite colour, followed by yellow, blue, and green. When shown pairs of colours and asked to say which they preferred, rather older children liked red best but yellow least of the four primary colours. By school age, blue was the favourite. Possibly yellow attracted the younger children more than did blue or green because it is lighter and brighter; but to the older ones it appeared insipid.

It may be that accurate perception and discrimination of colour do not develop until the child can name the colours, although he may be able to carry out simple matching of primary colours before this. When children of two years were required to match and to name the four primary colours, red, blue, yellow and green, it was found that they could match correctly in about half the number of trials, but name correctly in only about a quarter.[28] In general, naming of colours is developed later than naming of familiar objects. Red is the earliest to be named correctly. The name 'blue'

is also learnt early, but sometimes simply as the opposite of
'red'; thus all colours other than red may be named 'blue'.[29]
Names may tend to be associated with particular objects;
for instance, 'yellow like an egg'. Again, in their drawings
children of four to seven years habitually associate certain
colours with certain objects; the sky is always bright blue,
trees have brown trunks surmounted by masses of green, and
so on. This again indicates that the child is slow to abstract
colour as an independent and variable quality, and regards it
as an inherent characteristic of certain particular objects,
when he notices it at all.

Several experiments have been carried out to discover
whether children of various ages seem to attach more importance to the shapes or to the colours of objects. In one of
these experiments, they were shown two solid blocks of
different shapes and colours.[30] Then a third block was
presented resembling one of the pair in shape and the other
in colour; and the child was asked which of the pair the third
was like. The great majority of the youngest children, aged
two to two and a half years, matched the third block with the
one of similar shape. But the number who matched according
to colour increased up to four and a half years, when three-
quarters of them made this choice. After that age, the number
of colour choices decreased continuously until with adults
nearly all the matches were made according to shape. It
should be noted, however, that this is essentially an artificial
situation, at least for the younger children. They were
forced to make a choice between characteristics which they
do not usually notice clearly. If an experiment of this kind is
carried out with differently coloured pictures of real objects,
children almost invariably match according to the shape
characteristics upon which the identity of the objects
depends.[31] This substantiates the view that young children
pay comparatively little attention to colour as such when they

are concerned in the normal everyday life situation of identifying and reacting to things. This is essentially a different process from the primitive emotional reaction to colour.

CHAPTER 7

THE PERCEPTION OF SPECIAL TYPES OF MATERIAL

I · PICTURES

IN the civilized state, man makes so much use of shapes drawn on flat surfaces that his ability to comprehend these has reached a high degree of efficiency. In particular, he has developed the capacity to utilize such material *symbolically*, to suggest or indicate concepts and ideas which have become conventionally associated with it. But this capacity must be learnt, and the child acquires it only gradually, and sometimes only after much teaching. The more abstract and remote the connexion between the shapes drawn on paper and the meanings and ideas with which they are associated, the greater and more prolonged the effort to understand and utilize it. In this sense, the perception and understanding of pictures, printed words, and diagrams form a succession, each more difficult than the last.

We have seen that the child acquires the ability quite early in life to recognize and identify from pictures objects with which he is familiar, because he so frequently encounters such pictures. Thus by the age of two to three years he can identify and name correctly pictures of single objects; and pick out and name correctly three objects from the fairly complicated pictures used in the Terman-Merrill test of intelligence.[1] As he grows older, he learns to describe pictures in more detail, and by the age of seven he may be able to say something about the more obvious activities of people in the picture. But if the picture has a 'meaning' in the sense that it suggests events not actually depicted, he may not be able to understand this until he is about eleven years old. The Terman-Merrill test contains a picture of a telegraph boy whose bicycle wheel has come off, and he is waving to a car to stop and give him a lift. The average child is not able to give this meaning until he is twelve. Moreover, younger children do not always notice those items in a picture which appear to us to be important and central to the incidents depicted. They may ignore them, and yet notice relatively unimportant details. For instance, in a picture used by the author of a fight, beer spilt from a broken bottle on to the floor was one of the items most frequently mentioned by children of nine or ten, though this item was not of any particular importance to the main subject of the picture.[2]

These observations are discussed in some detail because of the importance attached in modern educational methods to 'visual aids'. Showing pictures of historical scenes or of people living in foreign countries to children aged under eleven may not give them any clear idea as to the incidents depicted. The children may be confused by the unfamiliar costumes and settings, and have no more than the vaguest notion of what the people are like or what they are doing. Or the children may notice only things which are familiar and comprehensible to them. Thus the teacher cannot assume that schoolchildren will really understand what she teaches them simply because she shows them pictures. It is necessary to explain what is happening in the pictures – still more to get the children to talk about them until they show that they really grasp the significant features.

An interesting example of the extent to which children take in information displayed in pictorial posters was given by a schoolmaster who asked groups of secondary modern schoolchildren questions on such information.[3] Some of these posters had been displayed in the school hall or corridors, some in the children's own classrooms. The children had not as a rule been specifically instructed to study the posters, and in some cases the amount they had noticed and remembered was very small. When they were asked to name a country shown on two posters which had been in the hall for three months, only thirty-six per cent answered correctly. Only about one per cent could answer the question: 'Of what modern city is there a photograph in the geography room?' However, when photographs in the geography room relating to the Oil Industry were actually discussed with two classes of children, a week later sixty-six per cent of these children could name the industry correctly; whereas among those who had not had their attention drawn to the photographs, only twenty-three per cent could do so. Of course in this investigation we are dealing with the effect of combined processes of perception, attention, and remembering. But we may perhaps conclude that the relevant information displayed in this way must be firmly impressed on the children's minds if they are to assimilate and remember this information.

2 · FILMS AND TELEVISION

Some caution is also necessary in the use of films and television programmes for instructional purposes. It is true that the movements depicted in films produce an impression of vitality and immediacy which is lacking in still pictures. Thus children are usually interested and attracted by films, and may therefore be stimulated to attend to them more closely than to material presented in other ways. As we shall see below, attention and motivation affect perception considerably. Clearly also living processes, actions, and scenes which the children could be shown in no other way, can be presented in this medium. But this does not guarantee that the children, and especially the younger ones, will really understand what is going on, particularly with quite unfamiliar scenes and events. Moreover, it has been found that in some cases isolated facts and events are noted and remembered – occasionally indeed irrelevant ones – but the children cannot reason about these, nor make inferences from them. Sometimes films of animal life are 'anthropomorphized' to make them more appealing; the animals are depicted as if they were people.[4] Such films are more readily remembered than purely factual ones; but the ideas derived from them may be distinctly erroneous.

Experiment has shown that the verbal commentary of a film is of the greatest importance to the understanding of its meaning, and to the gaining of any knowledge from it.[5] The commentary can pick out and emphasize important points in the film sequence, explain anything difficult or unusual, comment on the general ideas behind the film and on what has gone before, and discuss the relationship of the people in the film to one another, and why they behave as they do. In short, as we have emphasized before, the meaning of any pictorial material is inferred, and not directly stated as it can be in the verbal commentary. In using films for teaching, it is desirable for the teacher to introduce the film and discuss it afterwards with the children in order to ascertain whether they have in fact understood and remembered the important points. In one investigation on science teaching, films were shown which directly related to the children's text-books.[6] This procedure was most effective; the children taught in this way not only learnt more facts, but were also better able to reason about them and make inferences from them.

Adults also can gain information from films about topics with which they were previously unfamiliar. But intelligent interest is necessary to produce such learning. Furthermore, there is evidence to show that if the films are such as to arouse their emotions, their recollections may be distorted in that information towards which they are favourable is over-emphasized, whereas that which tends to arouse their dislike or hostility may be either ignored or forgotten.

It has often been advocated that films should be used for instruction in practical tasks – in manipulating and constructing objects, assembling and operating machinery, etc. The idea is that if someone actually sees a task being performed, he will be able to copy the procedure and then perform it himself. If the individual is intelligent and the task a simple one, then in fact he may be able to do this, particularly if he is shown the film more than once. But if any pieces of difficult manipulation are involved, or if intricate constructions or machinery are employed, he will be apt to miss the point, become confused, and be unable to carry out the task himself.[7] Again experiment has shown that the verbal commentary is of paramount importance in describing how these difficulties should be met, and in discussing the relationship of one part of the task to the next, or of one piece of the machinery to another. It has indeed been found that in some cases it may be more instructive to show still pictures or diagrams with a good verbal description than a film without one. This again is because the viewer has to formulate the 'meaning' or purpose of a sequence of operations in relation to the task as a whole, and to give himself instructions as to how to proceed when he is performing it himself. The commentary can be of the greatest assistance to him in doing this.

In television programmes, action and movement again produce a liveliness which readily interests and attracts attention.[8] By contrast, static scenes appear flat and dull, and may not be well perceived. An added advantage in many programmes may be an impression of reality and topicality which stimulates the viewer by making him feel that he is right in the centre of important events. But again unusually vivid and emotional incidents may distort the assimilation of the content of the programme as a whole; attention becomes focused on such incidents and they are liable to be remembered in isolation from the remainder, which is ignored or forgotten. As with films, a clear, coherent, and logical verbal commentary is essential, especially in programmes which require intelligent understanding and are not purely descriptive. It is also most important that the commentary and the visual material should exactly correspond and be integrated with each other; otherwise confusion and distortion are certain to occur.

3 · READING

The ability of the young child to understand fully simple pictures of actions and events may also be of some importance when he first begins to learn to read, since the commonest method of teaching reading nowadays is to attach words to pictures of objects and activities as names. In the first place, if the pictures are at all complicated, the child may not notice the significant features; or he may be accustomed to call them by some other name than the one shown, which naturally confuses him. Again explanation is necessary, and frequent repetition of the name shown, before the child can begin to associate what is spoken with what is printed.

But we have also seen that young children have much difficulty in perceiving the essential characteristics of meaningless shapes drawn on paper. Therefore it is not surprising that the process of teaching them to recognize the important features of printed letters and words may be protracted. In pursuance of the idea that children perceive 'wholes' rather than parts or details, the teaching of reading is often begun by presenting whole words rather than isolated letters for recognition. This method also has the advantage that the words can be spoken, and that these spoken words have meanings which are immediately familiar to the child; whereas letters by themselves are meaningless to him. But the characteristics of whole words are not at all clear and obvious, and thus it is difficult for him to remember them apart. The tendency is for the child to recognize words partly by means of their general outline and length, and partly by means of characteristic letters, such as the first and last letters, or letters of peculiar shape such as 'g' and 'y'. In this way, he learns to recognize a few whole words at a glance. But sooner or later, in order to perceive the essential structure of words he has to learn the characteristics of isolated letters and the manner in which they are combined in different words. This necessitates differentiating letters which are often similar in shape, particularly the reversed letters 'b' and 'd' and 'p' and 'q', and the inverted letters 'n' and 'u'. He then has to learn that each of the letters has one or more associated sounds; and that the sound of the whole word is made up of the appropriate letter sounds in the correct order. When, and only when, he has achieved the total word sound, he will know its meaning, given by its meaning in speech.

We noted that the perception of spatial position and of order or arrangement was itself difficult for the child; and the remembering of these characteristics is still harder. Thus confusions over order of letters in the word are even more difficult to eradicate than confusions over letter shapes. Even in normal children learning to read is a slow and arduous process, which requires considerable skill in teaching. And since the majority of children are taught to read in large classes, often by inexperienced teachers, it is not surprising that their particular difficulties are often overlooked. However, most children, when they are not handicapped in other ways, do learn at least to recognize words, even though slowly, while they are in the infant and junior schools.

But reading a continuous text in order to understand its

meaning is a much more complex procedure than recognizing the consecutive words one by one. We assume that the normal education of children is adequate to enable them to do this. But when studies are made of older children and adults, this often appears insufficient. They may retain the childish practice of reading one word at a time; hence their reading is so slow and laborious that they have some difficulty in relating together the meanings of separate words to arrive at the meanings of whole sentences and larger units.

It might be supposed, from this enumeration of the difficulties which the child encounters in learning to read, that even adult reading would be a slow process. In fact, as we know, for the literate adult it is nothing of the kind. Indeed, it has been shown in experiments in which letters and words are presented tachistoscopically that letters can be perceived more rapidly than meaningless figures.[9] Again, words can be read more rapidly than isolated letters in jumbled order. This is because we have become extremely familiar with the words of our native language and the kind of structure they possess. The probability of such structures occurring is high, and therefore once we have seen one or two letters, we expect the remainder. An experiment was carried out in which four groups, each of eight-letter nonsense syllables, were presented, one at a time, in a tachistoscope.[10] In the first group, the nonsense syllables consisted of letters selected completely at random; in the second, of letters selected from a written text, so that the commoner letters occurred more frequently; in the third, of pairs of letters selected from a text; and in the fourth, of sets of four consecutive letters found in a text. The number of letters perceived correctly increased regularly from the first to the fourth group. This showed that we acquire a notion of the probability of occurrence of certain letter sequences in words; and having seen the earlier letters in the sequence are expecting the later ones to appear. Whole words are of course even more familiar and therefore more easily perceived.

In reading a continuous text, the reader possesses in addition a knowledge of the familiar structure of the English language and of its most probable sequence of words. Thus once he has read a few words of the sentence, he can guess with fair accuracy what the remainder of the sentence may be. This is even more likely to occur in reading a continuous text on some familiar subject, since he then possesses expectations as to the general content. Thus we find that the literate adult does not even look at many of the words in such a text. Four or five brief glances at each line of the print are sufficient to produce enough perceptual impression to be filled out in the light of the meaning of the context. It is often a surprise to people to learn that in reading the eyes do not move smoothly and regularly along the line of print. In fact, they move in a succession of short jerks, stopping at one point after another along the line; and perception takes place only during the pauses, not during the movements. For rapid readers, the pauses may be relatively infrequent. At each pause, which lasts only a fraction of a second, not more than two or three words can be perceived directly. Thus many of the words, falling in the spaces between pauses, are not perceived at all, and others only marginally. A great deal of the text is thus inferred from what are little more than outline or skeleton percepts, filled out from the reader's knowledge of the text.

Sometimes it is true that the reader overreaches himself, loses the thread of the argument, and is forced to 'regress' or go back to look at the words again. If he encounters an unusual word, or a difficult passage, or even one which causes an emotional shock, he may pause and regress several times in the same area. In a slow inefficient reader, or one who has difficulty in understanding what he reads, pauses and regressions will be frequent. But this does not mean, as some people have claimed, that reading can be improved simply by forcing the reader to move his eyes at a regular pace – for instance, by using a device which exposes small groups of words successively at uniform speed, so that he can see only a few at a time and must then go on to the next group. He needs to acquire greater skill in grasping the meaning of sequences of words from the printed text; or in understanding the content of what he is reading. It is true that devices of this kind sometimes appear to have a stimulating effect, demonstrating to the reader that he can in fact, if he chooses, read much more rapidly than he supposed possible.[11] He may then, by making an effort, transfer the increase of speed to his ordinary reading; but there is always some danger, particularly with more difficult reading matter, that in doing so he will go too fast and fail to assimilate the meaning.

There is no doubt that adults, and even highly educated adults, vary greatly in the speed and efficiency of their reading. Some proceed very slowly throughout; others dash along too quickly and then have to regress. Poor readers in particular may lack the ability to vary their manner of reading according to the type of reading matter and to their intentions in reading it. A good reader can move at great speed through the text of a novel or similar light reading matter. He may be able to skim a page, picking up a word or two here and there, and gain a general idea of what the text is about without really reading it. In reading more difficult material, with the intention of taking in the whole of it, he will proceed more slowly; but even then he will vary his pace, concentrating on the key words and passages, perhaps rereading them several times, and passing more quickly over the remainder. A less efficient reader tends to maintain the same speed whatever the material he reads. Consequently even light reading matter gives him little pleasure because he reads it so slowly. But this pace may be too fast for really difficult material which requires special concentration at particular points.

A type of reading which necessitates careful attention to detail is proof-reading, in which the reader, in order to detect misprints, has to notice not so much the meaning of what he reads as the exact shapes and order of letters and words in the text. This is extremely difficult for most people, since they have become accustomed to overlook such details. In fact, considerable practice is required to perform this task efficiently; and it can be done only by reading very slowly, and by paying comparatively little attention to the general meaning of the text.[12]

4 · OTHER SYMBOLIC MATERIAL

There are other rather similar types of skill which we acquire in the perceiving and understanding of symbolic material; for instance, in reading numbers, equations, and formulae. Here also the highly trained individual develops a rapid speed of reading; whereas the tyro, or the individual who does not fully understand this material, makes numerous pauses and regressions.

Other types of symbolic material which are constantly used in scientific work, and which appear more and more frequently in everyday reading, are diagrams and charts of various kinds. Sometimes they are used in teaching children, again with the idea that they will learn more from seeing information displayed graphically than from merely reading about it. But even simple diagrams such as cross-sections of solid objects may be quite difficult for them to understand. Thus children aged ten to fourteen years were shown cross-sections of a doll and a stand, and required to match these to the three-dimensional drawings of these articles.[13] Only 8·4 per cent of all these children made perfect scores, and thirty-eight per cent scored little or nothing; though the older children did better than the younger ones. But after a period of instruction as short as ten minutes, even the youngest improved their scores considerably.

Again, it is customary to show children pictorial charts illustrating successions of historical events; or related geographical features; or technical processes in science or in manufacture. The meaning of these also is not always obvious to children. Many of the charts used in schools are too crowded and complicated for children to understand even after they have been explained. The same group of children who were tested with the cross-sectional diagrams were also shown a process-chart of the flow of wheat through a flour-mill, and were asked to mark the point of entry, direction of flow, and point of exit of the wheat.[14] Only twenty-five per cent of the whole group could do this; and though again the older children performed better than the younger ones, only about forty per cent of the former were completely correct. When various explanatory labels and arrows were added to the chart, performance was improved. But there were still many of the children who ignored these altogether.

Because people often fail to understand tables of numerical data – and indeed may find them definitely repugnant – such data may be presented to them graphically. For instance, information about population (births, diseases, deaths, occupations, etc.) or about financial and economic operations is often displayed in diagrams or graphs. These have a definite value in that they present a large amount of numerical information simultaneously in a small area of space. It also appears at first sight that the individual may perceive this information directly, without having to go through the series of arithmetical computations necessary to extract the information from a table of figures. But this is to suppose that immediate visual perception of the shapes of graphs and diagrams is the same as understanding the meaning that they are intended to convey. The author found that grammar schoolchildren, and even young adults, when shown material of this kind (see Fig. 25) could see that there

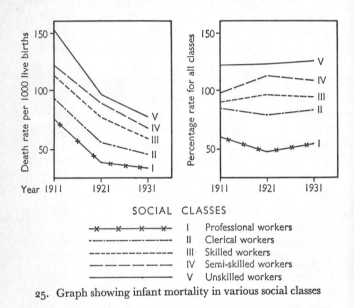

SOCIAL CLASSES

—x— x— x— x—	I	Professional workers
·—·—·—·—·—	II	Clerical workers
– – – – – –	III	Skilled workers
— — — — —	IV	Semi-skilled workers
————————	V	Unskilled workers

25. Graph showing infant mortality in various social classes

were lines and curves going in different directions.[15] But because they had not been taught to do so, they were unable to make out what these meant in relation to the data they presented. Sometimes people can be considerably misled by seeing graphs uncritically. Thus in the past Conservatives and Socialists came into conflict at a General Election over a graph the scale of which had been so graded as to make it appear that there had been an extremely steep rise in the cost of living under Labour Government. Plotted on a different scale, the graph showed only the slightest increase!

Some fifteen or twenty years ago, another type of graphical presentation was invented in which numerical data were shown in 'Isotype', as groups of little men, etc. Fig. 26a is a chart based on information in a Government White Paper showing the number of men employed in various types of occupation during the Second World War.[16] Fig. 26b shows the corresponding graph of the same data. These were used by the author in an investigation carried out to discover how well they were understood by people of different degrees of intelligence and amount of education. It had been supposed that because these charts somewhat resembled ordinary pictures, therefore anyone who studied them would be able to perceive and understand them, not as collections of little men, etc., but as data on the frequencies with which people performed the activities shown in the chart. It is true that, particularly when they first appeared, the novelty of these charts aroused people's curiosity, and therefore they possibly devoted more attention to them than they would have given to conventional diagrams or tables of figures. But, as the author found in her inquiries, a mere study of the charts and perception of the pictorial shapes they showed was no guarantee that their meaning would be understood. Such understanding necessitates a reasonable intelligence and some special training in how to interpret them.

It is not uncommon to make use of diagrammatic material in instructional television programmes, when it is desired to give a general scheme of events which cannot be directly illustrated; or when numerical data are to be presented. Very simple charts and block diagrams must be used, and they must be carefully explained, since the viewer has no time to study and think about them. But it has been found

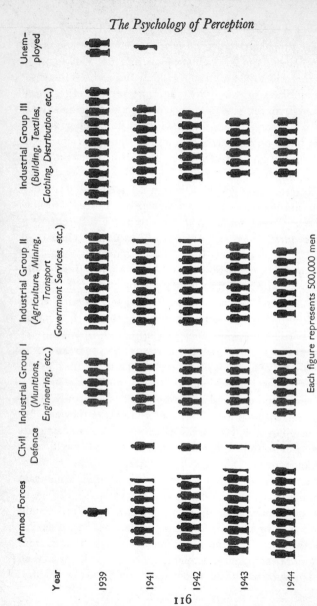

Each figure represents 500,000 men

26a. Chart showing number of men aged 16–64 years in various occupations

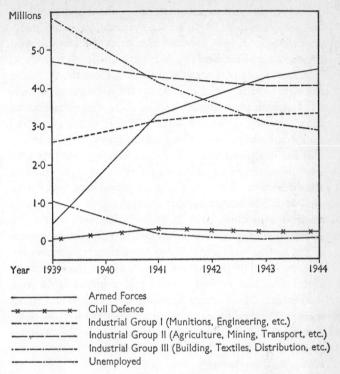

26b. Graph showing number of men aged 16–64 years
in various occupations

possible to enliven such diagrammatic material by introducing movement; for instance, moving arrows to indicate
direction; movement within the blocks to show change of
quantities; or even a speaker who moves pieces about and
fits them together as in a jig-saw puzzle.[17] All these devices
are effective in arousing attention which may produce more
accurate perception and remembering, provided that they
are simple enough to be readily understood.

Further data showing the necessity of teaching people to understand material which is not pictorial or immediately representational were obtained in a series of observations on the teaching of medical students as to how to perceive and interpret X-ray photographs of the hand and thorax.[18] The students were required to describe the differences between pairs of such photographs, and to make certain inferences from their descriptions. It was found that students who had no special training in making such observations frequently failed to describe accurately and objectively what they saw, but instead tended to make false inferences as to the source of the differences – for instance, 'A is a young hand and B is an old hand.' These were in fact assumptions which were based on irrelevant clues, such as the relative sizes of the two X-ray photographs. Classes were held in which the differences in description and inference made by different students were discussed, and the importance stressed of objectively accurate description and critical weighing of evidence in making inferences.[19] The students became more cautious and learnt to make fewer but more accurate inferences. It is clear, therefore, that they required training first in the accurate perception of material such as this; and secondly in reasoning about the data given.

However, it has been found that even experts may disagree in the inferences they make from visual material which is not directly representational. Experts in the diagnosis of tuberculosis from radiographs of the thorax were found to vary considerably in their judgements.[20] Thus one picked out fifty-six radiographs as indicating signs of tuberculosis, and another a hundred. There were also considerable discrepancies in the judgements made by the same men viewing the same photographs again two months later. These findings indicate that even when observers have been suitably trained, there is still considerable variability in the manner in which they select from a complex visual field, and in the significance they attach to what they select. We shall discuss these individual differences and variations in perception more fully in later chapters.

CHAPTER 8

THE PERCEPTION OF SPACE

WE must now consider an extremely important type of perception, the perception of the position of objects and their spatial relations to each other, to the perceiver and to the general surroundings. We noted above that people were more clearly aware of what was called the 'figure' than of the 'ground'. And indeed we are apt to take the 'ground' for granted, and with it our knowledge of the spatial relations of objects, and pay little conscious attention to these unless we wish to make a definite judgement – 'A is to the right of B' or 'C is about a hundred yards from here'. Yet in fact in all our actions we demonstrate that we perceive accurately the position of the body in space and positions of objects in relation to the body and to one another. Were it not so, we should have difficulty in remaining upright and also in avoiding objects as we moved about, and in gauging their movements in space.

I · HORIZONTAL AND VERTICAL ORIENTATION

To a great extent the conviction that we possess as to the permanence and stability of objects is due to the fact that we perceive them in a stable relation to the spatial background. They are distributed around us in space, above and below, to left or right, and at certain distances away from us. When we move about, they retain the same relative orientation – the same positions in relation to one another, to the horizon, and to the vertical co-ordinate perpendicular to the horizon, which we can perceive in upright objects such as buildings, trees, etc. We also relate the position of the body to the horizontal and vertical co-ordinates of space, not only through visual perception of the surroundings but also by means of certain sensations arising in the interior of the body through the pull of the force of gravitation. We possess in the ear an organ called the 'labyrinth' which registers accurately all movements of the head from side to side and up and down; and which indicates when the head is no longer parallel to the direction of gravitation. Again, whenever the body is tilted from the upright position, the gravitational pressure on the joints of the limbs is altered, and the tension of the muscles on either side of the body changed. The sense organs in the joints and muscles respond to these changes, sending appropriate sensory messages to the brain. Within the brain is co-ordinated the information given by sensations from the eyes, the labyrinth, the muscles, and the joints as to the position of the body in space in relation to gravitation. If this position is unstable, nerve impulses promptly proceed from the brain to the muscles, causing them to adjust the head, body, and limbs in such a way as to stabilize it. Thus if we are in a vehicle which tilts to one side, we automatically adjust the position of the body until it is vertical, by means of 'postural reflexes' – the immediate reflex responses to sensations of change of position. In this way we compensate for alterations in the position of the body caused by outside forces, or by the movements we ourselves make in running, climbing, swimming, skating, riding a bicycle, etc. And in addition we maintain the stability of our impressions of space and of the spatial position of objects through the information given us as to the orientation of the body to the horizontal and vertical co-ordinates of space. In other words, we assume that our bodies are moving, while the spatial surroundings remain motionless.

But there are circumstances in which we lose this impression of stability in our spatial surroundings, and our awareness of the position of objects and of the body in space. This may occur when the normal sensory data relating to spatial position are lacking, for instance in complete darkness. We may forget where objects are, especially if we ourselves move, or even think that stationary objects are moving. Thus if a small stationary point of light is viewed in an otherwise dark room, it may after a time appear to wander about irregularly, though curiously enough not to change its position. This so-called 'auto-kinetic movement' appears to be due to the fact that the eyes have no visual spatial 'framework' to which they can anchor themselves; and slight tremors of the eye muscles cause them to lose their fixation, resulting in perception of movement of the point of light.

Again, if in a dark room a stationary point of light is surrounded by a luminous rectangular outline which is moved to and fro, the point of light will appear to move and the rectangle remain stationary.[1] The rectangle has taken on the function of spatial framework; we assume that such a framework would normally be immovable, and therefore the movement is attributed to the small point of light. Sometimes the phenomenon is accompanied by sensations of movement of the body, even by disorientation and dizziness, because the normal relation between the position of the body and the perceived spatial framework has been interrupted. The perceived movement of the framework is attributed to the body also.

Similar effects may occur in daylight on board ship in a rough sea, in flying, and when being whirled round on a merry-go-round or other devices familiar to fair-goers! On board ship the body is exposed to unexpected oscillations and changes of position, and cannot adjust itself rapidly enough; hence the disorientation and sea-sickness. In flying, rapid and unfamiliar vertical movements of the body are experienced, like those produced by rapidly descending in a lift, when it feels as if the body has been 'left behind' in space. Moreover, when the aircraft turns or spins rapidly, centrifugal forces set up by this motion conflict with the vertical force of gravitation, and the total pull on the body is tilted and no longer vertical. Thus the sensations from the labyrinth, muscles, and joints tend to cause an adjustment of the body into a tilted position which is not at right angles to the visually perceived horizon. In order to compensate for this, the horizon may appear to tilt sideways, producing a feeling of disorientation. Sometimes pilots who are novices in flying will fly their aircraft in a tilted position in order to compensate for the tilted forces pulling on the body. Even greater disorientation may result when the body is rapidly whirled round a vertical axis. The centrifugal force is so much greater than the gravitational force that the latter ceases to be felt, and vertical surroundings may appear horizontal. But if the movement is maintained over a period of time, and especially if the visually perceived surroundings are not very clear (as for instance, in the large barrel-shaped structures in which people are whirled round on fair-grounds), the individual may become temporarily adjusted to this peculiar condition and no longer feel disorientated.[2]

Numerous experiments have been carried out to determine the extent to which an individual's perception of the horizontal and vertical coordinates may be affected by some interference with the normal position of the body in space, and the visual and bodily sensations to which it gives rise. For instance, in experiments carried out by Witkin and Asch, observers were shown a luminous tilted rectangular framework in an otherwise dark room, and asked to set a moveable rod in what they thought was the true vertical position.[3] Sometimes they were required to do this while sitting in a chair which tilted the body to one side. It was found that some people were able to utilize the sensations of bodily position in relation to gravitation; they continued to see the luminous framework as tilted, and they made fairly accurate vertical settings of the moveable rod. Others, however, seemed after a time to cease responding to the bodily sensations of position; they perceived the framework as moving into a vertical-horizontal position, and they set the rod parallel to it and therefore tilted from the vertical. Still others experienced a conflict between the two sets of impressions, and had great difficulty in making any setting of the rod.

Other experiments have been carried out in which over a considerable period of time observers have worn continuously spectacles containing prismatic lenses which inverted the field of view, and everything looked upside down.[4] Not unnaturally these observers were at first completely disorientated; when they reached for something which appeared to be below them, they found that they should have reached upwards, and vice versa, and their movements became quite uncoordinated. After a time they became accustomed to the inversion, and their movements became more accurate and coordinated. But the field of view still appeared upside down. In another experiment, lenses were worn which reversed the field from left to right, so that surroundings appeared as their mirror images.[5] Some observers wore these spectacles for several weeks; and though at first they were always turning to the left when they wanted to go to the right, in time they became accustomed to the reversal and could move normally. Moreover, the surroundings also began to look normal again, and they actually perceived objects on the right as being on the right, and not reversed. This re-reversal, however, took place piecemeal, some parts of the surroundings looking normal and others reversed. For instance, the inscription on a building might appear to be in mirror writing while the building itself was normally orientated. Or common and familiar words were perceived and read normally, but if they were considered carefully and critically, they became reversed. However, the observers differed somewhat from each other in what they perceived. Finally, when the spectacles were removed, the surroundings, or parts of them, tended for a time to appear reversed in the opposite direction.

In a similar set of observations, lenses were worn for rather shorter periods which tilted the field of view through 20°. After the observer had become accustomed to walking, he found that when he stood up, a broad path ahead of him appeared flat, whatever the direction in which he looked; whereas the remainder of the field continued to appear tilted. It also remained uniformly tilted as long as he was seated.

These observations seem to show that through long experience we develop a habitual integration of the visual impressions of our surroundings and the bodily sensations of the position and movements of the body in space. Ordinarily this integration is stable, and upon it are based our impressions of a stable world of objects, in which our bodies move about. But the integration may break down under the impact of unusual or conflicting visual and bodily sensations relating to spatial position. However, after a time it may be possible to adapt ourselves, particularly through action, and develop a new type of integration – at first less stable than the old one, but presumably in time able completely to replace it. Our actions provide us with information as to the 'real' nature of the environment undistorted by vision; and this corrects the visual distortion.

2 · DEPTH AND DISTANCE

It might appear that the position of objects in relation to the horizontal and vertical coordinates of space would be perceived naturally and accurately because they are precisely reproduced in the retinal image. Although the dimensions of the retinal image do normally correspond fairly accurately to the dimensions of the visual field, this correspondence is not necessarily retained in those parts of the brain to which the retinal impressions are conveyed. In the first place, a relatively much larger area of the occipital cortex of the brain is devoted to impressions from the central part of the retina, the fovea, than to impressions from the peripheral parts. Thus that part of the field of view towards which the eyes are directed is as it were spaced out, while surrounding parts are compressed. Again, as we have already seen, the correspondence between the actual spatial position of objects and their perceived position may be altered in certain circumstances. And finally, there have been cases of injury to the occipital area of the cortex in which parts of the visual field projected to the injured areas appear distorted and pulled out of shape. Thus the relation of actual to perceived position is acquired and subject to modification, not built into the physiological structures of eyes and brain.

When we come to consider perception of the third dimension of space, depth, or distance, we realize at once that there can be no aspect of the retinal image which directly reproduces this. We are obliged to infer this dimension from certain characteristics of the retinal images and do not perceive it directly from these. Nevertheless the appearance of distance, depth, and solidity is as much an inherent feature of our ordinary perceptions of our surroundings as is the appearance of above and below, left and right.

The perception of the third dimension in space depends principally upon the fact that the two eyes are in different spatial positions, and therefore the images on their retinas are somewhat unlike. This unlikeness is known as '*retinal disparity*'. Thus if we hold up a cube in front of the eyes, the right eye will see slightly more of the side face on the right, the left eye slightly more of the side face on the left. Normally we are quite unaware of this unlikeness, and become conscious of it only by shutting first one eye and then the other, when the differences of the two images become apparent. In binocular vision, when both eyes are open, we see, not a double image or a blurred image, but a solid object with its sides receding in depth, so that some parts are farther away than others.

Another demonstration of this effect is given by the stereoscope. Photographs of an object or a scene are taken from two different points in space situated at a distance apart equal to the distance between the two eyes. In the stereoscope these two slides are shown one to each eye; the resultant impression is of a three-dimensional object or of a scene with depth effects.

The perception of three-dimensionality in fused disparate retinal images appears to be spontaneous and unlearnt. It develops during the first six months of life, as the infant acquires the ability to coordinate the movements of the two eyes and focus them accurately upon an object in front of and fairly near to him. In adults, three-dimensional stereoscopic perception can be instantaneous, taking place during a single flash of light. However, stereoscopic perception may be as rapid as this only when figures containing a large number of disparate features are used, such as photographs of scenes or real objects. The three-dimensional effect can occur when pairs of dots or of lines at different distances apart in the two slides are shown; but it will be slower and less certain in appearance. Even if certain distributions of black and white patches are presented such that no pattern is apparent in either of the separate stereoscopic slides, a pattern with a depth effect may be perceived binocularly in the stereoscope.

If two objects are at different distances away from us, then the distance apart of their two images on one retina will be different from the distance apart of their two images on the other retina. This phenomenon can be directly observed by focusing the eyes on a pencil held close to the face, while at the same time consciously observing more distant objects. The latter will appear doubled, since their images are falling on different, or 'non-corresponding', points of the retinas. Normally we do not notice this doubling, because we attend consciously only to the object upon which the eyes are focused. The non-correspondence of the images of other objects is perceived as a difference of distance. In fact we can make astonishingly accurate estimates of the relative distances of two objects looked at with both eyes. It is possible to check this by trying to thread a needle with one eye shut; the task, which could be carried out with both eyes open, becomes impossible with one eye, because there is no retinal disparity of the images.

Accuracy in estimating distance in binocular vision is enhanced by means of the convergent and divergent movements of the eyes in focusing on objects at various distances. The eyes converge or look inwards to focus on a near object. As the object recedes, they gradually diverge until they look in parallel directions at far distant objects. Sensory impressions are conveyed to the brain from the muscles which rotate the eyeballs in convergent and divergent movements. These impressions of alteration in tension of the muscles are accurately related to alterations in distance of the object upon which the eyes are successively focused. But the impressions of disparity and convergence are effective only over a distance of about a hundred metres, since with objects at greater distances both eyes look straight forward in parallel directions, and there is no disparity between the retinal images. As we shall see, there are other perceptual data which we utilize in estimating the distances of objects which are far away, or which are viewed monocularly.

Though the perception of stereoscopic depth effects seems to develop spontaneously, the accurate estimation of distance from binocular cues does depend on learning from experience. However, even in the first months of life the infant demonstrates that he is learning to estimate near distances fairly accurately by the manner in which he reaches out to grasp near objects, but not distant ones. He coordinates his visual impressions of distance with the information he obtains by stretching out his arms, and later by moving his body to and fro, to arrive at increasingly accurate estimates of distance of objects which are within his reach. But he is much slower to acquire the ability to judge longer distances. That even the estimation of short distances from binocular cues must be learnt is shown also by individuals who have been almost blind from birth with cataract. When the cataract is removed, they take time to acquire the ability to make such estimates.[6] Since disparity does not operate at longer distances, or when one eye is closed, we might expect that in such conditions our spatial surroundings and the objects in them would look flat, and that differences in distance would be imperceptible. But of course this is not so. In fact there is a number of ways in which distance can be estimated from the manner in which the appearances of objects change as their distance varies. As distance increases, their retinal images become smaller; details of shape and surface texture become blurred and invisible; they recede behind objects in the foreground which partially cover them. At long distances their outlines become hazy and their colours change at length to a more or less uniform bluish-grey, as the result of the interposition of layers of atmospheric haze. Thus we learn by experience to perceive these features as characterizing distant objects; and to some extent to relate degrees of change to actual distance. In particular, we can often estimate change of distance quite accurately from change of size of the retinal image; and if we are familiar with the size of an object when it is close to us, we can also estimate its absolute distance from us from the size of its retinal image at that distance. As we noted in Chapter 4, a change in size of the retinal image with increase in distance is not perceived as a change in size of the object, but as a change of its distance. So compelling is this tendency that if an object is viewed monocularly in a dark room, where its relation to its surroundings is not apparent, and its size is gradually increased or decreased, it may appear to advance or recede and remain constant in size.[7] A similar effect may be produced by changing the brightness of a surface viewed monocularly in an otherwise dark room.[8] In normal daylight, however, we perceive the gradually decreasing sizes and brightnesses of the retinal images of objects as 'perspective'; and the distance of any object can be estimated by observing its position in relation to this perspective view of the spatial surroundings. Even then, an object in strong brightness or colour contrast to its background may appear nearer than one which does not stand out in this way.[9]

An important feature of our perception of depth and solidity of objects is constituted by the shadows which are cast upon parts of them by the general illumination. Normally, shadows appear on the receding parts of objects, and indicate recession and hence solidity. Changes in the appearance of depth can be produced by altering the direction of the incident light. Parts of a surface in relief may be made to appear as if they protruded by directing light on to it from below, instead of from above, as is normal. If the observer views the surface through a small hole in a screen so that he cannot perceive the manner in which it is being illuminated, the appearance of shadow and relief is destroyed, and the shadows will be seen as differently coloured flat dark patches on the surface.[10] Again, if objects are enclosed in a hollow sphere with luminescent walls, so that they are equally illuminated on all sides, and are then viewed binocularly through two small holes in the sphere, they may altogether lose their appearance of solidity; and a ball, for instance, may look like a flat disc.[11]

In certain circumstances, other factors may be utilized in the estimation of distance. Thus when the eye is fixed on an object at a certain distance, the lens of the eye is focused to produce a sharp clear image on the retina. If the object moves backwards or forwards, the image becomes blurred and the lens must be adjusted by means of the contraction or relaxation of the muscles by which it is attached to the eyeball. In monocular vision, the relative distances of objects can be estimated, though not very accurately, by the changes in tension of these muscles produced by looking from one object to the other.

If two objects at different distances move to and fro with equal velocities across the field of view in a direction at right angles to the line of sight, the angular velocity of the nearer object will be greater than that of the farther, because the distance moved by the nearer subtends a greater angle at the eye than does the distance moved by the farther. Even when no other perceptual evidence is available, an observer can usually perceive that such objects are at different distances, by virtue of these different velocities; and after some consideration he may be able to judge which is the nearer, and even estimate their distances apart.[12] The same effect may be obtained if the objects are stationary and the observer moves his head from side to side.

Although none of these cues, other than binocular disparity and convergence, gives complete or reliable evidence as to the distances of objects, in normal everyday life many of them combine together to produce corroborative evidence which enables us to make reasonably accurate judgements of the distances of near objects, and to have at least some idea as to the spatial positions of far-distant objects. In particular, retinal size, brightness, clarity, and colour of objects decrease gradually but regularly as distance increases. We perceive our surroundings as a continuous pattern of objects and landscape features, graded in this way as they recede from near to far distance in perspective. Any particular object can be located within this perspective pattern, and its absolute distance from us judged accordingly. The effect of perspective gradient can be observed clearly on a receding surface such as that of a carpet with a regular pattern, or even of a rough piece of ground. The elements in the pattern or the surface texture of the ground become gradually smaller, less clear, and more compressed as distance increases; and from observing the gradient it is comparatively easy to judge the distance of any one part of the surface.[13]

Sometimes in making judgements of distance, we may have to rely on a reduced number of factors, or upon factors which give us erroneous information; and in such circumstances our judgements are liable to be vague and faulty. Thus it is difficult to judge the height of aircraft at all accurately because there is no gradual recession in perspective of objects between us and the aircraft. Again, the sky looks flattened at the zenith by comparison with the sky at the horizon, because this recession is apparent at the horizon but not at the zenith. Estimates of the distances of objects may be faulty when the atmosphere is foggy or unusually clear, because the atmospheric haze is much greater than usual in the first case, and much less in the second. We can learn to make allowances for these factors; but only prolonged experience of them would enable us to perceive distance accurately when they were operating.

Clearly then perception of distance depends to some

extent on our knowledge of the situation, and what we expect to perceive in it. This is illustrated by the fact that if we place two stereoscopic slides of a landscape scene in the stereoscope in reversed position, normal recession of distance is perceived; whereas if the observer were relying entirely on binocular disparity, he would perceive depth as reversed, with far objects in the foreground and near ones in the background.[14]

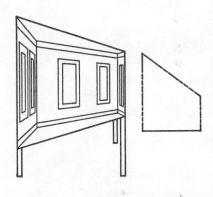

Seen from in front   Cross section
27. Diagram of the Ames 'distorted room'

Another instance of the effect of expectation has been demonstrated by Ames with the 'distorted room' (see Figs. 27 and 28).[15] This consists of a large structure made like the interior of a room; the observer looks at it monocularly through a peep-hole in one wall. In actual fact, the floor, ceiling, and end-wall of the room are sloped, and not at right angles to the other walls. Nevertheless, the retinal image produced in the single eye has the same dimensions as those of the image of a normal rectilinear room; and this is in fact what the observer perceives. But if the room is made large

28. Drawing of the appearance of the Ames 'distorted room'

enough for a child to stand in the nearer, down-slanted corner and a man in the further, up-slanted corner, the child actually looks larger than the man. Size is perceived in relation to perceived distance, which in this case is determined by the unequal dimensions of the room. This erroneous perception is extremely stable, and it requires prolonged practice before it can be corrected, by the observer touching the walls and ceiling with a pointer or bouncing a ball against them.[16] As in the experiments in which the distorting spectacles were worn (page 124), the observer has to establish new visual perceptions of space in relation to the movements he makes to estimate distance.

Since these perceptions depend upon learning from experience the relations between distances of objects and characteristics of size, brightness, colour, etc., it is understandable that children are relatively slow to acquire the ability to estimate long distances, since they cannot work out these relations for themselves by moving towards and away from far distant objects. They may 'cry for the moon' because for all they know or can perceive, it is no further away than a lamp hanging from the ceiling. However, when they become more mobile, and cover long distances in cars and trains, they perceive the gradual changes in the appearances of objects over long distances as they advance towards them or recede from them. At the same time, they also gradually acquire the ideas about the spatial relations of objects which we so commonly use in thinking about them. Thus when we learn to find our way about a neighbourhood, we develop a system of images and ideas about the relative positions and distances of roads, houses, and other natural features. For instance, we know that when we come to such-and-such a cross-roads we must then turn to the right and proceed until we reach a certain house (which we image), and then branch left – and so on. Most people can acquire such patterns of images and ideas; and they also learn to relate them to plans and maps which symbolize these topological relationships.

Yet there is evidence to show that a considerable degree of intellectual maturity is necessary before such ideas can be acquired. Piaget showed that children under the age of eight may have little idea as to the spatial relations of objects which they are not actually observing at the moment.[17] When younger children were shown a relief model of a landscape, with hills, trees, houses, etc., they were unable to choose from a number of photographs the one representing this model as it would appear if viewed from the other side. Again, when they were shown a similar model and asked to reproduce the arrangement of houses, etc., they could not place them in the correct spatial relationships to each other, before about ten years of age. Ability to reproduce by drawing even quite simple spatial arrangements was also acquired slowly. Objects situated on the side of a hill were drawn perpendicular to the hill, rather than vertical, up to the age of seven or eight years. Perspective drawings showed some change in the size of objects with distance, but nothing like the correct amount.

Some injuries of the brain prevent the development of normal perceptions of and ideas about spatial relations, or even destroy them when they have been acquired. Children suffering from cerebral palsy often have defects in their understanding of spatial relations, which seem to result from the disintegration of their percepts and their inability to relate parts to the whole.[18] In some adult cases of injury to the parietal area, which is adjacent to the occipital area, immediate perception of space and distance may be normal, but the capacity to think about spatial relations impaired. In one experiment, brain-injured patients were required to move about from one point to another in a room in accordance with the directions given in a simple map, such as those shown in Fig. 29.[19] Patients with injuries in the parietal area were less competent in performing this task than were other brain-injured patients. In other cases it has been found that a patient may be able to find his way about the ward of the hospital; he may even be able to find his way home from the hospital if he is sufficiently familiar with it.[20] But he may be unable to draw a simple plan of the beds in the ward, or a map of his route home. Even simple drawings of objects may show this lack of knowledge of spatial relations. Thus a

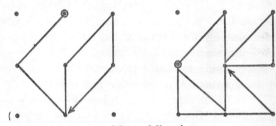

29. Maps of directions.
Nine points were marked on the floor. The patient
had to move as directed by the map

drawing of a horse had the neck separated from the body and the ears from the head. A drawing of a bicycle had the parts detached from each other and incorrectly juxtaposed. As the patient recovered, the drawings became more normal.

Thus the normal adult can extend and interpret his immediate perceptions of space by means of ideas and images which have become integrated with his perceptions. These he commonly uses without being aware of their value, which appears only when they have been lost, or failed to develop normally.

CHAPTER 9

THE PERCEPTION OF MOVEMENT

1 · THE BASIS OF MOVEMENT PERCEPTION

UP to this point we have considered mainly the perception of stationary objects of various kinds in relation to their surroundings. But in fact the perception of moving objects, and of various types of movement, is obviously vitally important not only to our knowledge of the world around us, but also to the preservation of life and safety. For this reason, it is not surprising to find that perception of movement constitutes a particular type of perception in itself, irrespective of the actual objects moving; and one which appears to be extremely primitive and very firmly ingrained among the perceptual processes. Almost as soon as he is born, the infant responds to the movement of objects close to his face, and, for instance, follows with his eyes the movements of something dangled in front of him when he appears to be unaware of the same object at rest.[1] The infant does this before he can focus his eyes accurately upon the moving object. So also when vision has been temporarily destroyed by injury to the occipital area of the cortex, one of the first types of perception to reappear on recovery from the injury is the perception of movement.[2] It is true that the retina itself is physiologically sensitive to changes in stimulation such as are produced by movements of retinal images. But this is not the sole explanation of the very rapid and immediate perception of movement as such. Psychologically, movement is of great significance to us, since any moving object may be potentially dangerous. Thus it is important that we should become aware of it at the earliest possible moment.

In this connexion, it should be noted that we very quickly become aware of movement at the margin of the field of vision, the image of which falls on the periphery of the retina. We noted in Chapter 4 that stationary objects were not at all clearly perceived when their images fell on the peripheral retina. But movement across this blurred field of view is perceived even when it is impossible to distinguish *what* is moving. And as soon as we become aware of such movement, we immediately turn the head and the eyes until its image falls on the centre of the retina. Then we can perceive clearly what has moved.

The perception of movement depends upon certain physical conditions. That is to say, the movement must attain a certain velocity before it is perceived as movement; at slower speeds, the observer will see an object in a succession of stationary positions, as with the moving hands of the clock. The minimum speed necessary for perceiving movement has been found to decrease with increasing intensity of illumination and also with increase in the time during which the moving object is exposed up to a duration of exposure of about eight seconds.[3] But if the observer views the object moving across a clearly perceived stationary background, the minimum speed for perception of movement is many times less than if he is shown simply a bright spot moving in a dark room, with no background perceptible. The contrast between moving object and stationary background makes the movement much clearer and more obvious.

Indeed, perception of movement is not produced primarily by the movements of the images of objects across the retina. We saw in the 'auto-kinetic' phenomenon (page 122) that movement was perceived when there was no movement or change of position of the object. Also the eyes are in fact always moving to and fro in the head, and thus images of stationary objects are constantly moving across the retina.

Even when we think that the eyes are at rest and that we are fixing them steadily on some point in the surroundings, they are making movements of three types: (1) a continuous small, very rapid, tremor; (2) a gradual slow drift across the field of view; this if continued indefinitely would alter the direction of the eyes, and therefore after a time it is followed by: (3) a rapid 'flick' bringing the eyes back approximately to their original position. The tremor is entirely involuntary and unconscious; but the drift and flick, although they are normally made unconsciously, can be to some extent controlled voluntarily.[4]

Why is it that our surroundings appear stationary although their images are always moving on the retina? It has been hypothesized that sensations to the brain from the muscles which rotate the eyeballs change continuously as the eyes move, and that these changing sensations offset and compensate for the changing retinal impressions. Another explanation is that the changing retinal impressions are compensated for in some way by an awareness of the motor impulses proceeding from the brain to the eye muscles which cause them to move the eyeballs. Whatever the explanation, it seems that we are able to differentiate between movements of the retinal images caused by movements of the eyes, and movements within the retinal image caused by movements of objects in relation to their surroundings, which appear stationary. It is these latter movements which we perceive and to which we attend with rapidity and ease, while remaining completely unconscious of the former. Also, we differentiate between the effects of to-and-fro parallel movements of the eyes, and convergent and divergent movements which, as we saw in the last chapter, are associated with changes in the distances of objects.

We may note in passing that the continual to-and-fro movements of the eyes have two important functions. The first is to preserve the sensitivity of the retinal cells, which is greater for changing than for unchanging stimulation. It has been found possible, by using a system of mirrors, to reflect on to the retina a small image of the field of view which moves as the eye moves.[5] Thus the image projected on to any one area of the retina remains unchanged. After a short time, as little as five seconds, this 'stabilized image' begins to fade from view; and then to regenerate and fade periodically. The retinal cells become adapted and cease to react; and cessation of response is followed by partial, but not complete, restoration of their sensitivity. In normal circumstances, the rapid tremor of the eyes produces sufficient variation in stimulation of the retinal cells to allow fairly adequate perception. But the 'flick' movements are even more effective; and it appears that they are necessary for maintaining the maximum sensitivity of the retina.

Longer movements of the eyes, and of the eyes and head together, have the second of the functions mentioned above. The area of the visual field which can be viewed at any one moment by the central area of the retina is very small. Other parts of the field are perceived with much less clarity, and as they gradually become more peripheral so they gradually shade off into invisibility. Yet we are not aware normally of any discontinuity in our view of the surroundings. We constantly scan the field, the eyes moving to and fro, and the successive images of different parts of the field are integrated together to produce a coherent impression of the whole surroundings, so that we think of them as consisting of a continuous series of objects in space all round us.

When an object begins to move across the field of view, the eyes will begin to move after it after a time interval of about 0·15 seconds, and will catch it up rapidly until they are centred upon it.[6] If the velocity of movement of the object is less than about 30° of arc per second, the eyes will then continue to follow the moving object smoothly, maintaining its image more or less in central vision. But at higher velocities these eye movements will be too slow, the image of the object will pass off the centre of the retina, and more rapid, jerky movements must be made in order to catch it up. If the head or the body is moved to and fro, then compensatory movements of the eyes are made in order to maintain their focus upon a fixed point in space. The giddiness and disorientations which occur in rapid forced movements of the body up and down or round and round appear to be related to the disordered eye movements made in unavailing attempts to focus the eyes upon some fixed point in space. Sometimes these become what is termed 'nystagmoid' – long, jerky, irregular, uncontrolled movements.[7] However, if the movement of the body is made regular and rhythmical, the eyes may then swing to and fro in comparatively smooth regular movements.

2 · PERCEPTION OF MOVEMENT IN RELATION TO THE SURROUNDINGS

We saw that the perception of movement was determined mainly by change of position of objects in relation to their background. This sometimes produces ambiguous effects, as when, for instance, the moon is seen among clouds moving across the sky; the moon may appear to move while the clouds remain stationary, because the latter form the general background in the field of view. Again, if we are sitting in a stationary train and another train to one side is moving past, we tend to perceive this latter train as stationary and the train in which we are seated as moving. This is particularly likely to happen if the moving train cuts out most of our view of the surroundings; it then forms the background which we assume to be stationary. Another instance of this phenomenon was given on page 122, in which a moving luminous framework surrounding a stationary point of light in an otherwise dark room was perceived as stationary while the point appeared to move. These examples demonstrate once again that perception of movement depends on the relative movements of objects and their backgrounds or surroundings, rather than upon the movement of images across the retina.

A complicated inter-relationship between the perception of the movement of the surroundings and the movement of the body is displayed in what is known as 'parallactic movement'. As we move forwards in a car along the road, the retinal image of the landscape in front of us expands, flows round on either side of us, and then contracts and becomes sucked in behind us.[8] This effect is not usually very noticeable in ordinary daylight, when the whole visual surroundings are perceived as rigid and stable while we ourselves move. But it may be apparent in driving at night, when the surroundings are not clearly perceived. Again, if we look at objects on either side of us, we may see them moving rapidly in the direction opposite to that in which we are moving; but the farther away they are, the slower the movement, and the horizon is stationary. In fact, the retinal image of the landscape is continuously distorted or deformed as we move. We are not consciously aware of this deformation, but perceive it in terms of our own movement across the landscape. But it is possible to utilize the deformation and the speed at which it occurs to estimate the distance of objects from us and the rate at which we are moving past them. This is a complex instance of the process described in the last chapter of estimating the relative distances of objects by perceiving their relative speeds of movement across the field. It seems possible that aircraft pilots can make use of these estimates to judge their height above the landing strip as they approach it. The point on the landing strip towards which the aircraft is directed in its downward glide will show no deformation; but surrounding areas will be deformed in a manner and at a rate depending on the height above the ground and the speed of the aircraft. The pilot can learn to perceive the deformation in terms of height and speed, and can thus regulate his approach accordingly.

We acquire the ability to judge the speed of moving objects with considerable accuracy in relation to our own movements. Thus we learn just when to intercept the flight of a ball; and how fast it is necessary to move in order to cross the road in front of an oncoming vehicle. However, it appears that these judgements do not depend only upon the actual speed of movement, but are also affected by the relation of the moving object to its background. Thus when an object moves across a homogeneous background, its velocity appears less than if it moves across a variegated background.[9] We noted above that the movement was also more easily perceptible. The movement is more readily contrasted with the stationary features of the variegated background, and is therefore more noticeable and appears faster. In a restricted field of view, perceived velocity may be related to the size of the object and the size of the field across which it moves. Thus if the size of the object is doubled and the field is also doubled in width, the speed may appear approximately double.[10] This phenomenon is rarely perceived in the large unrestricted fields of the everyday scene of life.

Although the perception of movement is so fundamental and primitive a phenomenon, it has been found that it is sometimes impaired by injury to the brain. In some cases of injury to the occipital cortex, it was found that the perception of the velocity of moving objects was quite inaccurate.[11]

3 · APPARENT MOVEMENT

But if there are circumstances in which real movement is not perceived in the normal manner, there is also a number of situations in which stationary objects are perceived to move. The most familiar example of this is to be seen in the cinema. The cinema camera photographs successive views of moving objects, each of these views recording the objects in slightly different spatial positions. The projector projects these photographs upon the screen at the same speed as the camera photographed them, and the succession of static views of the objects in different spatial positions is perceived as objects continuously moving. If the rate of projection is slowed down sufficiently, we can perceive the objects jumping from one position to the next. If the speed is greatly increased, the picture becomes blurred, because there is insufficient time for each successive view to clear up before the next one replaces it.

However, this phenomenon does not seem to depend simply on our familiarity with the movements of objects, and the fact that we are accustomed and expect to see objects moving rather than a succession of identical objects in different spatial positions. If two bright points or lines of light are exposed on a dark background at a certain distance apart, one immediately after the other, it is often possible to perceive a single point or line of light moving from the position of the first to the position of the second.[12] The movement will be clearer if the lines are alternated many times. The distance apart and the time interval between exposures of the two lights must, however, be arranged appropriately; and not everyone will perceive the movement, though they are more likely to do so if they expect it. Thus if successive exposures are given of a picture of a car crossing a bridge, movement is perceived more easily than if an oblong is shown in successive positions touching an arc shaped like the bridge.[13] Again, the perceived speed of movement may vary irrespective of the time intervals between successive stationary stimuli. A variation may occur in relation to the size of the field, just as in the perception of real movement.[14] An apparent movement vertically downwards tends to appear more rapid than a corresponding movement vertically upwards.[15] Silhouettes of darts and aircraft may appear to move more rapidly than silhouettes of discs.[16] A diagrammatic 'stick' man seems to move faster than a similar meaningless shape.[17] These variations parallel variations in apparent speed of really moving objects. If silhouettes of objects with a dynamic appearance, such as running people or horses, are pasted on a continuously moving strip of paper, their movement will appear faster than that of similar silhouettes of people and horses standing still.[18] This phenomenon is more marked with children and with imaginative adults than with other people.

A great deal of experimental work has been devoted to the study of the 'apparent movement' phenomenon, with the intention of showing that movement can be perceived as such – as a phenomenon in itself – depending only on the conditions of distance apart of the stimuli and time interval between them, and independent of the perception of any particular object in motion. It has been hypothesized that the necessary conditions for the perception of both real and apparent movement are changing patterns of retinal excitation occurring in the absence of the changing muscular sensations from the eye muscles which accompany a change of retinal stimulation produced by eye movement. Thus the physiological processes are much the same for real and apparent movement. In corroboration of this hypothesis, it has been found that adult brain-injured patients whose perception of real movement was impaired also found it difficult if not impossible to perceive apparent movement.[19] Children of eleven to fourteen years with brain lesions also had difficulty in perceiving apparent movement; and they ceased to perceive real movement when its speed was great, at a point at which it was still perceptible to children of the same age without brain lesions.[20]

Nevertheless, it seems that certain psychological factors may facilitate the perception of apparent movement. This phenomenon appears more obvious and impelling in circumstances in which it is expected to occur, as for instance when real movement of familiar objects is simulated; and this is apparent in brain-injured, as well as in normal, children. Again, it has been found that some people possess a tendency to adopt a critical or analytical attitude to the apparent movement phenomenon which precludes them from perceiving it in circumstances in which it would normally be seen.[21]

Another type of apparent movement which seems to be relatively independent of such psychological factors is known as the *after-effect of seen movement*. We are familiar with this in numerous everyday life situations. For instance, if we stare for a while at a rapidly moving river and then look away at the river bank, this may appear to move backwards in the opposite direction. Again, there is a laboratory demonstration of the phenomenon in which if a white disc with a black spiral pattern on it is rotated for a time and viewed steadily, the spiral will be seen to contract inwards. When the disc is suddenly stopped, the pattern appears to expand outwards. But the after-effect can be perceived also in a simpler arrangement in which a disc with a single radial line on it is rotated for about half a second and then stopped; experienced observers will then perceive the line moving backwards.[22] Curiously enough, the speed of this apparent movement is fairly uniform whatever the speed of the moving line. The effect appears to be produced by some form of adaption to the continuous movement of the stimulus; but its cause is not really understood.

4 · MOVEMENT AND THE APPEARANCE OF OBJECTS

Considered from another aspect, movement perception can sometimes be regarded as contributing to our awareness of real objects, in circumstances in which we might not otherwise perceive these. If a cinema film of people's activities is suddenly stopped, the people may appear not only motionless, but also flat and lifeless by contrast with the appearance of real life they possessed in the moving film. A simpler illustration of this phenomenon was demonstrated by casting the shadows of solid objects on a ground-glass screen which was then viewed from the other side.[23] When the objects were motionless, the shadows appeared to be those of flat shapes. But when the objects were rotated, so that their shadows moved continuously on the ground-glass screen, these were perceived as the shadows of solid objects. Moreover, if the objects then ceased to rotate, the shadows retained this appearance. It seemed as if the different aspects of the shadows perceived successively were integrated together into a pattern which was seen to correspond to the shadow of a moving solid. Another experiment showed that a flat illuminated surface rotated about an axis in an otherwise dark room retained a considerable degree of shape constancy; whereas the same surface when slanted sideways in a stationary position completely lost all shape constancy.[24] If the pattern on a surface was continuously transformed in such a way as to reproduce the kind of regular change in the pattern which would occur when the surface was rotated, then a tangible rotating surface was perceived; and its degree of slant at any one moment could be accurately estimated, especially if the pattern was a regular geometrical one.[25] The degree of slant of such a patterned surface when motionless could not be accurately estimated. If its pattern was completely irregular, the surface appeared to be at right angles to the line of sight. But if an irregular transformation was imparted to the pattern, the movement of certain parts being of a different type from that of other parts, an elastic distortion or bending of the surface appeared. This is the type of transformation we perceive in the movements of the face which occur in facial expression. If patterns were superimposed and each one transformed in a different manner, then there appeared to be two moving surfaces, one behind the other; whereas when there was no transformation, the patterns appeared to be intermingled. These observations all demonstrate the manner in which movement can suggest the existence of solid tangible objects which are not perceived in the absence of movement.

An illusory effect related to the continuous movement of a solid object was demonstrated by Ames. It was somewhat similar in nature to his illusion of the 'distorted room' (see page 133). A trapezoidally shaped framework with apertures like windows cut in it was rotated about a vertical axis in an otherwise dark room.[26] In general observers perceived it as an ordinary rectangular window frame oscillating to and fro. A rectangular frame would produce a trapezoidal retinal image when slanted; and the oscillation of such a frame would give rise to a succession of retinal images similar to those of the rotating trapezoidal frame. Since such a rectangular frame is much more familiar, the observers tended to perceive it in these circumstances. More curious, however, was the appearance of a tube which passed through one of the apertures in the trapezoidal frame; as the latter rotated, the tube appeared to bend to and fro. Presumably since it was the smaller of the two objects, its movements conformed to those of the larger and more inclusive frame.

It is interesting to note that African native boys living in rural areas were found to be somewhat less susceptible to this illusion than were white boys or Africans living in urban areas, presumably because the rural Africans were un-accustomed to perceiving rectangular windows and doors in their native huts.[27]

5 · IDEAS RELATED TO MOVEMENT AND SPEED

Up to this point we have considered the direct perception of movement. But, as with the perception of space, we acquire various concepts of movement associated with particular objects, and ideas about the speed and relative speeds of movements. Piaget found that children perceive movement at an early age, and also learn to estimate speed of movement in a practical way, so that they anticipate and avoid moving objects. But below the age of eight or nine the children were apt to be influenced in their judgements of the extent of movement by the total situation in which the movement occurred and were unable to analyse out its essential features.[28] Thus they sometimes said that the movement of the ascending car of a funicular railway 'went farther' than did that of the descending car because the former created the impression of greater effort. When two objects which started at the same point were moved, one along a straight path and the other along a very crooked path, a child asked to make the first one 'go as far' as the second usually stopped the former opposite to the latter, regardless of the different lengths of the two paths. Here he was unable to single out the features essential to making the judgement correctly. Relative speed was also little understood. One object was judged to move faster than another only when the former could be seen to go past the latter. Two objects arriving at the same place at the same moment were judged to move equally fast, no matter when or where they started. If two objects were made to rotate in concentric circles, starting and finishing at points opposite to one another, the children either thought that they moved at the same speed; or that the object on the inner circle moved faster because 'it had less to do'. These observations show that practical estimates of movement are not necessarily the same as abstract concepts and verbal formulations related to it.

6 · THE PERCEPTION OF CAUSALITY

The interplay between immediate perception and associated judgements also emerges in an interesting manner in connexion with the phenomenon of 'causality', and particularly with the perception of an object being 'caused' to move by the impact of another moving object. Piaget found that during the first year of life children were extremely interested in such phenomena, but that they had to learn by experience the conditions in which the phenomena appeared.[29] Probably the child first becomes aware of causality when he himself causes things to move by pushing, pulling, and shaking them. Such movements occur at first by chance, and then the child begins to produce them intentionally. Thus one of Piaget's children found at the age of three months that by kicking about in her cot she could make her dolls, which were suspended from a framework above the cot, move to and fro. This obviously pleased her, and she repeated the action many times. Another child, a month or so older, kicked the hanging doll when it was within reach of her foot and observed it swing. But she did not understand the necessity of some physical contact between the foot and the doll, for at another time she tried to make it move by wriggling and kicking without touching the doll. A boy of three months had a small rattle fastened to the framework over the cot, with a chain attached to it; pulling the chain shook the rattle. At first when the chain was put into his hand, he waved his hand about but dropped the chain. However, after a time he found that it was necessary to pull the chain in order to shake the rattle. At the age of seven months he saw his father drum with his fingers on a box. When his father stopped doing this, the boy tried to make the noise begin again by clapping and waving his own hands, as if to 'magic' the box at a distance. It was not until about a month later that he pushed his father's hand towards the box. Thus he was finding out that in order to cause events of this kind to happen, some sort of physical contact is necessary. But such events must be repeated again and again in different forms before the general principle is understood.

The realization that one must touch an object in some way to make it move precedes the understanding that one inanimate object must strike another, in direct physical contact, to make it move. Thus a little girl of one and a half years by accident pushed a chair which was touching an open french window and saw the window move; she then pushed the chair deliberately and obtained the same effect. But a little later she began pushing another chair some distance from the window, looking expectantly at the window as if waiting for it to move. Thus the impact of a moving body against another body, followed by the movement of the latter, is not at this age perceived directly as a causal phenomenon.

Yet it appears that in adults *mechanical causality* may be perceived from the contact of moving shapes even when no solid object actually strikes another one; just as in the perception of apparent movement, there is no moving object.

Michotte carried out an extensive series of experiments to determine the nature of the phenomenon of mechanical causality, and the conditions in which it appeared.[30] He used several ingenious devices, the essence of which was that a small coloured square was made to move across a screen and come in contact with another square which then moved in turn. When the speed of movement of the two squares was arranged appropriately, it appeared that the first square hit the second square and made it move away. The movement of the second square appeared to be caused by the impact of the first, though clearly there was no real impact as between two solid bodies. Michotte supposed that we have an innate tendency to perceive mechanical causality of this kind as a phenomenon in itself, irrespective of the nature of the moving objects, and indeed in the absence of any objects which could cause one another to move. To him, this type of perception was not simply an inference which we make on the basis of our experience of what happens when one object strikes another, because the situation in his experiments was so unlike those in which we normally perceive mechanical causality. Yet for causality to appear, the speeds and directions of movement of the two squares had to be similar to those which experience has shown are characteristic of the impact of a moving object on another object which causes the latter to move.

Later experiments have shown that, as with apparent movement, not everyone spontaneously perceives causality in situations such as those presented by Michotte, though they may do so when they expect it to happen. In one experiment it appeared that certain observers characteristically perceived causal phenomena in such circumstances, whereas others usually described objectively what happened.[31] Again, the phenomena were somewhat differently perceived by children of six to seven years.[32] In conditions in which adults perceived the first square hitting and propelling the second one, the children often saw the first square passing in front of the second one and proceeding ahead of it. Or in some cases the second square seemed to move backwards towards the first one, as in the apparent movement phenomenon. Piaget also found that in certain situations children of six to eight years perceived the causal phenomenon less readily than did adults.[33] In particular, adult observers sometimes obtained the impression that the first object was propelling the second even when they could see that the first object did not actually touch the second. For the children, perception of contact was essential. Thus the impression of causality is unlike the perception of apparent movement in that children appear to be more susceptible than do adults to the latter, but less susceptible to the former.[34]

Michotte found that other characteristic movement phenomena could be demonstrated by using similar techniques.[35] Thus if a black rectangle was shown moving across the field and expanding and contracting as it moved, it appeared to be propelling itself by its own movements. The phenomenon resembled that of a living object, such as a caterpillar crawling or a tadpole swimming. Other types of movement created the impression of human intention or purpose. Thus two squares moved towards a rectangle. When they were quite close, the leading square moved suddenly to the other side of the rectangle; both squares then closed in on the rectangle and moved backwards with it along the same path. The effect produced was of the squares purposively catching the rectangle, gripping it, and carrying it off. But this was not perceived by everyone who saw the phenomenon; and Michotte himself considered that the effect might be an inference based upon previous experience, rather than an immediate perception.

More elaborate patterns of movement of small circles or dots have also been studied, and it has often been found that the perceived pattern of movement differed very considerably from the actual physical movements of these objects.[36] Thus in a horizontal row of four dots, the first and fourth were made to move in circles, and the second and third to move up and down at the same time (see Fig. 30). But what observers perceived were synchronous up and down movements of all the dots, together with synchronous to and fro movements of the first and fourth dots. A number of complex movement patterns of this kind were shown; and it appeared that those in which movements were jerkier, with some dots

30. Apparent movement patterns

moving in directions opposite to those of other dots, were associated with mechanical movement such as that of piston rods in a machine; but smoother undulating types of movement were associated with the movements of living creatures. A small change in the relative directions of movement was thus sufficient to alter the type of movement perceived.

We may conclude from these various observations that for perception of movement certain physical conditions must exist – in particular, that it must be apparent to the observer that a fairly rapid change of position in some part of the field is occurring relative to the remainder of the field. But whether or not actual movement is perceived, and what type of movement is perceived, depend on the relation of this change to the general surroundings, or to other changes; and also on certain expectations on the part of the observers. In general these expectations are based upon the classification of types of movement which people acquire as they grow up. But there is some evidence to show that we have an innate and unlearned tendency to perceive the simplest type of movement; and that we may perceive this movement 'as such' and irrespective of any particular object in motion. The other more complex types of movement are, however, related to particular types of objects or situations of which they form characteristic features.

CHAPTER 10

ATTENTION AND PERCEPTION

1 · CONCENTRATION OF ATTENTION

WE have noted from time to time that what people perceive in any given situation may vary according to their previous experience, especially in so far as this affects what they expect to see. A very important instance of this variation arises in cases in which their attention varies. Attention is difficult to define; but we are all perfectly aware that when we wish to perceive something clearly and correctly, we concentrate our attention upon it. On the other hand, if we are idly contemplating the scene of view, with no great desire to perceive anything in particular, we may notice very little and overlook many things around us because, as we say, we are not attending.

In point of fact, the degree of attention may vary greatly from time to time, and with it the amount we perceive. We may concentrate upon a narrowly restricted view, as, for instance, in looking through a microscope, and perceive clearly and accurately almost everything within that field. If the field of view is wider, we may direct our attention upon one particular part of it, and in that case we are unlikely to notice much in the surrounding parts. Or we may look to and fro, deliberately picking out first one thing and then another. Or we may not be attending at all, but thinking of something other than the field of view. Then we perceive very little unless an event occurs which attracts our attention and forces itself upon our consciousness. We then concentrate on this event and endeavour to perceive it clearly. In all these cases, the total number of objects and events perceived varies, and the manner with which we perceive them.

Sometimes a pattern in the field of view may actually appear different when we attend to it 'figurally' and when we perceive it merely as the background of another figure. The *Gestalt* psychologists presented patterns made up of dots arranged in vertical columns and horizontal rows, and found that there was a tendency to notice either the rows or the columns according as to whether the dots were nearer together horizontally or vertically; that is to say, those in closer proximity to one another were grouped together. But it was necessary to make a considerable difference between the vertical and the horizontal separation of the dots before observers perceived the column or row structure. However, this structure was more readily perceived (with a smaller difference in separation) when the observers looked attentively at the dot pattern than when they perceived it merely as the background of another figure, superimposed upon it. This indicates that perceptual 'organization' of the field of view takes place more easily when it is attended to focally.

If the field of view is relatively unchanging, and we have plenty of time at our disposal, we may be able by glancing to and fro to perceive a great deal of it, though it is unlikely that we shall observe everything there. We tend to overlook anything relatively uninteresting and unimportant, unless it moves or changes in some way. But, as we saw, a sudden movement is likely to attract attention and stimulate us to try to perceive as clearly as possible what moved and how it moved. There are other events which produce a similar effect – bright lights or loud noises, for instance. As we shall see, these effects appear in part to result from certain concomitant physiological changes. Furthermore, they may be signals of something potentially dangerous to us. Therefore we are throughout life set, as it were, to become rapidly aware of such events, in order that we may respond to them and avoid them as quickly and effectively as possible.

There are other situations in which the time available to us for perceiving is extremely limited. If we know beforehand that this will be so, then we are able to concentrate our attention and make ourselves ready to perceive as quickly and accurately as possible. Obviously if we also know before-hand where to look, we shall perceive more than if we are obliged to waste time searching the field of view for the significant event. Moreover, the smaller the area which we are attempting to perceive, the greater the accuracy with which we shall perceive it. In experiments on tachistoscopic perception, such as those described in Chapter 4, the observer is directed to concentrate his attention upon what will appear within a limited area for a short interval of time. Thus he knows both where and when to look, and his perceptions within that area are maximally clear and accurate. But not unnaturally if attention is concentrated upon a particular point in the field of view, the perception of other parts of the field will be correspondingly less clear. Thus if letters or digits are presented in various positions in the field of view, and the observer instructed to direct his attention to one particular point in the field, what appears at that point will be perceived accurately; but letters appearing at other points are likely to be overlooked or reported inaccurately.[1] Thus a rough generalization may be made that the total amount which can be attended to at any one moment is constant. If attention is concentrated on a small part of the field, little will be perceived in other parts; if attention is diffused over a larger area, no one part will be very clearly and accurately perceived.[2]

So also if a complex field is viewed, to one aspect of which the observer's attention is directed by particular instructions, so that he has some idea or some expectation of what will be shown him, he will perceive it more quickly and accurately than if he has no such expectation. For instance, differently arranged groups of letters were presented, and different observers were instructed to report either the number of letters, or the positions of the letters, or what the letters were.[3] Each of these characteristics was reported most accurately by the observers who had been given the corresponding instructions. But in such circumstances the other characteristics tended to be disregarded. Again, sets of four nonsense syllables were shown printed in different colours and differently arranged in different sets.[4] The observers were given one of four tasks: to report the number of syllables, or their colours, or their arrangement, or the letters composing them. Afterwards they were asked to report all these characteristics; and it was found that those not mentioned in the task which had been set were overlooked or forgotten. In general, it appeared that the amount of information which could be obtained and reported from a given field of view was approximately constant; but it was differently distributed according to the instructions. Thus the greater the number of features an observer is required to perceive and remember, and the greater the complexity of these, the less his accuracy in doing so. The following results were obtained from the tachistoscopic perception of coloured shapes or letters: when only the number of shapes or letters were required, about eight were reported correctly; when numbers and names of letters were required, six to eight; with numbers and shapes of forms, four; with numbers, colours, and shapes of forms, three.[5]

However, there is some evidence to show that the limitation on perception of many features in a complex field is imposed less by the original intake of information than by the necessity of storing it in memory for more than a very short period of time. Thus when observers were shown various numbers of different shapes in various colours, and given instructions to attend primarily to number, or shape, or colour, it was found that the observers could report some information about the features to which they had not been directed to attend (or even told specifically not to attend), provided that this was done quickly.[6] But this information could not be retained in memory over more than a very brief period of time.

31. Classification of complex shapes

Again, in perceiving certain parts of a complex field and making judgements about the figures shown, the observer will be considerably affected if he does not know beforehand just which parts of the field will be relevant to his judgements. Observers had to classify a series of complex shapes primarily in accordance with the shape and size of the central figure (the ellipse in Fig. 31); but in certain cases they had also to take into account the inner figures (the crosses) and the outside border (the diamond).[7] When they were instructed beforehand which of these features were relevant and which irrelevant, they were quicker in making their judgements than when they were uncertain which features were or were not relevant. The time taken increased with the amount of irrelevant information presented. But it decreased with practice, which presumably enabled the observers to discard irrelevant information more rapidly and concentrate their attention upon the important aspects of the task.

In a situation in which it is difficult to perceive what is being shown, irrelevant and distracting information may be produced by the incorrect guesses of the observer. Thus a series of pictures was presented; the first of these were extremely blurred, but they became clearer as the series progressed.[8] Observers were liable to make incorrect guesses as to what the pictures represented and to stick to these as the series progressed. Thus they took longer to identify the clearer pictures than did other observers who had begun in the middle of the series, with less blurred pictures, and had not made the earlier incorrect guesses.

There are other cases in which the direction of attention towards the perception of some particular shape or object causes an observer to perceive what he expected to see rather than what is actually presented. Such a direction may be given by special instructions; or by what the observer has been accustomed to perceive in such circumstances and therefore he thinks will most probably appear in the present case. An experiment demonstrating the effect of instructions was one in which groups of letters were presented tachistoscopically, such as 'sael' and 'wharl'.[9] Observers who had been told that they would see words related to 'boats' perceived these as 'sail' and 'wharf'; while observers who had been told they would see words related to 'animals' perceived them as 'seal' and 'whale'. Such an effect may occur without any deliberate instructions being given and without any intention on the part of the observer. Thus in one experiment, observers were given to read a story of a feud between two families; a reconciliation affected by the betrothal of the son of one family to the daughter of the other; and the wedding feast which marked the uneasy truce.[10] Three days later the observers were shown some pictures including a reproduction of *The Village Wedding* by Pieter Breughel. They were asked to pick out from these the picture which depicted an incident described in the story; and they all selected *The Village Wedding*. On a subsequent occasion when they were asked to recall the picture, they stressed in their recalls the features most closely related to the story, and they sometimes introduced items which were in the story but not in the picture. In particular, they attributed to the picture the atmosphere of uneasiness which had occurred in the story. But another group of observers who had seen the picture but not read the story saw it simply as a scene of merriment and gaiety. Now it is true that this effect was in part a function of the remembering and recall of the picture; but it also seems probable that even in the first case the observers who had read the story must have perceived the picture in a somewhat different manner from those who had not.

More frequent are the cases in which an observer's general familiarity with a situation causes him to perceive what he expected would appear. Instances of this have already been given in Ames's two demonstrations of the distorted room which was seen as a normal rectilinear room (page 133); and the rotating trapezoidal window which appeared as an oscillating rectangular window (page 149). Another example is afforded by the experiment described on page 38 in which observers were shown playing cards with the colours of the suits reversed. Here their perceptions of the cards shown them were frequently falsified by their expectations based upon the familiar colours of playing cards. In everyday life an instance of this tendency appears in the so-called 'proof-reader's illusion', in which misprints in a text are completely overlooked, even when the reader is looking out for them, because he is so habituated to perceiving normally printed words.

However, in this and other cases observers may be trained, or given special practice, to acquire the ability to perceive something unlike that which they had previously perceived. Thus the professional proof-reader learns to perceive misprints, in part by ignoring to a considerable extent the meaning of what he is reading. So also by practice observers can learn to perceive the distortion in the Ames distorted room. We noted that one way of doing this was for the observer to touch the walls of the room with a stick, or to bounce a ball against them.[11] In this case, sensory data other than those of vision are used by the observer to modify his perceptions. A slower way of achieving the same result is to observe carefully the movements of an object of familiar size across the back wall of the room.[12] A cigarette packet, for instance, will at first appear to change its size as it moves. But after a time the observer perceives the size as remaining constant; and then he can see that the back wall slopes obliquely backwards. Again, in the experiments on the effects of wearing inverting or reversing spectacles, over long periods of time (see page 124), it was found that in time the observers saw the field of vision in its normal orientation; and that this occurred most quickly when they made voluntary movements. Thus again additional non-visual information was utilized in learning a new way of perceiving.

Many examples occur in ordinary everyday life of people learning to perceive particular aspects of the visual scene which they had hitherto overlooked. Thus botanists, zoologists, and geologists learn to notice flowers, animals, and geological formations which persons uneducated in these sciences do not perceive at all, and which in some cases they may be unable to perceive even when their attention is drawn to them. We noted instances of this in the perception of pictures and diagrams, and of X-ray photographs. An experiment which demonstrates this phenomenon was one in which students were shown pictures of medieval armour, and required to describe the armour afterwards.[13] Students who were instructed beforehand about how the armour was constructed were able to perform this task much better than the others, provided they had thoroughly understood and assimilated what they were told. But if they had not done so, they were merely confused.

In all these cases, it seems that an observer's perception of the field, or of any particular aspect of it, may be made more rapid and accurate in so far as his attention is directed towards it. The more narrowly and specifically attention is directed, the greater the improvement. Thus the greater the amount of training and experience, and the clearer and more defined it has been, the greater the effect is likely to be. It is also true, however, that in some cases the emphasis seems to lie more upon practice and training in a particular form of attending, rather than upon attending to a particular aspect of the field. In some cases, this may be the narrowly concentrated type of attention which is needed in tachistoscopic perception. Thus we saw that the practised observer could perceive up to eight separate dots, whereas the unpractised might see five to six dots only. This effect has sometimes been attributed to an actual widening of the perceived field, or 'span of apprehension' as it is sometimes called. But in fact experiment has shown quite definitely that training, for instance in perceiving shapes exposed in peripheral vision, does not produce any general widening of this span of apprehension.[14] However, concentration of attention upon a particular small field of view, exposed momentarily, may be improved, and probably also the capacity to disregard distractions.

Again, it was found that a training in the recognition of aircraft, pictures of which were shown for both long and short exposures, improved visual acuity as measured by the ability to detect a gap in the circumference of a circle (called the 'Landolt ring').[15] It seemed that the trainees learnt to look more closely at the finer points of detail of the aircraft and discriminate between them. This form of concentrated attention to detail they then transferred to the perception of the Landolt ring.

Rather different types of attention may be required for the performance of certain tasks, and this also may be improved by practice. In perceiving very dim lights, or in comparing the brightness of two very similar lights, a strong effort of highly concentrated attention seems less effective than a more detached and relaxed procedure, leading to an immediate judgement.[16] A prolonged examination and deliberate and careful consideration are not appropriate. However, the observer must of course keep his attention from wandering altogether. Moreover, as we shall discuss in more detail below, it is sometimes difficult for him to decide, with very dim light at the threshold of intensity, whether or not the stimulus light has appeared at all. For this reason it is usual to provide some kind of signal which warns the observer that he is about to be stimulated, thus bringing his attention back to his task.

It is customary to give the observer such a signal, a light or a sound, at a regular interval of time *before* presenting the stimulus of threshold intensity. Recent experiments have shown, however, that the lowest thresholds are obtained if the warning signal is given *simultaneously* with the stimulus; and also that thresholds may be lowered, though to a less extent, by a signal given *after* the stimulus.[17] Clearly the signal is not operating only in the usually accepted fashion of warning the observer to direct his attention towards something which is about to appear. It has been suggested that even after the stimulus has appeared, some uncertainty, some distracting perceptual and thought processes, are still occurring. The signal dispels these by emphasizing that the crucial event has just occurred or is occurring at this moment, and the observer then knows that he must select for attention the appropriate data from the total amount of information available to him.

There is, of course, a number of situations in which an observer may wish to perceive a wide field of view, or to notice the occurrence of certain events at positions in the field which are far apart from one another. It is not easy to perceive objects at the margin of the field of vision, since the natural tendency is to concentrate on the central region. We noted that, to perceive objects most clearly in very dim light, it is necessary to look slightly to one side of them, since in dark adaptation areas outside the centre of the retina are more sensitive than those within it. At first considerable effort is necessary to do this, but practice makes it easier.

Sometimes an observer may wish to perceive what is happening at several points in the visual field; for instance, the readings of instrument dials and gauges on an instrument panel. In this case he must look rapidly to and fro, from one to another. Often the tendency is to confine attention to the central parts of the panel and neglect those at either margin. This tendency can be overcome by practice; and some observers seem to be more skilled than others in acquiring the capacity.[18] The same tendency to overlook parts of the field occurs when an observer wishes to scan the whole of it in order to perceive something which might appear in any part of it. In recent work, the eye movements were recorded of observers searching a field for some small figure somewhere in it.[19] The actual pattern of eye movement adopted varied with the size and appearance of the field and with the size, brightness, and type of object to be spotted. It also differed characteristically in different observers. Naturally figures in strong contrast to the background tended to attract the eyes; other figures were often not perceived even when the eyes passed over them. Moreover, in every case the field was not evenly scanned; some parts of it were covered much more exhaustively than were others. This type of task is of particular importance in scanning maps or aerial photographs; and it is clear that it will not be carried out efficiently unless instructions are given on how to perform it.

It is sometimes supposed that highly gifted individuals can attend to more than one activity at once; for instance, they can perceive simultaneously two or more different series of events. There do appear to be cases in which two series of events can be combined in some way which enables the observer to perceive both of them, though this happens more commonly in auditory than in visual perception. Thus a listener can sometimes hear two different messages conveyed to him simultaneously provided that they are differentiated in some way – for instance, they are spoken by different voices.[20] But since the eyes are more narrowly directed in space than are the ears, simultaneous perception of different visual stimuli is harder to carry out. Thus what usually happens is that the observer's attention alternates rapidly between the two series of events. Indeed, it has been shown that absolutely simultaneous perception of a visual and an auditory message was impossible.[21] An observer was required to locate places on a map in accordance with information about their positions, part of which was presented visually, four words at a time; and part of which was spoken. The places could be located accurately only if both these sets of instructions were received. It was clear that when the words of the spoken message coincided exactly with the visual presentation, one of the messages was always overlooked. Some observers received the visual messages correctly, others the auditory messages; on the whole, the visual messages were perceived better than the auditory ones. Now it is true that this experiment did not make use of simple percepts but of the perceiving and understanding of quite complex information. Also, the information was presented through two different sensory modalities, vision and hearing. There is some evidence that two series of visual events may be combined to some extent; for instance, an observer may be able to count the number of lines in two series presented simultaneously.[22] But it is not clear whether in this case the observer may not be alternating his attention rapidly between the two series.

Other evidence has been given that if two visual events occur in very rapid succession in the same position, one of these may not be perceived at all. Or there may be some modification of the percept of the one by the perception of the other, although the observer is not aware of the existence of the latter. In one experiment, two bright fields, one containing a black cross, were presented.[23] When the length of exposure of the unfigured field exceeded that of the figured field, the black cross was wholly or partially obscured, whether the figured field preceded or followed the unfigured. But interposing a dark field for ·02–·06 seconds between the two bright fields prevented the effect. Presumably when the figured field preceded the unfigured, there was insufficient time for perception of the former to develop before it was blotted out by the latter. When the figured field followed the unfigured, perception of the latter continued to operate and did not allow the former to develop. In any case, it was clear that there was an inhibitory effect of one event on the other, and not a summation as might have been predicted.

Other experiments have been carried out in which two figures have been exposed, one after the other, with an interval of about ·01 seconds between them.[24] The first was not perceived as a separate figure; but some part of it was nevertheless registered in some way such that it modified the perception of the latter. Thus when a picture of a smiling face was shown before a picture of a non-smiling face, the

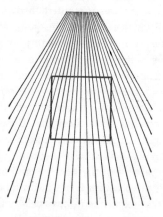

32. Effect of successive exposure of radiating lines and square

latter was perceived to be smiling to some extent; and the smile increased in clearness as the time interval of exposure of the smiling face was increased. Again, a square was preceded by a series of radiating lines. When such lines are super-imposed on a square, the latter tends to appear distorted and to become trapezoidal in shape (see Fig. 32). This effect is similar to those shown in Fig. 9 (page 56). In the experiment, the time interval between presentation of the lines and the square was increased from ·003 seconds upwards. The square appeared increasingly distorted until the lines became fully visible. In another experiment, observers were shown three rows of shapes for a period of 0·3 seconds, and asked to name the two shapes which appeared in all three rows.[25] For half the observers, one of these shapes was flashed on alone at an interval of ·03 seconds before the rows were shown. These observers were significantly more accurate in their judgements with regard to the previously exposed shape than were the other observers, although they were not aware that they had been shown it. These effects resemble those obtained in 'subliminal perception', which we shall discuss below.

In general, then, these experiments indicate that it is not possible to perceive and attend to two events separately and independently if these coincide too nearly in time or space. Either one will cancel out the other, or they will be combined in some way if this is at all possible. It appears that a time interval of the order of one fifth of a second is necessary to transfer the direction of attention from one event to another, in the sense of perceiving them as different.[26] This time appears to be about the same whether attention is being transferred from one part of the visual field to another, or from a visual to an auditory stimulus. So also it has been shown that if an individual thinks he may have to modify his reaction to a given stimulus in the light of information given him by another stimulus, he can react correctly when the latter appears at an interval of one fifth to two fifths of a second before the former; that is to say, he can perceive both stimuli correctly when they are separated by this interval of time.[27] However, the time is lengthened if the observer is uncertain whether or not the second stimulus will appear.

2 · FLUCTUATION OF ATTENTION

Up to the present we have been considering in the main how observers perceive events upon which their attention is focused. However, we noted that although such events were perceived more clearly than any others, yet things to which attention was not principally directed were perceived, and remembered, for at least a short period of time afterwards. Now it is clear from everyday experience that we do in fact perceive many things and many aspects of the visual field without directing attention upon them. In fact, the theory has been put forward that there is a large number of 'levels of attention', varying from the highest, at which attention is focused and narrowly concentrated upon a particular part of the field, to the lowest, a bare consciousness of the marginal parts of the field. It would perhaps be preferable to say that our awareness of our surroundings varies continually, from place to place and from time to time, from a maximal to a minimal amount. We have seen that much is known as to the conditions of maximal awareness. Far less is known with regard to lower degrees of awareness.

In discussing the effects of the background upon perception, for instance of size, shape, colour, etc., it was noted that our perceptions of this background did in fact affect considerably the manner in which objects attended to were perceived. In these cases, the background in itself might not be perceived at all; it merely formed a setting or framework for the objects. But it also seems that parts of the background may be perceived as such, without attention being directed upon them, at least at that moment; though it may pass to them subsequently.

It is clear that events sometimes occur in the first place outside the central focus of attention, and then rapidly become focal. It was noted that we may be scarcely conscious of a familiar scene in which little or no movement or change is occurring. But if some aspect of this scene or some object in it is altered, and particularly if the change is sudden and involves movement, we immediately become aware of it, and *then* direct our attention upon it, investigating it and responding to it as rapidly as possible. Such events are said to force themselves upon our consciousness.

So also when we are endeavouring to direct awareness, with the maximum degree of concentration, upon a task on which we are engaged, irrelevant events may intrude into consciousness which we call distractions. Whether or not this happens depends in part upon the nature of these events. Sudden loud noises or sudden blows are almost invariably distracting. Bright lights and moving objects are also distracting if they happen to 'catch the eye'. But we are better able to preserve the direction of attention in visual than in auditory or tactile perception because of our capacity voluntarily to control the sense organs themselves. However, we know that it is impossible to maintain the direction of attention, even in visual perception, for an indefinite period of time upon a single aspect of the visual scene. After a period, a shorter or longer time, the direction alters and attention 'wanders' spontaneously to something else. In an intermediate period, events become distracting which at an earlier period would have been ignored. But all these fluctuations of attention depend to a greater or less extent upon conditions within the individual himself – his general health, his state of fatigue, his interest in his task, and the strength of his motivation for maintaining attention.

Let us consider first some cases in which attention seems to fluctuate very readily. When a stimulus, a light or a sound, of very low constant intensity is exposed for some length of time, and the observer is required to say whether or not he perceives it, he may report that it appears at one moment and disappears the next. In other words, the perception of stimuli at threshold intensity fluctuates.[28] If two stimuli are presented, one very slightly more intense than the other, and the observer is asked to adjust their intensity so that one is perceptable and the other is not, it is found that his adjustments vary regularly over a certain range of intensity.[29] No amount of effort of attention on the part of the observer can prevent the stimulus at threshold intensity from disappearing from time to time. This phenomenon probably depends on certain physiological processes which we shall discuss below.

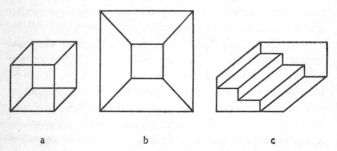

a   b   c

33. Alternating perspective figures

Other instances of fluctuation are given by the phenomena of the alternating 'figure' and 'ground', alternating perspective and retinal rivalry. We discussed the alternating 'figure' and 'ground' on page 42. If the sectors of the cross shown in Fig. 2a are equal in size, the observer may by making an effort of attention and concentrating on one cross rather than the other maintain its figural aspect for some time. But sooner or later it will be replaced by the other cross as 'figure'; and the observer cannot prevent this.

The same type of effect occurs in alternating perspective figures, some of which are shown in Fig. 33. In these, one part of the figure appears to stand out in front of the rest of the figure; but there is alternation, first one part standing out and then the remainder. Thus Fig. 33a may be seen with the cube alternately facing to the left and to the right. Fig. 33b can be seen as a receding hollow or a protruding boss; and Fig. 33c as a staircase or an overhanging cornice. Again, voluntary direction of attention to one aspect may make it predominate in awareness, but cannot altogether suppress the other aspect. Introducing complicating details, such as windows, a door, and other objects, in Fig. 33b, tends to make it look like a receding passage and increase the dominance of that aspect, but this seldom altogether suppresses the other aspect.

These effects have been attributed by some psychologists to an effect called 'satiation'. This is little more than a name for this effect, in which an observer seems unable to attend to one aspect for more than a limited period of time. However, as we shall see, there is some possibility that events in the central nervous system may be responsible for the effect. It cannot be due to any form of retinal fatigue. Nor can binocular retinal rivalry be attributed to retinal factors, in spite of its name. In this phenomenon, different fields of view are presented simultaneously to the two eyes, for instance, two differently coloured fields. If these are fairly similar in brightness and wave length (i.e. they are neighbouring colours in the spectrum), the two fields may fuse and a mixture of the colours be perceived.[30] But if their unlikeness is increased, they will tend to alternate with each other; though sometimes a black and a white field will produce a shimmering or lustrous effect. If one field is figured and the other plain, the former will dominate and the latter may be altogether suppressed.[31] The same things occur if one field is more structured or brighter than the other, or if one is more 'meaningful'. Thus it was found that if the photograph of a face was presented to one eye, and the same photograph upside down to the other eye, the upright photograph tended to dominate and the inverted photograph was sometimes completely suppressed.[32] Again, pairs of photographs were presented stereoscopically, a Mexican scene to one eye and an American one to the other, to Mexican and American observers.[33] The Mexican scenes tended to dominate for the Mexican observers, the American ones for the Americans. The more nearly equal the degree of figuration of the two fields, the greater the tendency to alternation between them. Voluntary direction of attention towards one field may increase its dominance, but seldom produces complete suppression of the other field. However, the rate of alternation can be increased by voluntary effort.

Somewhat similar effects have been demonstrated recently in the 'stabilized image' phenomenon which was described on page 141.[34] When shapes of different kinds were projected continuously on to the central area of the retina, the speed and amount of fading and regeneration varied according to the nature of the figure. In the first place, meaningful figures faded less. With a line and a profile face side by side, the latter faded more slowly and remained for a larger proportion of the time than did the former. A letter with an irregular line across it remained when the line disappeared. Specific attention to any part of a figure would restore it to awareness. Again, different parts of meaningless figures faded in different ways; but curved figures remained as a whole to a greater extent than did straight line figures. With a square, certain lines might disappear while others remained; in particular, parallel lines tended to fade and regenerate together. These observations are interesting as showing that the fading tendency is affected firstly by attention and interest; and secondly by some of the *Gestalt* factors of 'goodness' of form which were described on page 52.

But the 'wholes' into which parts of a complex shape were organized appeared to be somewhat different from those postulated by the *Gestalt* psychologists.

These effects may at first sight seem to have little relevance to everyday experience. Nevertheless they all appear to be related to fluctuations in attention. What does occur frequently in everyday life is that, if the field of view contains a number of objects all of which are interesting and attractive to the observer, his attention is likely to alternate between them. He will automatically glance to and fro, looking first at one and then at another. In such a situation also he may find it difficult to concentrate and maintain his gaze on one object or part of the field, although voluntary effort may assist him up to a point.

In all these cases, interest in and attractiveness of objects play an important part in the direction of attention. Experiments have shown that variation, surprise, and incongruity are also liable to attract attention.[35] Observers were shown sets of pictures containing one or two items which were quite incongruous with the others, and told that they could prolong the exposure of any of the items as long as they were interested in looking at it. They spent more time in looking at the incongruous items than at the others; and also in looking at irregular figures among a series of regular ones. Other figures were presented in pairs, one a regular and the other an irregular figure; or one a picture of a normal animal and the other an animal with incongruous parts. Again, the irregular and incongruous figures were studied for a longer time than were the regular and familiar ones. Presumably longer time was required to perceive the exact nature of the unusual and irregular items than of the normal ones.

It is true also that lack of interest makes attending more difficult and distraction easier. An important instance of this appears in the kind of boredom which results from lack of change or variety in the environment, and especially from the monotonous repetition of an event at intervals over a considerable period of time. If a stimulus pattern is repeated sufficiently often and unchangingly, at length the observer may cease to be able to attend to it; or if he has to respond in exactly the same way, he may be unable to continue doing so. It seems, however, as if it is the perceptual activity which breaks down, before the response. A test called the 'clock test' was designed by Mackworth to find how long observers could go on perceiving a repeated event.[36] A pointer rotated round a dial like that of a clock, in successive small jumps, one every second; and at irregular and comparatively infrequent intervals it made a double jump. The observer had to notice and signal each of these double jumps. After only about half an hour observers began to miss these; and the number of omissions increased steadily throughout a two-hour period. In another experiment, observers had to signal the occurrence at intervals of an 'echo' on a mock-up radar screen.[37] There was a marked increase in omissions when the echo was dim and difficult to see, but relatively little when it was bright and clear. Thus attraction of attention by the more striking perceptual event was effective in preventing wandering of attention from the task. So also was lengthening of the time over which the signals were visible, in another similar task. Keeping the observer continuously active in the clock test, by requiring him to press a key at every one of the smaller jumps (as well as another key at the larger jumps) did not keep up his efficiency. And if a continuous loud sound was maintained throughout the period of testing, this enhanced the decline. Thus clearly there are certain conditions of perceptual stimulation which make it particularly difficult for the observer to maintain attention, of which the most important are low intensity, short duration, and repetition.

These effects may however be counteracted in various ways by making the situation more interesting and more generally stimulating. Having another observer in the same room, or alternating one observer with another, prevented increase of failures to respond. So also did signalling to the observer whenever a double jump occurred, whether he responded to it or not. But also an increase in the rate and regularity at which signals appeared sometimes seemed effective, by increasing the probability of their appearance and hence the observer's expectancy. Clearly, however, the factors involved in the maintenance of attention to tasks of this kind are complex.

It is of course well known that a state of fatigue is liable to make it harder for an observer to maintain his attention on any task, even a complex and variable one. Indeed, performance of such tasks may itself engender states of fatigue which make it more and more difficult for the performer to keep up his efficiency. This was strikingly demonstrated by experiments carried out during the war on aircraft pilots in an experimental cockpit.[38] The pilots had to make co-ordinated movements of the hand and feet, as in flying an aircraft, in response to the readings on a series of dials similar to those on the instrument panel of an aircraft cockpit. In addition, distracting lights were introduced at intervals. Towards the end of a two-hour period, certain characteristic changes appeared in the mode of responding: (a) the pilots became relatively indifferent to small changes in dial readings, attended to them sporadically and unsystematically, and sometimes not until they had passed a 'danger' reading; (b) the pilots tended when they did respond to make correct responses but in the wrong order; (c) there was a funnelling of attention towards those dials to which response was most frequent, with a consequent failure to notice other dials less frequently used, for instance, the petrol gauge; (d) the distracting stimuli, which in earlier stages could be ignored, or allowed for, became increasingly obtrusive and annoying. In general the fatigued individuals were seldom aware of the deterioration in their performance, but thought that they were attending and responding quite adequately. If because of the deterioration in efficiency, something went wrong, they tended to attribute this to faults in the machinery and not to their own actions.

It is clear therefore that there are several situations in which the power to attend is only partially under voluntary control, and in which the observer cannot deliberately maintain his attention for an indefinite period. It appears to become temporarily inhibited, and his strongest efforts cannot preclude this happening. Some strong interest or other motive may prevent it for a time, but not indefinitely. The principal condition in which this failure of attention occurs is that of lack of change or variation in the perceptual situation; the more pronounced the invariability, the greater the deterioration. We shall now consider some particularly striking instances of this.

Under the direction of Hebb, at the University of MacGill, experiments were carried out to investigate the effects of keeping people for periods up to five days in a completely homogeneous and unvarying environment.[39] In a small room they lay on a bed; they heard nothing but the monotonous buzz of machinery; they had translucent goggles over their eyes so that they could see only a blur of light; and they wore long cuffs which came down over their hands and prevented them from touching anything. Some observers were able to stay in these surroundings continuously for five days; others could not endure them for more than two days, in spite of the very high rate at which they were being paid for performing the experiment. Although at first they slept a great deal, after about a day they were unable to sleep except in snatches. They became bored and restless, and could not think in any concentrated fashion about anything. In fact, when their intelligence was tested, it was found to have deteriorated. They frequently suffered from visual and auditory hallucinations. When they emerged from their incarceration, their perceptions of their surroundings were impaired. Objects appeared blurred and unstable; straight edges, such as those of walls and floors, looked curved; distances were not clear; and sometimes the surroundings moved and swirled round them, causing dizziness.

In another rather similar experiment, the observers were kept in a completely silent room.[40] Here few hallucinatory phenomena were experienced. But after a period of sleepiness, there was again an increasing disturbance of thought, beginning with loss of power of concentration, and progressing in some cases to complete disorganization. Thoughts became incoherent, and the observers developed erroneous ideas about their own bodies including feelings of unreality and depersonalization. These were accompanied by growing anxiety leading to states of panic such that they were compelled to give up the experiment. But no after effects were noticed.

Somewhat similar phenomena were experienced by observers who placed themselves in the tank type of respirator used for poliomyelitis patients.[41] In these, they were kept motionless, and could perceive little of their surroundings. They experienced hallucinations and loss of concentration, accompanied sometimes by acute anxiety such that many of them could not endure the experience for more than thirty-six hours. Similar hallucinatory phenomena have been experienced by poliomyelitis patients themselves, and also by patients immobilized for fractures and cardiac disorders, when their environment was restricted and monotonous.

The effect of lack of variation in the perceived field has

been demonstrated in other ways. We discussed on page 141 the manner in which the 'stabilized image' falling continuously on the same area of the retina soon fades, and then regenerates and fades periodically.[42] It was found also that from time to time the whole field of view became completely black; and the experience was sometimes extremely unpleasant, and was accompanied by a feeling of disorientation. There was evidence to show that this effect was not due to retinal adaptation, as was the fading of the image; and it appeared to result from a failure in the central nervous system to respond to the unchanging homogeneous visual field. Somewhat similar effects were obtained by covering each eye with a hemisphere made from half a ping-pong ball.[43] The observer perceived a homogeneous field of light which soon became darkened and might then cloud over altogether. Again the experience was an unpleasant one. Rapid eye movements or flickering light restored its original brightness. If coloured light was used, the colour disappeared and was replaced by a neutral grey. In another set of experiments, the observer looked with one eye into the interior of a uniformly illuminated white sphere, which constituted his whole field of vision.[44] At first it appeared as an impenetrable fog. But after a short time it faded altogether from view to a uniform blackness, and the observer did not even know whether his eyes were open or closed. When figures were introduced into the field, vision was restored but only slowly. It was from one to three seconds before the observer perceived them, and even then they might appear distorted and wandering about in space. After a succession of exposures of three minutes each to these conditions, observers often became extremely fatigued, dizzy, and uncoordinated.

Recent studies have indicated that the behaviour of infants may be affected if they are kept for a period of time in surroundings which lack variation.[45] The infants were under seven months of age, and were in hospital for periods of one to two weeks. On removal from hospital, they appeared to be almost unaware of objects and people, even their mothers, and spent their time continually gazing around them with blank and bewildered expressions on their faces. This behaviour might continue for a few hours, or as much as two days. It did not appear while they were in hospital unless they were moved from one ward to another. The behaviour seems to have been caused by their prolonged exposure to monotonous and unchanging surroundings in the hospital, where they could see little, and were seldom lifted up and played with. Thus apparently they became as it were rigidified and set in the unchanging perceptual environment. When they were moved, this rigid environment was disrupted; and they had difficulty in adapting to the change and becoming orientated to the more normal type of varying surroundings. Hence their prolonged inspection of these. Moreover, the resulting stress often produced disorders of eating and sleeping.

Thus we must conclude that normal consciousness, perception, and thought, can be maintained only in a constantly changing environment. When there is no change, a state of 'sensory deprivation' occurs; the capacity of adults to concentrate deteriorates, attention fluctuates and lapses, and normal perception fades. In infants who have not developed a full understanding of their environment, the whole personality may be affected, and readjustment to a normal environment may be difficult.

3 · MARGINAL AWARENESS

Even when attention is not maintained, and perception becomes so vague and unclear that we are uncertain as to what we perceive, or indeed may be unaware that we perceive anything, nevertheless some degree of marginal awareness may persist. Moreover, in much of our habitual and automatic behaviour it is clear that we do indeed perceive our surroundings and are able to react to them appropriately without being consciously aware of what is present. Thus we cannot equate perception or even attention with consciousness. Perception may occur at a very low level of attention, when awareness is marginal and not fully conscious. In some cases we may become conscious that we remember certain events after they occurred, without having attended to them or being fully aware of them at the time. Instances of this were given in the experiments described above (page 161), in which observers were able to describe parts of a complex field towards which their attention had not been directed; but although perceived, it was not remembered for long.

But we also have evidence of cases in which people have apparently perceived things without *ever* being conscious that they did so. In one of the first experiments carried out on this phenomenon, observers were shown coloured shapes resembling a banana, an orange, a lemon, and a leaf, in very dim light.[46] They were told to look at the screen on which these shapes were projected, and at the same time imagine each of them in turn. They then thought that what appeared was in fact a visual image, and were not conscious that they perceived them at all. However, if they were instructed beforehand that they would perceive these objects, they did so normally.

In later experiments, shapes were shown at an intensity supposed to be below the absolute threshold of vision.[47] Subsequently it was calculated that in many cases in which the observers were not conscious of having perceived these shapes, their guesses as to what had been presented were nevertheless more often correct than could have been expected by chance – provided that the intensity was only slightly below threshold. This phenomenon has been termed 'subliminal perception', since apparently the observers did in fact perceive at least some of these shapes without being conscious that they did so. But some observers did much better than others; and it has been claimed that some small part of the shapes may be perceived, although the figures as a whole cannot be identified. Another 'subliminal' effect was produced by projecting a background of lines such as that in Fig. 9 (see page 59) at below threshold intensity, and presenting a square upon it at normal intensity for a quarter of a second.[48] It then appeared that the observers perceived the square distorted in somewhat the same way as it would have been distorted had the observers seen the background normally.

Other experiments have indicated that the ideas and actions of observers may be influenced by 'subliminal' perception of material of which they are not consciously aware. Dixon presented a series of words, some of which were related to sex, at intensities of illumination just below the absolute threshold of vision, signalling to the observer each time one of these was shown.[49] The observer was instructed that when he received the signal, he should say the first word that came into his head. Though none of the observers were ever conscious of having seen the stimulus words, and did not in fact report any of them correctly, yet there were many cases in which the response word had a definite association with the stimulus word. With the sex words, the response words had sexual connotations or exhibited some type of Freudian symbolism of the sex words. The observers were later asked to make free associations to their own response words, and in some cases produced the original stimulus word, or a synonym of it, by association. However, throughout these experiments individual differences in response tendencies were marked.

As each stimulus word was presented, the observer's psychogalvanic reflex response was measured. This response is obtained by passing a constant electric current through a person's hand, the two electrodes being fastened to the palm and the back of the hand. Any kind of emotional shock is liable to produce a sudden reduction in the electrical resistance of the skin, and hence a sudden increase in the recorded current strength. The effect appears to be due to one of the responses to emotional shock of the autonomic nervous system, which causes increased sweating in the skin and hence a reduction in its resistance. Now in Dixon's experiments it was found that the psychogalvanic response when the sexual words were presented was significantly greater than when the other words were presented. Thus he concluded that in fact they were perceived, and an emotional shock resulted, although the observers were not conscious of it, or of having perceived sex words. We shall discuss some further evidence on this question in Chapter 11.

Furthermore, experiments of Dixon's showed that a response made to a subliminal stimulus must be based upon some old and well-established association; it would not occur if the associations were weak and temporary. The observers were shown, in normal vision, a series of lines in different positions, and were instructed to respond by saying 'Up', 'Flat', or 'Slant' to vertical, horizontal, and slanted lines respectively. When the lines were then presented subliminally, and the observers instructed to guess their positions, there was no tendency to say the correct word. When the observers were presented subliminally with the digits 1, 2, and 6, and asked to guess the name of the digit presented, the digit 6 was reported with greater than chance frequency; but there seemed to be a tendency to say '2' instead of '1'.

This effect was greatest when the intensity of the stimuli was only just below threshold. It occurred only when the observers were instructed beforehand that there would be subliminal stimulation, and not in the absence of this instruction.

It is difficult to demonstrate these effects without introducing supra-liminal stimulation, since as we pointed out above, the absolute threshold of vision is not constant, but continually fluctuates. However, Dixon evolved an ingenious technique for raising and lowering the intensity of the subliminal stimuli *pari passu* with the rise and fall of the threshold, so that the former was always just below the latter.[50] He then obtained effects with digits similar to those quoted above. It may be concluded that it is possible to perceive such stimuli, though not very accurately, provided that the observer's attention is directed towards their occurrence. It is also possible that stimuli with some emotional significance are more readily perceived than those which have none. They may in fact act as a kind of warning signal, before the observer is fully aware of them. We shall discuss this possibility more fully in the next chapter. But a recent experiment showed that quite ordinary unemotional words could be guessed correctly, when presented tachistoscopically, before the observer was conscious of actually perceiving them, especially if he was required to select the word which had been presented from among a group of five given him to read subsequently.[51] Our final conclusion, therefore, must be that it is extremely difficult to delimit the range either of perception or of attention, or to state exactly what will or will not be perceived in any given set of physical conditions.

4 · THE PHYSIOLOGICAL BASIS OF ATTENTION

In recent years, certain physiological processes in the brain have been discovered and investigated which appear to be related to the arousal, direction, and maintenance of attention. In general, sensory impulses from the sense organs in various parts of the body are transmitted by the main sensory nerve tracts, through the brain stem and the nuclei of nerve cells at the top of the brain stem, to the cerebral cortex (see Fig. 34). In one of the nuclei, the optic thalamus. these impulses are, as it were, sorted out, and those from different

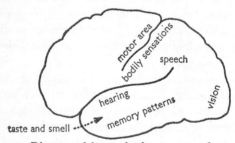

34. Diagram of the cerebral cortex, seen from the side; showing the main receptor areas and the motor area

senses transmitted to different receptor areas of the cortex, for vision, hearing, touch, and so on. Surrounding the receptor areas are areas in which the sensory messages appear to be elaborated by thought and memory processes on which depend our meaningful perceptions of the world around us. Nerve impulses from these areas are transmitted to the motor areas, the principal area being shown in Fig. 34; and from the motor areas impulses pass down through the brain stem in the motor nerve tracts to the muscles. An area on the underside of the cortex appears to be responsible for regulating motivational and emotional processes, and the activities of the autonomic nervous system related to these.

Recently, physiological investigations have suggested that the nervous tissue within the brain stem and in the region of the thalamus, called the 'reticular formation' (see Fig. 35), also plays a part in regulating the passage of sensory impulses to the cortex.[52] Collateral or branch nerves from the main sensory tracts pass to the reticular formation, so that it is stimulated by sensory impulses, elaborates them within itself, and sends on further impulses to the cortex.

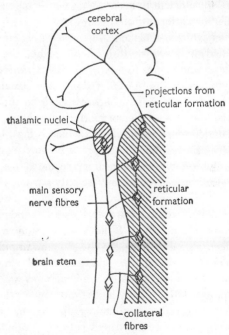

35. Diagram of the reticular formation and its nervous connexions

These are concerned in the first place with arousing the cortex of a sleeper to wakefulness. Electrical records have been made of the nerve impulses which flow to and fro in the cortex; such a record is called the electroencephalogram (EEG). During sleep, the EEG shows a set of large slow regular rhythmical waves. This rhythmical discharge appears to be an inherent property of the brain, which continues throughout life whenever there is no waking consciousness. There was also some evidence of its occurrence in the hallucinatory states experienced in the 'sensory deprivation' experiments (see page 180 ff.). But when a sleeper receives some kind of stimulation sufficient to arouse him, nerve impulses from the reticular formation inhibit the slow rhythmical discharge of the cortex, which is replaced by a more rapid nervous discharge called the alpha rhythm. Finally, when the sleeper opens his eyes and begins to attend to his environment, the alpha rhythm also disappears and a set of small rapid irregular waves appears which corresponds to the diffuse and incessant activity of the cortex during waking life.

It is a sudden sensory stimulation which is most likely to produce this arousal effect, and it may be only temporary. If the stimulus is not repeated, or if it is repeated in a regular monotonous fashion, arousal may be only partial; impulses will cease to be transmitted from the reticular formation, and sleep will be restored. However, the nature and meaning of the stimulus is important. If, for instance, someone whispers the sleeper's name in his ear, the reticular impulses will produce a greater arousal effect than occurs with a meaningless stimulus. Moreover, the autonomic nervous system may also be stimulated to action by such stimuli during sleep, and a psychogalvanic reflex response set up. Again, however, these processes may occur without complete waking; or if the sleeper does wake, he may not remember what stimulated him.

The function of the reticular formation in arousal from sleep has been demonstrated by experiments on animals in which it has been injured, so that it ceases to function normally. Such animals then remain in a condition of lethargy or coma from which it is difficult if not impossible to arouse them.

But the reticular formation is also concerned in the perceptual processes of waking life. It appears possible that these functions proceed from another section of the reticular formation than that concerned with arousal from sleep. It seems that in general the reticular formation, having received sensory impulses through the collateral fibres from the sensory nerve tracts, sends on further impulses which enhance the sensitivity of certain parts of the receptor areas of the cortex, and facilitate their nervous discharges particularly in relation to percepts which are novel or interesting to the individual, and to which it is important that he should pay attention. On the other hand, cortical responses to repeated or uninteresting stimulation, to which there is no need to attend, are inhibited.

The type of sensory impulse which most quickly stimulates the reticular formation is that of pain; and on the whole auditory impulses affect it more than do visual ones. It is of course true that awareness of pain is more immediate and compelling than that of any type of sensation. Also on the whole we attend more quickly to sudden noises than to sudden visual stimuli. But the discharges from the reticular formation do not depend automatically on the type of sensation; they are also modified and regulated in accordance with the meaning and significance of these. Thus what appears to happen is that impulses passing directly up the sensory nerve tracts to the cortex are conveyed directly and rapidly, whereas the discharges from the reticular formation are delayed through elaboration there of the impulses from the collateral fibres. There is time therefore for the cortex to evaluate the sensory impulses it receives in terms of their importance, interest, etc., and to send impulses downwards to the reticular formation, modulating its upward discharge before this begins. This discharge in turn facilitates or inhibits the cortical responses according as to whether it is desirable to attend, to continue attending, or not to attend to the sensory impulses. The effect may be to heighten discrimination of impulses towards which attention is directed. Thus it was found that direct electrical stimulation of the reticular formation in man increased the power to discriminate between two flashes of light, one exhibited at a short interval of time after the other. With such stimulation, the observer could perceive the two flashes as separate with a shorter time interval than normal between them. On the other hand, repeated stimulation of a monotonous character with little significance for the individual seems to result in inhibitory discharges from the reticular formation, so that he ceases to attend, or even to be aware of, such stimuli. Some such effect may occur in the cases of 'sensory deprivation' described above.

An important application with regard to the influence of the reticular formation on discrimination is demonstrated in the effect of barbiturate drugs. The activities of the reticular formation are depressed or inhibited by concentrations of these drugs too small to affect the direct sensory stimulation of the cortex. Thus people under the influence of these drugs may continue to be aware of their surroundings after they have lost the power to attend to or discriminate accurately any part of them.

We noted that one part of the cortex was specifically concerned with awareness of and response to motivation and emotion. This area, when it is aroused by stimuli of a potentially emotional character, also sends impulses to the reticular formation which in turn seems to play a large part in organizing responses to them. General 'alerting' results, specific attention is directed towards the stimuli, and searching with the eyes takes place. Experiments were carried out on the electrical stimulation of certain parts of the reticular formation in monkeys. An electric shock of mild strength aroused sleeping monkeys and alerted waking animals, inhibiting their movements. A stronger shock produced reactions typical of fear, such as cowering and avoidance; still stronger shocks resulted in panic flight.

It was found in other experiments that strong shocks in the cortical area associated with motivation and emotion might produce profound blocking of the activities of the reticular formation for as much as two seconds. This seems to parallel the states of stupefaction, amounting to loss of consciousness, which may occur as the result of violent emotional shock. Again it seems that in some cases the general alerting discharges of the reticular formation are over-activated, and the specific discharges responsible for attention and discrimination suppressed. These effects may produce the violent activity together with loss of discrimination which also occur in some emotional states.

It seems therefore that we possess physiological mechanisms upon the activities of which are based the capacity to direct and heighten attention to particular aspects of the perceptual field which are of significance to the individual, while at the same time distracting and irrelevant aspects may be suppressed from awareness. Some perception of parts of the field outside the focus of attention still takes place; but they are not discriminated accurately or in detail. Indeed, the observer may not be conscious of having perceived them. Any sudden change in the field rapidly alters the direction of awareness, and the observer searches until he has explored the field and perceived the nature of the change. In all these processes the significance of perceived objects to the observer and their appeal to his emotions and motives play an important part. We shall now consider the evidence as to the psychological effects on perception of these.

CHAPTER II

THE RELATION TO PERCEPTION OF MOTIVATION AND EMOTION

I · EFFECTS OF DESIRES AND NEEDS ON PERCEPTION

WE have frequently noted that the objects perceived in a complex field, and the clarity and accuracy with which they are perceived, appear to be related to the observers' 'interest' in perceiving them. 'Interest' is a comprehensive and ill-defined term; but it usually possesses the implication that there is some strong and persistent motive in the observer which has impelled him to observe, investigate, and acquire knowledge about some set of objects or ideas in the world around him. Thus when we say that an observer perceives something because he is interested in such things, we imply both that he is knowledgeable about them, and also that he is eager to perceive and learn more about them. Therefore it is not immediately apparent whether it is the previous knowledge or the impelling desire which has the greatest effect in directing and facilitating perception – or whether both together are necessary. Furthermore, it is clear that the observer's purpose in furthering his interest will be served only in so far as he perceives accurately. If he does not do so – if he imagines things which are not actually there – he is in danger of entering the world of phantasy, or 'autistic thinking' as it has sometimes been called. Thus if perception is affected not only by interests but also by other motives and desires, it is important to distinguish between the perception of something which actually exists in the environment which might appeal to these motives and satisfy these desires, and the incorrect or fanciful perception of something which does not exist there, which can lead only to disappointment.

In the last fifteen years, a large amount of experimental work has been carried out to investigate the relationship between motivation and perception. But the subject-matter of these investigations has not always been clearly defined and conceptualized. There has been inadequate discrimination between the effects on perception produced by knowledge acquired in the furtherance of an interest or need, and the direct effects of need where acquired knowledge is not involved. Again, the experimenters have not always distinguished between the facilitation of accurate perception which could further need satisfaction, and the imaginative or phantastic distortion of perception which in ordinary everyday life situations would soon be discarded because it led only to dissatisfaction and frustration. Indeed, we shall see that these illusory perceptions occur as a rule only in situations in which it is difficult for the observer to perceive with any clarity or certainty, and in which he is therefore necessarily thrown back to a greater or less extent upon his imagination.

These comments are particularly apposite to some of the earliest experiments which were carried out upon the relationship of perception to need, namely the perceptions of hungry observers. In one experiment, observers were shown blurred pictures of articles related to food, and of other household articles, at varying periods after their last meal.[1] There was an increase in the number of food related objects perceived up to about six hours after the last meal, but thereafter there was a decrease, and also an increase in the number of failures to give any response at all. In another experiment in which pictures of food and other objects were shown at first very dimly and then increasingly brightly, the brightness at which the food objects were perceived decreased up to about three to four hours after the observer's last meal, and then increased again.[2] There was no corresponding effect with the non-food objects. It appeared therefore that there was at first a tendency for food and related articles to be perceived more readily, but that as hunger increased the observers became increasingly frustrated, and ceased to take the trouble to respond. When, instead of pictures, words related to food or drink were projected momentarily to observers who had been deprived of food or drink for varying periods, there was a decrease in the time taken to perceive the appropriate words up to ten hours deprivation, but an increase after twenty-four hours.[3] This again suggests that the observers became apathetic and unresponsive after long periods of deprivation. However, these effects were also related to what the observers expected to perceive. Different expectations were created by first showing different groups of observers sets of skeleton words to fill in, some of which were related to food, for instance, LUN – H, while others were not.[4] Those who had not received the food suggestions were less likely to perceive food-related words subsequently, however hungry they were, than those who had received them. But among the latter, the more hungry gave more food words than the less hungry. Clearly there was a complex inter-action between need and expectation. The individual in a state of need is more likely to perceive something which will satisfy his need if he thinks that it will probably be there. If the perceptual situation is ill-defined, he may imagine for a time that he perceives something appropriate to his need; but he ceases to do this after prolonged frustration.

Somewhat similar effects have been demonstrated in experiments relating to more enduring types of motivation which are not temporarily unsatisfied needs. Thus individuals who were judged from a personality test (the

Thematic Apperception Test) to possess a high degree of aggressiveness were quicker to perceive pictures showing aggressive acts than were those with a low degree of aggressiveness.[5] Those who appeared from the same personality test to possess a strong desire to strive for success and mastery perceived words related to such achievement at a lower intensity of illumination than those with a less strong desire.[6] The same type of effect appeared with those who possessed a strong desire for security. A similar result was obtained in relation to anxiety. Student observers, some of whom appeared from their answers to a questionnaire to be highly anxious individuals, perceived a set of hostile faces more quickly than they perceived friendly faces – provided that their anxiety had been stimulated by informing them that their personalities were being evaluated. From these experimental findings, therefore, it seems fairly clear that perceptual material which relates to some inherent motive in the personality may be perceived more readily, other things being equal, than will unrelated material.

2 · EFFECTS OF VALUES AND INTERESTS ON PERCEPTION

A similar conclusion to the above may be drawn from experiments on less simple and clear-cut motives. One of the earliest and best-known of these was an experiment by Postman, Bruner, and McGinnies, in which the observers first of all answered a questionnaire known as the 'Study of Values Test'.[7] By his answers, the individual questioned indicates the relative extent to which he possesses aesthetic values, religious values, social and charitable values, scientific and philosophical interests, and so on. After answering the questionnaire, the observers were shown tachistoscopically a series of words related to the above values. It was found that they perceived most readily the words corresponding to the particular values which the questionnaire had shown them to possess. Moreover, when they made incorrect guesses as to what the words were, other words of synonymous meaning were given in response to the 'valued' types of word; and words of different or contradictory meaning were given for the 'non-valued' types of word.

Certain criticisms have been made of this experiment which recall the introductory comments in this chapter. It was pointed out in the first place that the words presented were not all equally familiar, and that different degrees of familiarity had probably affected perception of different words.[8] In particular, those who possessed a particular value or interest might very well be more familiar with related words than those who did not. Some attempt was then made to control the degree of familiarity by equating the frequency with which the words appeared in printed literature.[9] It then appeared that there was no difference in the rapidity of perception of words in the valued and non-valued categories. However, a further experiment indicated that perception of relatively infrequent words in the 'valued' categories was more rapid than perception of equally infrequent words in the 'non-valued' categories.[10] We must therefore conclude that in fact people do acquire a special vocabulary of words relating to the topics in which they are interested, and for that reason are able to perceive such words more readily. This is particularly likely to happen with topics such as those covered in these experiments, most of which have a considerable literature of their own. Here direct motivational effects are probably of much less importance than the effects of special knowledge.

A rather different type of interest and value the effects of which have also been investigated is that which relates to people's social relations to one another. It seems quite probable that such relations would affect the manner in which they perceive those whom they like or dislike. Some interesting studies of this kind were made in relation to Negroes. Thus Seeleman found that white students whose attitudes were favourable towards Negroes perceived and recognized correctly a significantly larger number of photographs of Negroes than did students whose attitudes were unfavourable.[11] The former perceived the photographs as those of individuals with distinguishable personal characteristics. The latter, however, tended to regard Negroes as a homogeneous group, without differentiating their individual characteristics.

The supposed attributes of such social groups, however, may be over-emphasized. Observers were asked to rate photographs of Negroes and whites as to the degree they showed of certain Negro characteristics such as width of nose, fullness of lips, etc.[12] These characteristics are related to the stereotyped notion of Negro appearance. Those observers who were prejudiced against Negroes exaggerated the degree to which these characteristics appeared in the Negro photographs, by comparison with the less prejudiced observers. So also in a study of anti-Semitic prejudice, it was found that those with a high degree of prejudice differentiated more accurately than those with a low degree between photographs of Jews and non-Jews.[13] The differences between ethnic groups were over-emphasized, those between individuals under-emphasized. The same effect appeared when groups of white South Africans (some English-speaking and some Afrikaans-speaking), Indians, Africans, and Coloured People (mixed white and African), were shown photographs of people of different races, in a binocular stereoscope.[14] To one eye was presented a photograph of a member of one race (European, Indian, African, or Coloured), and to the other eye a photograph of a member of another race. In general, each group was most accurate in picking out its own members. But the Afrikaaners were distinguishable from the other groups in that they tended to differentiate their judgements more sharply into either Europeans or Africans, and gave comparatively few intermediate judgements, of Indians or Coloured. That is to say, they exaggerated their differentiation between whites and Negroes.

In another study, Negroes themselves were asked to rate the colour of their own skins, and those of other Negroes known to them, on a scale from light to dark colour.[15] It appeared that the preferred skin colour was not the lightest of all, but a medium colour; and that individuals tended to rate both their own skin colour and that of girls they thought attractive closer to the preferred colour than it actually was. However, all these experiments except the first, by Seeleman, involved the making of judgements. Although these were based in the first place upon direct percepts, it seems quite possible that the distortions occurred during the process of deliberation over the judgement, rather than in the original perception. It is not possible, however, to arrive at any definite conclusion on this point.

Rather different again are the studies in which is demonstrated the influence on perception of suggestions from others in the individual's immediate social group. One of the earliest of these related to the perception of the auto-kinetic movement – the illusory perception of movement of a stationary point of light in a dark room.[16] It was found that when several observers were together asked to judge the direction and extent of this movement, these judgements were extremely similar to one another, and differed considerably from those of the same individuals when they were tested alone. It is true of course that one can scarcely consider the auto-kinetic movement to be 'perceived'; it is more in the nature of those imaginative effects which are particularly prone to modification through motivational influences.

Several other studies have been made in which it is apparent that individuals modify their judgements of perceived objects, such as lengths of lines, to conform to the judgement of a social group, or the opinions expressed by other members of the group. One interesting example of this type of experiment was the following:[17] A series of drawings was presented to twelve-year-old children, which began with a face scribbled over (see Fig. 36). In successive drawings, the face was gradually changed into a bottle. Each child was tested separately, and was asked to say what each

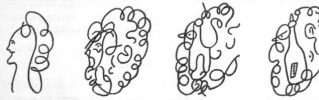

36. Examples of figures changing gradually from a face to a bottle

of the successive drawings represented. He was accompanied by another child who had been 'briefed' beforehand by the experimenter to say that in every case he saw a face. The children tested in this way continued to report a face for much longer than did other children who were tested alone, without any suggestion being made to them. A somewhat similar set of drawings, in which a dog was gradually transformed into a cat, was shown to children aged eleven to sixteen years who appeared to have rigid and stereotyped personalities, mainly as the result of their constricted and authoritarian upbringing.[18] Although there was no confederate to offer suggestions, these children also were slow to perceive the transformation from one figure to the other, presumably because they were afraid of guessing at something new, and prone to cling to what they had already perceived. However, it is by no means certain in these experiments also whether the observers really *perceived* these modifications. It may be that they were in any case doubtful of their judgements, and preferred to rely either upon the judgement of others, or upon judgements which had previously proved correct. Experiments described on page 225 indicate the manner in which results may be affected by individual differences in the nature of judgement rather than of perception.

Numerous experiments have been carried out to demonstrate the effect of various forms of valuation upon the perception of certain particular qualities of objects – their size, brightness, distance, etc. The earliest and best-known of these experiments was one performed by Bruner and Goodman, in which ten-year-old children were required to adjust the size of a disc of light to equal the sizes of coins and cardboard discs.[19] In general, it was found that they over-estimated the sizes of the coins by comparison with the sizes of the cardboard discs; and the more valuable the coins, the greater the degree of over-estimation. Moreover, children from poor homes over-estimated to a greater extent than did those from well-to-do homes. This experiment has been repeated more than once, in a similar manner, but with varying results.[20] However, the general conclusion appears to be that the absolute sizes of the coins are not always over-estimated to any greater extent than are the sizes of the discs. But although there is some tendency to over-estimate the larger discs than the smaller ones, it is not so great as the tendency to over-estimate the sizes of the more valuable coins by comparison with those of the less valuable. The effect may be due to the greater value of the larger coins; thus size is perceived as varying with value. Or it may be that when differences in size between objects is a matter of importance, for instance in discriminating between coins of different values, then the difference is exaggerated. This was indeed found to occur with florins and half-crowns. Finally, some experimenters have found these effects to occur only when judgements are made from memory, and not from immediate perception of the objects.

Other studies have been made to investigate the effect of 'value' on perception. But the results of these have also been variable. Some have appeared to show that discs bearing dollar signs, or dollar bills, were over-estimated in size, or their distances under-estimated, by comparison with discs or pieces of paper bearing meaningless figures. Other experiments have contradicted these findings. But in an experiment with children it was found that pictures of foods which they liked were perceived as being relatively larger than pictures of foods they disliked.[21] In an experiment on adults, hungry and thirsty observers perceived pictures of articles of food and drink as being relatively brighter than those of objects unrelated to food or drink.[22] The estimates of brightness increased steadily in amount until the observers had been eight hours without drinking. They were then allowed to drink all they wanted; and immediately the estimated brightness of the pictures fell to the same value as it had at the beginning of the experiment.

In other experiments, certain objects were given a value by the experimenter. Thus a group of children was given the task of turning a crank handle, and rewarded with poker chips which they could subsequently put into a slot machine to obtain candy.[23] They over-estimated the size of the chips; but the over-estimation disappeared when they had to perform the task without reward. The effect of reward and punishment on judgements of length and weight by adults has been investigated.[24] The observers were rewarded with money whenever they were shown the longest lines or the heaviest weights in series of lines and weights; and were punished by forfeiting money whenever they were shown the shortest lines or the lightest weights. When subsequently they were required to make judgements of length and weight, they tended to over-estimate both of these by comparison with estimates made before the rewarding and punishing. In a similar experiment, the observers were rewarded for both the heaviest and the lightest weights in a series.[25] The tendency subsequently was to extend the range of judgement of the series, relatively more being judged very heavy or very light.

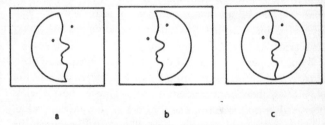

a   b   c

37. Effect of reward and punishment on perception
of juxtaposed faces

In one remarkable experiment, it appeared that observers perceived a previously rewarded percept more readily than a previously punished one.[26] This experiment was carried out with sets of two juxtaposed 'faces', as shown in Fig. 37c. In the first part of the experiment, only single faces were presented. Whenever one of them, Fig. 37a for instance, was presented, the observer was rewarded with money; whenever the other, Fig. 37b for instance, was shown, he was punished by having money taken away from him. The observers were encouraged to learn to name and recognize these faces, but their attention was not drawn to the fact that one was punished and the other rewarded; indeed it was claimed that in no case were the observers aware of the connexion. (Other faces of the same type as those shown in Fig. 36 were also presented.) Finally, the observers were shown the juxtaposed faces; and in the combined figure (Fig. 37c) the rewarded face was perceived in the great majority of cases rather than the punished one. This experiment has been repeated several times. In general, the original results were confirmed, but there were considerable individual differences in susceptibility to the effect.[27] Children showed it more markedly than did adults. Observers who reported that they did not mind much whether they won or lost money did not tend to choose the rewarded faces. If a rewarded or a punished face was combined with one which had neither been rewarded nor punished, this latter was chosen less frequently than either the rewarded or the punished face.

Thus the general conclusion from all these experiments is that, especially in rather ambiguous situations, qualities of objects which are independent of their value are nevertheless distorted or biased in some way as a function of that value. It is more doubtful whether such effects would occur in the clearer and less ambiguous perceptual situations usually encountered in everyday life, especially in circumstances in which correctness of perception is important. Indeed, some evidence for this view is given by an experiment in which were shown groups of varying numbers of dots, the observers being required to estimate the numbers.[28] They were rewarded proportionately to the number estimated, provided that the estimate was correct; but penalized for incorrect estimates. Up to the twentieth trial, they produced more incorrect responses and more over-estimates than did other observers who were rewarded for correct responses irrespective of the number estimated. After the twentieth trial, however, the number of over-estimates and of incorrect responses of the former observers began to decrease, and eventually they gave more correct responses than did the latter. Thus at first the rewards stressing numerousness produced over-estimation; but when this was found not to be effective in winning the reward, over-estimation disappeared.

3 · EFFECTS OF SUCCESS AND FAILURE ON PERCEPTION

It is not surprising to find that success or failure in a task has some effect on the performance of that task itself, and may also affect tasks performed immediately afterwards. When people have succeeded, they tend to feel lively and elated; when they have failed, they may be depressed or apathetic. These feelings may be prolonged, and influence the performance of other tasks, for instance, perceptual tasks, carried out subsequently. Thus observers who had been set difficult tasks which they had failed to perform satisfactorily were slower than those who carried out the tasks adequately to perceive ambiguous pictures, shown them afterwards.[29] A similar effect was found when tachistoscopic perception of sentences was preceded by attempts to perceive pictures which were practically invisible because of the low intensity or short exposure with which they were exhibited.[30] In addition, the observers were reproached with their failure to perceive these. Not only were they slower subsequently to perceive sentences correctly, but they also made more wild and irrelevant guesses. Again, observers were given a series of blurred pictures which gradually increased in clarity, and were reproached with their failure to perceive the very blurred pictures at the beginning of the series.[31] Other observers were reassured. The former began guessing what the pictures were sooner than did the latter, but were slower to recognize them correctly.

Rather different results were obtained, however, in experiments in which observers were first required to solve anagrams, and then afterwards to perceive the anagram words presented to them tachistoscopically. In one experiment, the observers perceived the words in which they had failed to find the anagrams more quickly than the words with which they had succeeded.[32] This effect was enhanced when the observers were praised for their successes and reproached for their failures. Other experiments showed individual differences.[33] Some observers perceived relatively more easily words which they had succeeded in solving as anagrams, whereas other observers perceived relatively more easily words with which they had failed. It was then found that the latter effect was characteristic of observers shown by means of a personality questionnaire to possess a high degree of anxiety; the former effect characterized those low in anxiety.[34] In another ingenious experiment, observers were asked to estimate how well they thought they would do a perceptual task.[35] After the task, half of them were told that they had surpassed their estimates, and half were told that they had fallen short of them. Subsequently, a series of words was presented, four of which related to success (excellent, succeed, perfection, winner), four to failure (unable, failure, obstacle, defeat), and four to striving (improve, achieve, strive, compete). The 'success' words were recognized relatively more quickly by the 'success' group and the 'failure' words by the 'failure' group. There was no significant difference for the 'striving' words. It was suggested that the observers who had succeeded or failed labelled the situation as one of success or failure, and formed appropriate hypotheses about the type of words shown them.

There is at first sight a good deal of disagreement between

these findings. But it is of course true that people differ in their reactions to failure in a task. Some people, in certain circumstances, may be stimulated to try harder and show that they are not beaten. Others may begin to feel anxious at their failure, especially if they are naturally prone to anxiety; and this is more likely to occur if they have been made to feel, as in some of these experiments, that failure was due to their own inferiority of intelligence, perceptual abilities, and so on. Then again, anxiety and inadequacy make some people try wildly and stupidly to do anything which might remove their failure; others are inhibited, pull in their horns and do nothing, to avoid further failure. The most interesting of the above experiments is the last one which showed that after success or failure people might be not only quicker or slower, more or less correct, in their perceptions; but also that the actual nature of what they perceived might be affected.

5 · EFFECTS OF PAIN ON PERCEPTION

Some of the experiments described above attempted to investigate the effect on perception of unpleasant experiences such as failing in a task or losing money. Other experiments have been performed to study the effect of a really painful experience on perception. The technique employed most frequently has been to require observers first to learn words or nonsense syllables, some of which are accompanied by a painful electric shock; and then to compare the speed or ease with which these words or nonsense syllables are perceived with those for the non-shocked words or nonsense syllables.

Again a good deal of disagreement between different experiments was demonstrated. In the first place, it was found that when nonsense syllables had been memorized, those which had been associated with shock were subsequently perceived more quickly than those which had not.[36]

Another technique was sometimes to terminate the shock, during the preliminary learning, as soon as the observers responded with the correct syllable, whereas in other cases the shock was continued throughout the learning.[37] A control group of observers received no shock at all. The first group perceived the nonsense syllables about as quickly as the control group; whereas the second group perceived them more slowly. Thus in one experiment, association with pain appeared to accelerate perception; in the other, it tended to disrupt it.

A surprising effect was obtained by Lazarus and McCleary, that the effect of shock was to alert observers in such a way that they reacted emotionally to previously shocked nonsense syllables before they consciously perceived them.[38] Psycho-galvanic responses were first established to certain nonsense syllables which were accompanied by shock. Subsequently both shocked and unshocked syllables were presented tachistoscopically; and although the observers failed to perceive consciously many of the previously shocked syllables, nevertheless they gave an appreciable psycho-galvanic response to them. It appeared therefore that there was some capacity to differentiate between shocked and non-shocked syllables before these were consciously perceived. However, it was shown later that observers who were unable to report the syllables correctly at the first guess could sometimes do so at the second or third guess.[39] There-fore it seems possible that the observers, before they fully perceived the syllables, yet had sufficient knowledge of what they were to place them in the shock or non-shock category.

Other experiments have been carried out to investigate the effect on perception of shock administered during the perceptual task. As might be expected, the most common effect was to distract the observers' attention, and to disrupt performance. However, in one case in which observers had to estimate the sizes of discs, and at first a shock was given whenever an estimate was made, there was no tendency to make incorrect estimates.[40] When the shock was discontinued, however, estimation became less correct, as if the release from pain had made the observers less careful. When, during the discrimination of size, the shock was given at random intervals, the effect was to make estimates less variable, more rigid, and stereotyped, but on the average neither more nor less accurate. Again, in the tachistoscopic perception of nonsense syllables, one group of observers was given a shock for every incorrect response, which was terminated as soon as they responded correctly; another group was shocked at random.[41] By comparison with a control group which received no shock, the first group perceived the nonsense syllables more quickly, the second more slowly.

Variation in the severity of the shock may produce different effects. A series of ten drawings were presented, similar to those shown in Fig. 36 (page 202) in which a face changed gradually in successive drawings to a bottle, observers having to report in each case what they saw.[42] Subsequently some of them were shown photographs of faces accompanied by either mild or severe shock; others were shown photographs of bottles, also accompanied by mild or severe shock. When the original drawings were again presented, those who had received mild shocks perceived the shocked face or bottle more readily; but those who had received severe shocks perceived these less readily. However, in another experiment shapes such as an arrow, the number eighty-eight, etc., were presented, at first incompletely and then with increasing degrees of completeness; and different observers were given different degrees of shock at random during presentation.[43] The stronger the shock, the slower were the observers to perceive and name the shapes. Thus it appears that a painful association may in some cases accelerate perception or draw attention to particular material, especially if the observer can avoid or lessen the shock, by perceiving rapidly. On the other hand, if the shock is severe, or if he can neither anticipate nor avoid it, it is more likely to retard or disrupt perception. But there are individual differences in these effects. And in the experiment of Lazarus and McCleary it appeared that material with painful associations was sometimes anticipated before it was fully perceived. In circumstances in which such anticipation would enable the individual to avoid the painful situation, this response would clearly be valuable.

6 · PERCEPTUAL SENSITIZATION AND PERCEPTUAL DEFENCE

Finally, we must consider a large group of experiments designed to investigate the effect on perception of presenting material of such a nature as to be likely to produce considerable emotion of a conflicting type in the observers. The greater number of these experiments employed material with some sexual connotation, which tended to arouse not only sexual feelings but also some degree of anxiety and guilt such as are often associated with sexual feelings because their expression is socially tabooed. It is not surprising to find that the results of these experiments were as variable and as much in disagreement with each other as any we have discussed heretofore. One explanation of this disagreement is, as we noted in connexion with the experiments on the effects of failure, that the reactions of different people to objectively the same situations may be different, not to say diametrically opposed.

These experiments began with one by Bruner and Postman in which was measured the time for free association to each of ninety-nine words.[44] For each observer, the six words were selected to which the reaction time in free association was quickest, the six to which it was slowest, and six with intermediate reaction times. A fortnight later, these words were presented for tachistoscopic perception. It was found that for some observers the words with the longest reaction times, which were assumed to produce the greatest emotional shock, were most quickly perceived. These were often sexual words, tabooed in ordinary conversation. But other observers perceived these words more slowly than the others. The first set of observers were said to exhibit 'perceptual sensitization' or 'vigilance', the second set, 'perceptual defence'. The latter therefore appeared to be able to guess at the nature of the taboo words before they could perceive exactly what they were; or at least before they were able, or willing, to report what they were.

A great deal of criticism was aroused by these and similar experiments, since it appeared that the experimenters were claiming that observers were perceiving something in order *not* to perceive it; just as in the experiment of Lazarus and McCleary the observers perceived the shocked syllables sufficiently to react to them in the psychogalvanic reflex before they could perceive them consciously. In spite of the apparent absurdity of this claim, it is not impossible that such a process might occur. People may be capable of perceiving that there is 'something nasty in the woodpile' before they perceive exactly what it is. However, it was argued that the observers did in fact perceive the taboo words as quickly as, or even more quickly than, the neutral words, but that they were shy of uttering them. Or else they guessed what the words were, but did not act on their guesses because it seemed to them unlikely that anyone would have shown them words of this kind.

There is indeed some experimental evidence for these arguments. In one case, some outraged comments were reported on the presentation of words of this kind. Again, it was shown that there was no 'perceptual defence' if the observers were allowed to write the words down instead of saying them out loud. It was also found that the defence effect occurred only with the first of the taboo words.[45] It could be eliminated by warning the observers that words of this type would be shown them. However, other experimenters found that even when observers had been alerted to the appearance of sexual words, these were still perceived more slowly by the majority, who also reported that they did not consciously stop themselves from uttering them.[46]

Another factor which may have introduced variability and unreliability into the results of some of these experiments was the variation in the familiarity of the taboo words. Some attempt was made to compensate for this by selecting words of measured frequency in written English (based on the Thorndike-Lorge word count).[47] It was then claimed by some experimenters that the emotional effect of the sexual words on perception could be demonstrated independently of the effect of their frequency.[48] Other experimenters found that relatively infrequent sexual words were perceived more readily than equally infrequent neutral ones, especially when the observer had been shown several of the former and had come to expect them.[49] For more common words, there was no difference in speed of perception of sexual and neutral words. But it is of course extremely difficult to estimate the actual familiarity of individual observers with such words from their frequency in written English. Several of the words used were sexual slang words, such as 'balls' and 'screw'; and whether or not observers are familiar with them must depend on their particular social experience.

Some attempts have been made to discover whether any effect similar to the above occurs with words of less ambiguous meaning and emotional effect. The speed of perceiving words with pleasant meanings (brave, honest, loyal) was compared with that for words with unpleasant meanings (agony, shame, cheat, guilt).[50] The effects of these appeared to vary in different experiments; in some cases there was little effect, in others the pleasant words retarded perception as much as did the unpleasant ones, by comparison with neutral words.[51] Again it was found that only observers who were characterized by possessing a high degree of anxiety were much affected.[52] No doubt in many cases these words produced little emotional effect, and this accounted in part for the variability of the results.

Some attempt has been made by the defenders of the 'perceptual defence' hypothesis to differentiate between those who characteristically show defence or retardation of perception, and those who show sensitization or acceleration. Thus words and pictures relating to aggressiveness and homosexuality were shown to mental hospital patients.[53] Those patients who gave long reaction times in free association to these pictures, caused presumably by inhibition of these desires, also perceived them more slowly than neutral words and pictures. There did not seem to be any specific relation between repression of a particular desire in certain patients, and slower perception of the related words and pictures. But patients known to be openly aggressive perceived the aggressive pictures more quickly than the neutral ones. In another investigation, it was found that individuals guilty of sexual offences were quicker to perceive pictures of the sex organs than were individuals guilty of other offences.[54] The former also made more aggressive responses as well as more sexual ones. To university students were presented parallel sentences, the second clause of each of which was related to sex or to aggression.[55] In general, these were found more difficult to perceive than were neutral sentences; but male students were relatively slower with the sexual ones, female students with the aggressive. It was supposed that the men possessed more repressed sexual desire, the women more repressed aggression. In another experiment, normal adults were required first of all to complete sentences relating to sex, hostility, or feelings of inadequacy; and their responses were assessed according as to whether these indicated sensitizing (preoccupation, over-reaction, etc.) or repression (blocking, avoidance, etc.).[56] Subsequently words relating to sex and hostility were perceived more rapidly than neutral words by the 'sensitizers' and less rapidly by the 'repressers'. The effect did not hold for words relating to feelings of inadequacy; but apparently this type of response was less clearly differentiated in the original sentences.

These experimental results seem to indicate that the general performance of individuals in such situations is disintegrated to some extent by perceiving material likely to produce emotional conflict. But they do not show clearly whether in fact the material is partially perceived and then excluded from consciousness. Some further light was thrown on this problem by a series of experiments in which the observers' psychogalvanic reflex responses were measured. Sexual and neutral words were exposed tachistoscopically, and at the same time as each one was presented, the observer's psychogalvanic response was recorded.[57] Not only were the observers slower to perceive the sex words than the neutral words; but also the psychogalvanic response to the former was greater than that to the latter, and it appeared before the words were correctly perceived. It was therefore concluded that, just as in the experiment of Lazarus and McCleary, the sexual words were partially perceived, to a sufficient extent to set up the psychogalvanic reflex, before they were perceived with sufficient clarity to be reported. However, another experimenter found that the rise in the psychogalvanic response did not occur until after the words had been perceived.[58] But, as we saw in the last chapter, Dixon showed that a rise in the psychogalvanic response was produced by sexual words which were never consciously perceived, since they were presented at an intensity below the absolute threshold.[59] However, judging from the observers' associations, they did gain some idea as to the nature of the words, although they were not conscious of this.

Thus it may be hypothesized that in the experiments on 'perceptual defence' there is some awareness, though of a rudimentary character, which has the effect of retarding or accelerating fully conscious perception. Which of these processes in fact occurs seems to depend on the inhibitions, or freedom from inhibitions, of the observer. Many experiments on personality qualities have demonstrated differences between those who freely admit emotional experiences to consciousness and conscious expression, and those who repress or avoid them.

What general conclusions can we draw as to the effects of motivation on perception? These must necessarily be speculative, since few if any of the experiments described show with any certainty the type or degree of motivation or emotion which was actually experienced by the observers. Curiously enough, the effects of positive and pleasurable emotions aroused by the satisfaction of needs seem to have been less thoroughly investigated than the effects of frustrated needs and unpleasant emotions. This is unfortunate, since pleasurable emotions could be directly effective, and would not be repressed. However, it is possible that they are less easy to create in laboratory situations. In general, it seemed that those who were rewarded, or who had experienced success in a task, had some tendency to attend preferentially to the rewarded or successful situation, or related material such as pictures or words associated with reward or success, and to perceive them more readily. Positively valued material may also be perceived, apparently, in such a way as to accentuate certain irrelevant qualities of the material, such as size. This type of inaccuracy may occur to a small extent in everyday life. But it is doubtful if it would persist in any unambiguous situation in which the observer could check his judgements, since its inaccuracy might lead to the frustration rather than the satisfaction of need.

There does not seem to be much direct evidence as to whether need, satisfaction, and pleasurable emotion facilitate perception, making it more rapid or more accurate. One might suppose that perception would be facilitated in so far as it led directly to need satisfaction. Also, pleasurable feeling might produce a general state of elation which would stimulate the observer to perceive more efficiently. It seems possible that activity of the reticular formation would facilitate attention and discrimination in such circumstances. The experiment of Postman, Bruner, and McGinnies (see page 198) and other similar experiments, do suggest that in the furtherance of interests, which are undoubtedly highly motivated (even if the nature of the motive is not always clear), special knowledge is acquired which in itself facilitates perception of relevant material.

The most extensive data have been obtained from experiments in which unpleasant emotions have been aroused, by some form of painful experience, by frustration of needs and desires, or by arousal of emotional conflict over sex. There seems little doubt that with many people these states are liable to disrupt the process of perception, as they disrupt other activities, making it slower or more uncontrolled and inaccurate. However, some people appear to be stimulated by these experiences to try harder. In all probability, a severely painful experience is likely to have a prolonged disruptive effect. Indeed, we know that violent needs and emotions tend to monopolize attention completely, making the observer incapable of perceiving anything in his surroundings unless it, or some distorted perception of it, can be related to his need. A mild degree of pain or unpleasant emotion may make the observer more cautious and hence slower; or may stimulate him to attend with greater concentration, hence producing in some cases more rapid and accurate perception. This latter result would be most likely to occur in situations in which rapid and accurate perception would enable the observer to avoid the pain or unpleasantness. This may indeed have occurred in the experiments in which the observer could terminate the electric shock by giving the correct response.

Can we conclude, however, that in addition to a general effect on perception, unpleasant emotions also result in a specific change in sensitivity to unpleasant material, or that individuals are able to avoid perceiving material which is likely to cause them pain, frustration, or shame? We saw in the last chapter that it was extremely difficult to define the limits of perception, which sometimes appeared to take place when observers were scarcely aware of what they had in fact perceived. Most people brought up in a civilized society are adept at rapidly repressing sexual impulses which they cannot gratify, and which are socially tabooed. It seems possible therefore that these repressing tendencies do in fact come rapidly into operation as soon as sexual suggestions appear, and for many people preclude, at least for a time, fully conscious awareness of their nature. People who, on the other hand, appear to possess a heightened awareness of such material presumably lack repressive tendencies, and are even pleasurably stimulated by it. But the ambiguous results obtained with other forms of unpleasant material suggest that retarded perception is a function of repression, rather than of the mere disagreeableness of the material. It is possible of course that the inhibitory effect of emotion which, it appears from the increase in psychogalvanic response, was in fact aroused before complete perception occurred, may have disrupted the discharges of the reticular formation responsible for specific attention and discrimination, as we described in the last chapter.

These problems, however, can be solved only by a fuller and more detailed understanding of the motivational and emotional processes themselves, and of their effects on the earlier behaviour and the acquired knowledge of the individual observer.

CHAPTER 12

PERCEPTUAL 'TYPES' AND THEIR RELATION TO PERSONALITY

WE noted in the last chapter that the effect of motivational factors on perception often seemed to vary with the type of personality, and in particular with individual tendencies towards repression and inhibition on the one hand, and expansiveness and over-action on the other hand. In fact, a considerable number of experiments has been devoted to studying individual differences in perception. These differences have often been attributed to certain persistent methods of perceiving, sometimes called 'attitudes', which are supposed to operate in different situations and with different types of material. Often these methods have been classified into two contrasting types, for instance, the 'synthetic' and 'analytic'. Again, these and other typical ways of perceiving have been related to inherent characteristics of personality, which again have been classified into two opposed types, such as the 'introvert' and 'extrovert'. In so far as perceptual characteristics are concerned, there seems little doubt that some of these differences are well established; though it is more doubtful whether they are as simple, clearly defined, and persistent as their protagonists represent them to be. But the evidence as to the association between perceptual differences and personality typologies is far more dubious. Even if personalities can validly and usefully be classified into two contrasting types, which is as yet unproven, the relation to these of typical modes of perceiving is by no means clear nor well-established.

Nevertheless, there appears to be a persistent fascination in the postulation of 'perceptual types', and the results of the great majority of the experiments which have been carried out to demonstrate characteristic methods of perceiving have been classified in this manner. Such experiments have a long history. Though it is scarcely worth while to detail them all, some of the earlier experiments are worth comment. It should be noted that not all experimenters have supposed that such methods of perceiving appear in every situation. They have recognized that observers may vary in their manner of perceiving according to circumstances.

Perhaps the most popular and best known classification is into the '*synthetic*' and '*analytic*' methods of perceiving. As the names indicate, the observer who adopts the first method tends to see the perceptual field as an integrated whole, whereas the observer who adopts the second breaks up the field into its constituent parts or details, studying each one separately and perhaps overlooking the effect of the whole. In the synthetic method visual illusions appear more compulsively;[1] apparent movement[2] and causality[3] are readily seen; size, shape, and colour constancy are high.[4] The analytic method is more appropriate when small details must be attended to and certain qualities isolated from the whole, for instance, in judging the brightness or colour of a surface independently of its other qualities, or those of the remainder of the field. Also it must be utilized in making judgements of perspective size. But though these two methods of perceiving can be clearly distinguished from each other, it is more doubtful to what extent they are consistently adopted throughout a single experiment, or a series of experiments. It has been claimed that in the estimation of brightness constancy, some observers tend consistently to be more synthetic in their approach, others more analytic.[5] When instructions are given to adopt either the synthetic or the analytic procedure in size constancy experiments, some observers find the former easier, others the latter. In the comparison of sensory qualities such as brightness, loudness of sounds, and roughness of touch, it was found that whereas some observers could readily change on instruction from the analytic to the synthetic method, others found one of these methods considerably easier to maintain than the other.[6] We shall return to this point shortly.

Closely related to the distinction between analytic and synthetic methods of perception is the contrast of *objective* and *subjective* types, first propounded in connexion with reading, particularly the reading of words and short sentences presented tachistoscopically.[7] The objective type of reading was accurate but limited in scope; in the subjective type, more was read but less accurately because the reader filled in the gaps in what he saw by means of inferences as to what he thought might be there. Again there is some doubt as to whether these methods were consistently maintained; though they did operate fairly persistently in the tachistoscopic perception of real objects.[8] In the tachistoscopic perception of pictures by children similar procedures were found to occur, but they were to a considerable extent functions of age, education, and intelligence.[9]

Bartlett, in his experiments on perceiving, distinguished between those who tried to perceive the whole of a complex figure at a single glance, were *confident* that they had seen the whole, and often thought it contained more detail than was in fact the case; and the *cautious*, hesitating observers, taking one thing at a time, who tended to decrease the amount of detail.[10] Now though at first sight this dichotomy appears to resemble the synthetic-analytic, it does not correspond exactly. Moreover, temperamental factors seem to have been associated with the confident and cautious methods. But Bartlett did not note whether his observers were consistent in these throughout the experiments. A recent experiment on the perception of ambiguous material – blurred pictures – indicated that when the observers made incorrect guesses as to what this represented, some did so tentatively and hesitantly, and others rapidly and confidently.[11] These types of procedure were consistent throughout the experiment, with different types of material. But again we do not know if such methods operated in other perceptual situations.

As we noted above, there has often been a tendency to link the method or procedure used in perceiving with some basic attribute of personality. In recent years, this tendency has reappeared in experiments in which observers are classified into the *'introvert'* and *'extrovert'* types, usually on the basis of a questionnaire or personality inventory. The perceptual performances of the two types are then compared. It was found that extroverted individuals tended to show a higher degree of size constancy than did introverts, but this may have been because the former responded more easily to 'synthetic' instructions, the latter to 'analytic'.[12] With 'analytic' instructions, the difference between judgements of introverts and extroverts was greater than with 'synthetic' instructions.[13] Shape constancy was also lower for introverts than for extroverts when the instructions were analytic in bias.[14] Presumably therefore the analytic method of procedure is more difficult than the synthetic for the extrovert to adopt. The differences in measured judgements are always small; and it is probable that there is a large class of people who can adopt either the synthetic or the analytic approaches equally well.

A number of experiments was carried out by Klein on the classification of different types of procedures of perception; and these were also related to types of personality. The first classification was into *'sharpeners'* and *'levellers'*.[15] Observers were shown successively sets of squares of varying sizes which they were asked to estimate. At each successive projection of a set of squares, the smallest square was replaced by one larger than any in the previous set. Though some observers, the 'sharpeners', made accurate size judgements throughout, others, the 'levellers', lagged behind the change in size and made estimates which became increasingly too small. The 'levellers' also perceived less clearly than the 'sharpeners' the contrast between grey squares surrounded by contour lines and placed on a background of a different grey. Reports on the personalities of these observers were obtained from psychotherapists; and it appeared that in general the 'sharpeners' were active, energetic, competitive, and sometimes aggressive; whereas the 'levellers' were more passive and dependent, and tended to drift and to retreat inwards into themselves.

Another investigation showed that extreme 'levellers' gave responses on the Rorschach ink-blot test which indicated a strong tendency towards repression of emotion.[16] In straightforward estimation of size, however, observers who were objectively accurate in their estimates were less apt to behave emotionally, as shown by their emotional reactions to pictures and their answers to a questionnaire on emotional reaction, than were observers who were less accurate in their estimates.[17] There seems to be an unresolved contradiction between these findings.

Recent experiments have produced results which seem to qualify these conclusions to some extent.[18] It appeared that in making judgements of changing numbers of dots and lengths of lines, some individuals tended to make narrowly limited classifications of responses, excluding doubtful cases; others to make broader categories of a more inclusive type. The former, who seemed to prefer the risk of saying 'no' incorrectly to the risk of saying 'yes' incorrectly, adapted their responses to changes in the stimulus material more adequately than did the latter. But neither type was essentially more accurate than the other. These two types corresponded roughly to Klein's 'sharpeners' and 'levellers'. But it was clear from the experimental results that the actual percepts varied with the nature of the situation and the stimulus material.

In another investigation by Klein, twenty people were selected on the basis of their responses to the Rorschach ink-blot test.[19] Ten were said to be '*form-bounded*'; they gave constricted and stereotyped responses showing objective accuracy and little imaginative interpretation. The other ten were termed '*form-labile*'; they gave much freer and less restricted responses showing much imaginative, not to say bizarre, interpretation. The 'form-labile' in general perceived the apparent movement phenomenon over a wider range of conditions (with greater variation in time interval between stimuli) than did the 'form-bounded'. When a flickering field of light was shown them, the 'form-bounded' tended to see the flickering light disappear into fusion more readily than did the 'form-labile'. Klein considered that the 'form-bounded' were insecure individuals, 'intolerant of perceptual ambiguity', who preferred not to see the uncertainty and movingness of the apparent movement and flickering field.* They resembled the children described on page 202. However, the 'form-labile' group included not only people of an imaginative trend of mind, but also those who produced bizarre responses quite out of touch with reality.

A somewhat similar investigation of the relation between perceptual tendencies and personality qualities was that carried out by Witkin and his colleagues.[20] We noted on

---

*Recent investigations have indicated that neurotic patients appeared to possess the same 'intolerance of perceptual ambiguity' in perceiving shifting figures like those in Fig. 36; and the neurotics also perceived the apparent movement phenomenon less readily than did normal persons (Hamilton, V. 'Imperception of Phi.' *Brit. J. Psychol.*, 1960, 51, 257).

page 123 that it was found by Witkin and Asch that there were characteristic differences in the procedure of observers shown a tilted luminous framework in an otherwise dark room, and asked to set a rod in the vertical position. Some observers tended to rely on their bodily sensations of gravitational forces; whereas others were more influenced by their visual sensations and tended after a while to judge the tilted framework as being vertical. The latter observers were also found to have some difficulty in extracting 'hidden figures'. In personality tests such as the Rorschach tests and the T.A.T., these observers showed passivity, readiness to submit to authority, little self-esteem, and a tendency to anxiety. The first group of observers, on the other hand, were much more active, independent, self-reliant, and self-confident. Witkin hypothesized that the passivity of the one group of observers was displayed in their '*field dependent*' tendency to cling to the external environmental framework of the visual field, whereas the self-reliance of the other '*field independent*' group was demonstrated by their ability to rely on their own bodily sensations. However, these two groups formed the polar extremes of a continuous distribution, the majority of adults lying in the middle ranges. Witkin has since extended his observations to children, and has found that, although 'field independence' tends to increase with age, it is also differently distributed in different children. 'Field independent' children show a greater capacity than do 'field dependent' for active analysis and differentiation and for imposing a structure on the field in a number of tasks involving perception and thinking (including some of those in the Wechsler Intelligence Scale for Children). But these capacities are independent of general intelligence.

Recently Gardner and his collaborators[21] have made further extensive studies of certain general methods of perceiving, and have subsumed their results under a number of principles of '*cognitive control*'. There are four main principles, more or less independent of each other, which are related to types of approach to complex perceptual tasks; and these Gardner considers to be associated with certain personality qualities, and especially to methods of 'ego defence'. They are:

(1) *Levelling* and *sharpening*, which were discussed above; the former relates to the tendency to perceive things as they actually are at the moment, the latter to a tendency to assimilate percepts to the memory traces of previous percepts. These tendencies are demonstrated in the experiments already cited, and also in experiments on the comparison of pairs of lights, sounds, etc., in which the judgement of the second of the pair may be affected by the interpolation of a much more or less intense light, sound, etc. The 'levelling' tendency is considered to be related to ego-defence through repression.

(2) *Field articulation*, covering Witkin's 'field dependence' and 'field independence'. This type of control relates to the selectiveness of attention: the capacity to direct attention actively and appropriately to the significant features of the field, disregarding irrelevant ones, as against the passive acceptance of what is given.

(3) *Scanning control*, relating to a tendency to deploy attention over a wide field, as against concentrating it narrowly upon a small area. This type of control is related to Piaget's 'centration' (see p. 93); and it produces individual differences in the extent to which numerous visual illusions are perceived. It has been claimed that wide scanning is related to the ability to isolate knowledge and ideas from any emotional connotations, and thus to preserve the accuracy of these from emotional influence.

(4) *Tolerance of unrealistic experiences*, which replaces 'tolerance of perceptual ambiguity' and the 'form-labile' and

'form-bounded' classification. This control is exercised when individuals continue to perceive the surroundings normally while viewing them through distorting lenses. It is considered to be related to the ability to maintain the balance between objective reality and subjective ideas based on motivation.

It is impossible in this book to expound these principles of control at all fully, to cite all the relevant experiments, and to discuss the methods by which the principles have been related to personality qualities. Although Gardner and his collaborators have not yet fully established the existence of these controls, still less their relationships to personality, yet this work provides a more hopeful approach to these problems than any other work of this nature. Perceptual differences also seem to appear in individuals with *neurotic* or *psychotic* tendencies. Thus when sets of letters were shown them tachistoscopically, *obsessional* individuals were very accurate in perceiving them; and they always began with letters in the same place and reported them according to a consistent and rigid pattern.[22] Cases of *anxiety* and *hysteria* were fluctuating, inaccurate, and inconsistent in their perceptions, often substituting other letters for those actually shown. Normal individuals were intermediate between these two extremes. Again, it was found that normal persons were able to perceive correctly pictures exhibited tachistoscopically at a lower brightness than could either neurotics or psychotics.[23] The neurotics made many premature and irrelevant hypotheses as to the content of the pictures, which delayed correct recognition; and in anxiety patients particularly these hypotheses often reflected their own personal preoccupations. The psychotics made relatively few meaningful hypotheses, tending to report instead the shapes and brightnesses in the pictures. But once they had produced a meaningful hypothesis, they tended to stick to it and refuse to change it even when, as the pictures became clearer, it was manifestly incorrect. Another experiment showed that people with *paranoiac* tendencies were slower than others to identify schematized drawings of real objects, the parts of which were shown successively.[24] In other words, they were less ready to guess the identity of the objects from partial cues.

The tendency of *schizophrenics* to isolate themselves from their surroundings has been demonstrated in an experiment on the perception of the relative velocity of two spots of light moving across a screen.[25] Schizophrenics related the velocities together to a lesser extent than did normal individuals. The isolating, self-orientating attitude to this phenomenon appeared also, though to a lesser degree, in markedly unsocial and introverted individuals who were not schizophrenic. The schizophrenic's slowness in organizing the field and inter-relating its parts was also demonstrated in experiments in which shapes were presented tachistoscopically grouped in pairs or sets of three.[26] Schizophrenics were able to perceive the shapes as quickly as did normal observers, but were significantly slower in perceiving the grouping.

Again, it has been hypothesized that since schizophrenics tend to be out of touch with reality, they might show less size constancy than the normal; they would be less aware of the 'real' and more aware of the formal characteristics of the field. When the experimental instructions stressed the 'analytic' procedure, it was indeed found that size constancy was less among schizophrenics than among normal persons.[27] In addition, there was a stronger tendency among the former to make very literal 'form-bounded' responses in the Rorschach test. But in another experiment in which the instructions favoured the 'synthetic' procedure, paranoid schizophrenics were found to have a higher size constancy than normals, non-paranoid schizophrenics being intermediate though not significantly different from normals.[28] It might be suggested that paranoids tend to exaggerate, and therefore over-estimated size. But also these results indicate that schizophrenics can adopt a synthetic procedure just as well as can normals. The same type of result was obtained with neurotic patients; their size constancy was lower than that of normals with 'analytic' instructions, but not significantly different with 'synthetic' instructions.[29]

Even when schizophrenics are not completely isolated from their environment, their perceptions of it may be fragmented and lack the integration of perceptual experiences in normal persons. Schizophrenic and normal observers were asked to describe the behaviour of an individual who was trying to solve a difficult manipulative problem, for instance, to drop a ring over a stick beyond his reach.[30] The schizophrenics tended to report isolated actions rather than sequences of related actions directed towards the solution of the problem. This behaviour may, however, reflect a disorder in thinking rather than in immediate perception.

We have advanced the criticism that in many of these experiments insufficient data are obtained as to the different methods adopted by different individuals in a variety of perceptual situations. Experimenters have been apt to classify the observers into 'perceptual types' on the basis of a single experiment; or to study the methods employed by different types of personality in one or two experiments only. No such criticism can be made of a very extensive investigation carried out by Thurstone.[31] He administered to 170 students forty different tests of perceptual performance, including their perceptions of visual illusions, alternating perspective and retinal rivalry, auto-kinetic and apparent movement, shape and brightness constancy, various *Gestalt* figures (including 'hidden' figures), pictorial material, and words. Performance in these tests was scored quantitatively, and the scores were submitted to statistical procedures known as correlation and factorial analysis, by means of which it was possible to demonstrate that certain observers performed particularly well or badly on certain groups of tests. One group of tests which showed these individual differences required observers to pick out and identify quickly the main 'figural' aspects while disregarding distracting parts of the field. This type of perception, which was related to intelligence, seems to be somewhat similar to the objective method, described above. In another group of tests, the main requirement appeared to be the ability to be aware of two figures simultaneously, or to move easily from one to the other. It seemed to be related to 'spatial aptitude' – the ability to manipulate shapes in imagination, to know how one shape will fit into another without actually putting them together. This type of perception seems to have some resemblance to that adopted in the analytic procedure. There were in addition certain characteristic individual differences in speed of perception and susceptibility to visual illusions. No relationship was found to exist between any of these characteristic differences and performance on the Rorschach test. The most important and interesting conclusion which can be drawn from this study is that no one pair of dichotomous 'perceptual types' will cover all the variations in performance which occur in perceiving in numerous different situations. But there do appear to be certain fairly consistent methods or types of procedure; and certain persons are more adept in adopting some of these, whereas other persons are more apt with others. It is not at all easy to define the exact nature of these different methods, nor the possible aptitudes upon which they are based.

Again, were it possible to describe and assess the methods adopted by different persons in an infinite number of different perceptual situations, many other characteristic methods and aptitudes might appear. Clearly intelligence, and probably also previous individual experience, have considerable influence on the actual performance in these perceptual tests, which makes it even harder to differentiate and segregate purely perceptual factors. But it is curious and interesting that no relationship was established between perceptual performance and Rorschach test responses which are supposed to demonstrate the personality characteristics which determine our perceptual reactions to our environment. However, the interpretation of Rorschach test responses is always a difficult and debatable problem, and it may be that the particular responses and interpretations employed by Thurstone did not in fact provide a good estimate of relevant personality factors.

That the particular procedures or methods of perception adopted by different individuals depend upon the perceptual situations studied was indicated in an investigation carried out by the author.[32] A variety of perceptual material, including simple and complex shapes, letters and digits, dial faces and pictures, was presented both in a short exposure tachistoscope and also by increasing brightness gradually until they were fully visible through an obscuring mottled grey field. It was found that in general two main types of characteristic appeared: (1) the ability to perceive rapidly pure shape and pattern, and to discriminate these from their background; (2) the ability to interpret shapes in terms of what they represented, as in pictures, letters, digits. Though at first sight the first ability seems to bear some resemblance to Thurstone's first type of perception, it was not however related either to intelligence or to 'spatial aptitude'. The second ability did not function in an all-or-none fashion; some observers were better at perceiving certain types of representational material than others. Intelligence, imagination, and previous experience, including education, undoubtedly influenced their perceptions. Although the distinction did not appear very clearly, there were some who were more cautious and objectively accurate in their responses to the pictorial material, and others whose responses were more imaginative and subjective. Again, in an earlier series of experiments by the author, differences were found in the perception and remembering of pictures between 'verbalizers', who tended to be more objectively accurate about detail, and 'visualizers' who often gained a better impression of the whole picture but overlooked or modified detail. The results of the later experiments were also affected by certain specific factors connected with the two different methods of presentation of the material. The difference between these methods and those employed by Thurstone may in part account for the difference between the characteristics demonstrated here and those obtained by Thurstone.

It is clear, however, that the greater the variety of perceptual situations, including variations both in what is presented and also in the manner in which it is presented, the less possible it is to attribute individual differences in perception to simple 'types' of perceptual method or ability. Indeed, such a typological classification can be made only by glossing over the multifarious individual differences that appear in such varying situations. The relationship to other personality characteristics is even more obscure. What is perceived has been shown in several experiments to be affected by the age and sex of the observer.[33] It is also influenced by his intelligence and previous experience. Thus it has been shown that observers with some training in mathematics perceive diagrams more accurately than those without such a training;[34] and that artists have a lower degree of size constancy than other people.[35] In the tachistoscopic perception of pictures, grammar schoolchildren were found to be more objectively accurate than children from other types of school.[36] Indeed, it may be that only well-educated persons, who have been taught to work accurately and pay attention to detail, are capable of exact analytic perception. Thus it has been found that more intelligent people may show a lower degree of size constancy than less intelligent;[37] and in particular that the less intelligent are seldom able to perceive the 'projected' size under 'analytical' instructions.[38] Again, there may be differences between those with a literary education and those with a scientific or mathematical education. Results obtained in a recent study made under the author's guidance suggest that this is so.

Finally, we cannot differentiate satisfactorily between the effects of these factors upon what is actually perceived from their effects upon direction and concentration of attention. Most of the experiments described in this chapter were aimed at enforcing a high degree of concentrated attention, rather than diffuse or prolonged attention. But 'one can bring a horse to water; one cannot make him drink'. Many of the performances indicating 'synthetic' or subjective perceptions may have resulted from inattention on the part of the observer, due to his lack of interest or of the trained ability to concentrate. On the other hand, a recent study of size-constancy indicated that more suggestible observers might try so hard to cooperate with the experimenter to give very accurate judgements that they over-compensated for distance, and judged the more distant object to be larger than it really was.[39] Again, accurate judgements may have been made in other experiments because the observer was interested in this type of material, and had therefore acquired knowledge of and familiarity with it, which in turn enabled him to concentrate upon its important and relevant features. It is difficult therefore to judge whether in fact what is actually perceived, granted that the observer is attending to it, is modified by personality characteristics, since these influence the nature of his attention and of his judgements, and the amount of relevant information and experience he possesses. The best approach to these problems is perhaps provided by the studies of Gardner and his colleagues described on p. 228.

CHAPTER 13

CONCLUSION

IT has become abundantly clear from the preceding discussion that perception is by no means always a simple, straightforward, and unambiguous process, but is in fact liable to many variations and interruptions. These are caused partly by the great complexity of the perceived field of view as constituted by our normal surroundings; and partly by limitations in the perceptual capacity of the observer. He can view only a small part of his surroundings at any one moment; and even when he scans them deliberately, there is much that he tends to overlook or to perceive incompletely or inaccurately. Undoubtedly during the course of his life he learns to perceive more, and more correctly, especially when he has an interest in so doing, or when he has received special training. But the effects of knowledge and experience are in themselves liable to produce selective perception and the funnelling of attention to objects and events about which special knowledge and experience have been acquired. The consequence is that no two observers may perceive a given scene in exactly the same manner, and that they may disagree considerably as to its nature and contents.

Fortunately we appear to possess certain 'built in' devices which enable us to perceive and respond rapidly to highly significant events. The most noticeable of these is a change in the environment; and the greater and more sudden the change, the more likely it is to attract attention and to stimulate the observer to perceive it to the utmost of his capacities. Any change, such as a sudden rapid movement, which may be potentially dangerous, is thus unlikely to be completely overlooked. However, it may be that the comparatively peaceful and undemanding nature of our normal existence has to some extent lulled us into apathy and carelessness. It may even, as in the states of sensory deprivation set up by a homogeneous environment, have robbed us to some extent of our capacity to attend quickly to the significant features of a rapidly changing environment and to perceive them correctly. Thus in rapidly moving traffic drivers may genuinely fail to perceive oncoming vehicles or straying pedestrians. Not realizing the constant state of danger they are in, they are insufficiently alert to all the significant changes in their surroundings. Nevertheless it is also true that many, if not the majority, acquire a 'traffic sense' and learn to expect and perceive such events.

Our perceptions must always strike a balance between rapidity and ease on the one hand, and accuracy on the other. If we are too quick, we may overlook important events; if we are too accurate, perception is retarded to such an extent as to be inaffective. However, the more intelligent individual at least can learn to modify his manner of perception according to circumstances. Thus although in general his perceptions may be quick and rather superficial, in certain particular situations he learns to search carefully and attentively and to study closely; and to select particular details for examination irrespective of the whole field of view of which they are a part. One of the functions of education is to teach the observer how to do this; and if he has not been taught, we must not blame him if he is inefficient in this type of perception. We have the capacity to perceive our surroundings with different degrees of accuracy and clarity, and different amounts of conscious awareness. Thus we may perceive marginally events and aspects of the environment to the extent that we are able to respond to them appropriately without the necessity of employing the full effort of deliberate and conscious concentration upon all their details. Nevertheless, our capacity for continuous perception is limited. We cannot maintain prolonged awareness of a relatively uninteresting and featureless environment, and sooner or later awareness lapses and we are distracted by irrelevant events or by our own thoughts.

What, in addition to sudden changes, are the features of the environment which we perceive most readily and accurately? Undoubtedly, the objects which we see daily and which we use habitually. In these perceptions, we are assisted to a great extent by our capacity to overlook unimportant details, and to classify these objects into broad general categories related to their appearance and their use. Thus we readily perceive and identify these objects.

However, there are also classes of situations or events, as well as of objects, which we perceive throughout our lives, usually with considerable efficiency. Of these the most important are our spatial relations to our surroundings, and the spatial relations between different parts of these surroundings. We may not be very clearly conscious of these relations, until something happens to change them in an unusual manner. Then our disorientation, and the bewilderment it produces, indicate promptly how much we had perceived marginally. So also we acquire the ability to perceive accurately events in their temporal relations, such as sequences of movements and activities; and the capacity to integrate such series of events into the total patterns, spatial and temporal, characteristic of meaningful scenes, people's behaviour, moving objects, and the like. We even impose on such patterns explanatory concepts such as causality. In fact, as Bartlett pointed out, these and all our perceptions are continually characterized by 'an effort after meaning'; the extraction of some significance or relevance to our knowledge, behaviour, and desires.[1]

One of the many controversial topics in the psychology of perception is the extent to which everyone perceives their environment similarly, and the degree of divergence between their percepts. We may agree that many of the types of perception we have considered are indeed very similar for most people. Perception of brightness, colour, shape, size, numerousness, distance, movement, is to a considerable extent determined by the activities of the sense organs and nervous system. So also it seems is the capacity to attend and the manner in which attention is physiologically determined. Then again much the same objects and events are perceived at least by most people belonging to any one human society, and the uses accorded to them are often very similar. Thus people in childhood acquire the capacity to perceive such objects and events clearly and accurately, to classify them in accordance with socially accepted nomenclature, and to react to them in much the same way. Equally we are all bound to learn something about the spatial and temporal relationships of these objects. Thus much of our perceptual experience is common to all of us.

But also we have seen that individual differences do exist, both in the manner of perceiving and in what is perceived. In many cases these differences may be wholly or partially concealed by what has been called 'redundancy of information'. In the normal environment there are so many different aspects and qualities of objects and events which can be perceived, all of which corroborate to enable identification. One individual may make use of certain of these aspects in perceiving the nature of his environment, and another may utilize others. Thus it is only in the artificially simplified, impoverished, and constrained conditions of laboratory experiments that individual differences may appear clearly. There we do find that people notice and perceive differently. Not only are there differences between the perceptions of different people; but also between the perceptions of the same person at different times. However, the evidence as to the nature of these differences is often hard to obtain, since invariably when they are unable to perceive clearly, people tend to fill out or make inferences from their immediate perceptions by using their reason or imagination. And since these are not closely tied to uniform physiological processes, they vary to a much greater extent. As we have seen, even in cases in which desire and emotion appear to modify perception, it is never quite certain whether it is the immediate perception which varies, or the use which the observer makes of it.

It is natural to suppose that people do vary in their capacity to perceive, or at least to cognize, their surroundings, just as they vary in their other psychological capacities. This variation may be merely one of efficiency; some people perceive more quickly and accurately than do others. Undoubtedly some people are better able than others to control the direction and concentration of their attention. These variations are to a considerable extent functions of training and experience, but they may also have an innate basis, like intellectual efficiency. Indeed, there is considerable evidence that this is so. But at the same time the evidence, for instance, from Thurstone's investigation, suggests that there is no such thing as an all-round perceptual efficiency or inefficiency, but rather that people tend to be relatively more efficient in some types of perception and in some perceptual situations than in others.[2]

Have we any reliable evidence as to whether perception varies qualitatively in a consistent manner in different persons? Again Thurstone's investigation suggests that this is so; but we cannot be sure to what extent these variations are caused by differences in training and experience. They may indeed be a function of differences in intelligence, or in certain other qualities of personality. Or again it may be what the observer makes of his percepts and how he utilizes them which are affected by such qualities. Clearly there is a great deal still to be discovered before these problems can be solved.

NOTES AND REFERENCES

CHAPTER 2: How the Child Learns to Perceive the World Around Him.

1. There is a large number of books by Gesell and Piaget, and their collaborators, presenting the information described in this chapter, of which the most important are: Gesell, A., Ilg, F. L., and Bullis G., *Vision: Its Development in Infant and Child* (Harper, New York, 1949); Piaget, J., *The Child's Construction of Reality* (Routledge & Kegan Paul, London, 1955); Piaget, J. and Inhelder, B., *The Child's Conception of Space* (Routledge & Kegan Paul, London, 1956).
2. Piaget, J., *The Child's Construction of Reality*.
3. ibid.
4. Lewis, M. M., *How Children Learn to Speak* (Harrap, London, 1957).
5. Lewis, M. M., *Infant Speech* (Kegan Paul, London, 1936).
6. Werner, H., *Comparative Psychology of Mental Development*, 2nd Ed. (International Universities Press, New York, 1948).
7. ibid.
8. Lewis, M. M., see note 4.
9. Werner, H., see note 6.
10. The following are quoted from Werner, loc. cit.

CHAPTER 3: The Perception of Objects by Adults.

1. For a fuller discussion of these processes, see Vernon, M. D., *A Further Study of Visual Perception*, Chap. III (2) (Cambridge University Press, 1952).
2. Carmichael, L., Hogan, H. P., and Walter, A. A., 'An Experimental Study of the Effect of Language on the Reproduction of Visually Perceived Form,' *J. Exper. Psychol.*, 1932, 15, 73.
3. Herman, D. T., Lawless, R. H., and Marshall, R. W., 'Variables in the Effect of Language on the Reproduction of Visually Perceived Forms,' *Percept. Motor Skills*, 1957, 7, 171.
4. Brain, W. Russell. 'Visual Object-Agnosia with Special Reference to Gestalt Theory.' *Brain*, 1941, 64, 43.
5. Senden, M. von., *Raum- und Gestaltauffassung bei operierten Blindegeborenen vor und nach der Operation* (Barth, Leipzig, 1932).
6. Bruner, J. S. and Postman, L. 'On the Perception of Incongruity,' *J. Pers.*, 1949, 18, 206.

CHAPTER 4: The Perception of Shape by Adults.

1. Liebmann, S., 'Über das Verhalten farbiger Formen bei Helligkeitsgleichheit von Figur und Grund,' *Psychol. Forsch.*, 1927, 9, 300.

2. Koffka, K. and Harrower, M., 'Colour and Organization,' *Psychol. Forsch.*, 1931, 15, 193.

3. This phenomenon, first demonstrated by Rubin, forms an important feature in Gestalt psychology, which is discussed more fully below (Rubin, E., *Visuellwahrgenomme Figuren*, Copenhagen, Gyldendal, 1921).

4. Cheatham, P. G., 'Visual Perceptual Latency as a Function of Stimulus Brightness, Shape and Contour,' *J. Exper. Psychol.*, 1952, 43, 369.

5. Gelb, A., 'Über den Wegfall der Wahrnehmung von "Oberflächenfarben",' *Zschr. f. Psychol.*, 1920, 84, 193.

6. Perkins, F. T., 'Symmetry in Visual Recall,' *Amer. J. Psychol.*, 1932, 44, 473.

7. A fuller discussion is given by Koffka, K. in *Principles of Gestalt Psychology* (Kegan Paul, London, 1935).

8. Kristofferson, A. B., 'Visual Detection as Influenced by Target Form,' in *Form Discrimination as Related to Military Problems,* edited by Wulfeck, J. W. and Taylor, J. H. (National Academy of Science, Washington, D.C., 1957).

9. Attneave, F., 'Physical Determinants of the Judged Complexity of Shapes,' *J. Exper. Psychol.*, 1957, 53, 221.

10. Osterrieth, P. A., 'Le Test de copie d'une figure complexe,' *Arch. de Psychol.*, 1945, 30, 205.

11. Gottschaldt, K., 'Über den Einfluss der Ehrfahrung auf die Wahrnehmung von Figuren,' *Psychol. Forsch.*, 1926, 8, 261.

12. Orbison, W. D., 'Shape as a Function of the Vector Field,' *Amer. J. Psychol.*, 1939, 52, 31.

13. Krauskopf, J., Duryea, R. A., and Bitterman, M. E., 'Threshold for Visual Form,' *Amer. J. Psychol.*, 1954, 67, 427.

14. Crook, M. N., 'Facsimile-Generated Analogues for Instrumental Form Displays,' in *Form Discrimination as Related to Military Problems.* See note 8.

15. Rock, I. and Heimer, W., 'The Effect of Retinal and Phenomenal Orientation on the Perception of Form,' *Amer. J. Psychol.*, 1957, 70, 493.

16. French, R. S., 'Identification of Dot Patterns from Memory as a Function of Complexity,' *J. Exper. Psychol.*, 1954, 47, 22.

17. Boynton, R. M. and Bush, W. R., 'Recognition of Forms against a Complex Background,' *J. Opt. Soc. Amer.*, 1956, 46, 758.

18. Johansen, M., 'An Introductory Study of Voluminal Form Perception,' *Nordisk Psykologi's Monograph Series*, 1954, No. 5.

19. Johansen, M., 'The Experienced Continuations of Some Three-Dimensional Forms,' *Acta Psychol.*, 1957, 13, 1.

20. Michotte, A., 'Perception et Cognition,' *Acta Psychol.*, 1955, 11, 70.

21. Nadel, S. F., 'A Field Experiment in Racial Psychology,' *Brit. J. Psychol.*, 1937, 28, 195.

22. Leeper, R., 'A Study of a Neglected Portion of the Field of Learning – the Development of Sensory Organization,' *J. Genet. Psychol.*, 1935, 46, 41.

23. Bartlett, F. C., *Remembering* (Cambridge University Press, 1932).

24. Goldscheider, A. and Müller, A., 'Zur Physiologie und Pathologie des Lesens,' *Zschr. f. klin. Med.*, 1893, 23, 131.

25. Thouless, R. H. 'Phenomenal Regression to the Real Object,' *Brit. J. Psychol.*, 1931, 21, 339.

26. Brunswik, E., 'Distal Focusing of Perception,' *Psychol. Monogs.*, 1944, 56, No. 1.

27. Leibowitz, H. and Bourne, L. E., 'Time and Intensity as Determiners of Perceived Shape,' *J. Exper. Psychol.*, 1956, 51, 277.

28. Hastorf, A. H., 'The Influence of Suggestion on the Relationship between Stimulus Size and Perceived Distance,' *J. Psychol.*, 1950, 29, 195.

29. Slack, C. W., 'Familiar Size as a Cue to Size in the Presence of Conflicting Cues,' *J. Exper. Psychol.*, 1956, 52, 194.

30. Joynson, R. B., 'An Experimental Synthesis of the Associationist and Gestalt Accounts of the Perception of Size,' *Quart. J. Exper. Psychol.*, 1958, 10, 65.

CHAPTER 5: The Perception of Colour.

1. Eysenck, H. J., 'A Critical and Experimental Study of Color Preferences,' *Amer. J. Psychol.*, 1941, 54, 385.

2. Kouwer, B. J., *Colors and their Character* (Nijhof, The Hague, 1949).

3. Rorschach, H. *Psychodiagnostics* (Grune & Stratton, New York, 1942).

4. See Evans, R. M., *An Introduction to Colour* (Chapman & Hall, London, 1948).

5. Brown, R. W. and Lenneberg, E. H., 'A Study of Language and Cognition,' *J. Abn. Soc. Psychol.*, 1954, 49, 454.

6. For a full discussion of the different appearances of colours, see Katz, D., *The World of Colour* (Kegan Paul, London, 1935).

7. Helson, H. and Jeffers, V. B., 'Fundamental Problems in Color Vision,' *J. Exper. Psychol.*, 1940, 26, 1.

8. Tudor-Hart, B., 'Studies in Transparency, Form and Colour,' *Psychol. Forsch.*, 1928, 10, 255.

9. Ishihara, S., *Tests for Colour Blindness*, 7th Ed. (Kanahara, Tokyo, 1936).

10. Gelb, A., 'Über den Wegfall der Wahrnehmung von "Oberflächenfarben",' *Zschr. f. Psychol.*, 1920, 84, 193.

11. Myers, C. S., 'A Case of Synaesthesia,' *Brit. J. Psychol.*, 1911, 4, 228.

12. Birren, F., *Color Psychology and Color Therapy* (McGraw-Hill, New York, 1950).

13. Myers, C. S., 'Two Cases of Synaesthesia,' *Brit. J. Psychol.*, 1914, 7, 112.

14. Birren, F., op. cit.

15. Wheeler, R. H. and Cutsforth, T. D., 'Synaesthesia in the Development of the Concept,' *J. Exper. Psychol.*, 1925, 8, 149.

CHAPTER 6: The Development of Shape and Colour Perception in Children.

1. Ling, B. C., 'Form Discrimination as a Learning Cue in Infants,' *Compar. Psychol. Monogs.*, 1941, 17, No. 2.

2. Gellerman, L. W., 'Form Discrimination in Chimpanzees and Two-year-old Children. I. Form (Triangularity) *per se*,' *J. Genet. Psychol.*, 1933, 42, 3.

3. ibid., 'II. Form versus Background,' *J. Genet. Psychol.*, 1933, 42, 28.

4. Terman, L. M. and Merrill, M. A., *Measuring Intelligence* (Harrap, London, 1937).

5. Granit, A. R., 'A Study on the Perception of Form,' *Brit. J. Psychol.*, 1921, 12, 223.

6. Piaget, J. and Inhelder, B., *The Child's Conception of Space* (Routledge & Kegan Paul, London, 1956).

7. ibid.

8. Gesell, A. and Ames, L. B., 'The Development of Directionality in Drawing,' *J. Genet. Psychol.*, 1946, 68, 45.

9. Slochower, M. Z., 'Experiments on Dimensional and Figural Problems in the Clay and Pencil Reproductions of Line Figures by Young Children. II. Shape,' *J. Genet. Psychol.*, 1946, 69, 77.

10. Rupp, H., 'Über optische Analyse,' *Psychol. Forsch.*, 1923, 4, 262.

Notes and References

11. Bender, L., *A Visual Motor Gestalt Test and its Clinical Use* (American Orthopsychiatric Association, New York, 1938).

12. Osterrieth, P. A., 'Le Test de copie d'une figure complexe,' *Arch. de Psychol.*, 1945, 30, 205.

13. Walters, A., 'A Genetic Study of Geometrical-Optical Illusions,' *Genet. Psychol. Monogs.*, 1942, 25, 101.

14. Piaget, J. and Stettler-von Albertini, B., 'Observations sur la perception des bonnes formes chez l'enfant par actualization des lignes virtuelles,' *Arch. de Psychol.*, 1954, 34, 203.

15. Ghent, L., 'Perception of Overlapping and Embedded Figures by Children of Different Ages,' *Amer. J. Psychol.*, 1956, 69, 575.

16. Piaget, J., *Les Mécanismes perceptifs* (Presses Universitaires de France, Paris, 1961).

17. Strauss, A. A. and Lehtinen, L. E., *Psychopathology and Education of the Brain-Injured Child* (Grune & Stratton, New York, 1947).

18. Cobrinik, L., 'The Performance of Brain-Injured Children on Hidden Figure Tasks,' *Amer. J. Psychol.*, 1959, 72, 566.

19. Cruikshank, R. M., 'The Development of Visual Size Constancy in Early Infancy,' *J. Genet. Psychol.*, 1941, 58, 327.

20. Beyrl, F., 'Über die Grössenauffassung bei Kindern,' *Zsch. f. Psychol.*, 1926, 100, 344.

21. Zeigler, H. P. and Leibowitz, H., 'Apparent Visual Size as a Function of Distance for Children and Adults,' *Amer. J. Psychol.*, 1957, 70, 106.

22. Dukes, W. F., 'Ecological Representativeness in Studying Perceptual Size-Constancy in Childhood,' *Amer. J. Psychol.*, 1951, 64, 87.

23. Lambercier, M., 'La Configuration en profondeur dans la constance des grandeurs,' *Arch. de Psychol.*, 1946, 31, 287.

24. Piaget, J. and Lambercier, M., 'La Comparaison des grandeurs projectives chez l'enfant et chez l'adulte,' *Arch. de Psychol.*, 1951, 33, 81.

25. Honkavaara, S., 'A Critical Revaluation of the Color and Form Reaction,' *J. Psychol.*, 1958, 45, 25.

26. Chase, W. P., 'Color Vision in Infants,' *J. Exper. Psychol.*, 1937, 20, 203.

27. Staples, R., 'The Responses of Infants to Color,' *J. Exper. Psychol.*, 1932, 15, 119.

28. Cook, W. M., 'Ability of Children in Color Discrimination,' *Child Devel.*, 1931, 2, 303.

29. Malrieu, P. 'Quelques problèmes de la vision des couleurs chez l'enfant,' *J. de Psychol.*, 1955, 52, 222.

30. Brian, C. R. and Goodenough, F. L., 'The Relative Potency of Color and Form Perception at Various Ages,' *J. Exper. Psychol.*, 1929, 12, 197.

31. Ségers, J. E., 'Recherches sur la perception visuelle chez des enfants âgés de trois à douze ans et leur application à l'éducation,' *J. de Psychol.*, 1926, 23, 608.

CHAPTER 7 : The Perception of Special Types of Material.

1. Terman, L. M. and Merrill, M. A., *Measuring Intelligence* (Harrap, London, 1937).

2. Vernon, M. D., 'The Relation of Cognition and Phantasy in Children,' *Brit. J. Psychol.*, 1940, 30, 273.

3. Foster, R. J., 'Those Posters!' *Visual Education*, 1955, p. 22.

4. Allen, W., 'Readability of Instructional Film Commentary,' *J. Appl. Psychol.*, 1952, 36, 164.

5. Laner, S., 'Some Factors Influencing the Effectiveness of an Instructional Film,' *Brit. J. Psychol.*, 1955, 46, 280.

6. Rulon, P. J., *The Sound Motion Picture in Science Teaching* (Harvard University Press, 1933).

7. Laner, S., see note 5; Laner, S., 'The Impact of Visual-Aid Displays Showing a Manipulative Task,' *Quart. J. Exper. Psychol.*, 1954, 6, 95.

8. Vernon, M. D., 'Perception and Understanding of Instructional Television Programmes,' *Brit. J. Psychol.*, 1953, 44, 116.

9. Goldscheider, A. and Müller, E., 'Zur Physiologie und Pathologie des Lesens,' *Zschr. f. klin. Med.*, 1893, 23, 131.

10. Miller, G. A., Bruner, J. S., and Postman, L., 'Familiarity of Letter Sequences and Tachistoscopic Identification,' *J. Gen. Psychol.*, 1954, 50, 129.

11. Morton, J., 'An Investigation into the Effects of an Adult Reading Efficiency Course,' *Occup. Psychol.*, 1959, 33, 222.

12. Vernon, M. D., 'Characteristics of Proof-Reading,' *Brit. J. Psychol.*, 1931, 21, 368.

13. Malter, M., 'The Ability of Children to Read Cross-Sections,' *J. Educ. Psychol.*, 1947, 38, 157.

14. Malter, M., 'The Ability of Children to Read a Process-Diagram,' *J. Educ. Psychol.*, 1947, 38, 290.

15. Vernon, M. D., 'Learning From Graphical Material,' *Brit. J. Psychol.*, 1946, 36, 145.

16. ibid.

17. Vernon, M. D., see note 8.

18. Johnson, M. L., 'Seeing's Believing,' *New Biology*, 1953, No. 15.

19. James, D. W., Johnson, M. L., and Venning, P. 'Testing for Learnt Skill in Observation and Evaluation of Evidence,' *Lancet*, 1956, 271, 379.

20. See Johnson Abercrombie, M. L., *The Anatomy of Judgment* (Hutchinson, London, 1960).

CHAPTER 8: The Perception of Space.

1. Duncker, K., 'Über induzierte Bewegung,' *Psychol. Forsch.*, 1929, 12, 180.

2. Gibson, J. J. and Mowrer, O. H., 'Determinants of the Perceived Vertical and Horizontal,' *Psychol. Rev.*, 1938, 45, 300.

3. Witkin, H. A. and Asch, S. E., 'Studies in Space Orientation,' *J. Exper. Psychol.*, 1948, 38, 325, 455, 603, and 762.

4. See, for instance, Stratton, G. M., 'Vision Without Inversion of the Retinal Image,' *Psychol. Rev.*, 1894, 4, 341 and 463; and Ewert, P. H., 'A Study of the Effect of Inverted Retinal Stimulation upon Spatially Co-ordinated Behaviour,' *Genet. Psychol. Monogs.*, 1930, 7, 177.

5. Kohler, I., 'Rehabilitation in Perception,' *Die Pyramide*, 1953, parts 5, 6, and 7.

6. Senden, M. von., *Raum- und Gestaltauffassung bei operierten Blindegeborenen vor und nach der Operation* (Barth, Leipzig, 1932).

7. Ittelson, W. H., 'Size as a Cue to Distance: Radial Motion,' *Amer. J. Psychol.*, 1951, 64, 188.

8. Ames, A., *Some Demonstrations concerned with the Origin and Nature of our Sensations* (A Laboratory Manual, Dartmouth Eye Institute, 1946).

9. Mount, G. E., et al., 'Distance Judgment of Colored Objects,' *J. Gen. Psychol.*, 1956, 55, 207.

10. Katz, D., *The World of Colour* (Kegan Paul, London, 1935).

11. Wagner, R., 'Über die Wahrnehmung schattenloser Objekte,' *Zschr. Biol.*, 1941, 100, 421.

12. Graham, C. H., 'Visual Perception,' in *Handbook of Experimental Psychology*, ed. by S. S. Stevens (Wiley, New York, 1951); and Gibson, E. J., Gibson, J. J., Smith, O. W., and Flock, H., 'Motion Parallax as a Determinant of Perceived Depth,' *J. Exper. Psychol.*, 1959, 58, 40.

13. Gibson, J. J., *The Perception of the Visual World* (Houghton Mifflin, Boston, 1950).

14. Eaton, E. M., 'The Visual Perception of Solid Form,' *Brit. J. Ophthalmology*, 1919, 3, 63.

15. Described in Ittelson, W. H., *The Ames Demonstrations in Perception* (Princeton University Press, 1952).

16. Kilpatrick, F. P., 'Two Processes in Perceptual Learning,' *J. Exper. Psychol.*, 1954, 47, 362.

17. Piaget, J. and Inhelder, B., *The Child's Conception of Space* (Routledge & Kegan Paul, London, 1956).

18. Strauss, A. A. and Lehtinen, L. E., *Psychopathology and Education of the Brain-Injured Child* (Grune & Stratton, New York, 1947).

19. Semmes, J., Weinstein, S., Ghent, L., and Teuber, H. L., 'Spatial Orientation in Man after Cerebral Injury,' *J. Psychol.*, 1955, 39, 227.

20. McFie, J., Piercy, M. F., and Zangwill, O. L., 'Visual-Spatial Agnosia Associated with Lesions of the Right Cerebral Hemisphere.' *Brain*, 1950, 73, 167.

CHAPTER 9: The Perception of Movement.

1. Gesell, A., Ilg, F. L., and Bullis, G. E., *Vision: its Development in Infant and Child* (Harper, New York, 1949).

2. Riddoch, G., 'Dissociation of Visual Perceptions due to Occipital Injuries, with Especial Reference to Appreciation of Movement,' *Brain*, 1917, 40, 15.

3. Brown, R. H., and Conklin, J. E., 'The Lower Threshold of Visible Movement as a Function of Exposure Time,' *Amer. J. Psychol.*, 1954, 67, 104; and Brown, R. H., 'Velocity Discrimination and the Intensity-Time Relation,' *J. Opt. Soc. Amer.*, 1955, 45, 189.

4. Ditchburn, R. W., Fender, D. H., and Mayne, S., 'Vision with Controlled Movements of the Retinal Image,' *J. Physiol.*, 1959, 145, 98.

5. ibid.

6. Miller, E. F., 'Effect of Exposure Time upon the Ability to Perceive a Moving Target,' Research project *NM 1701 11 Report No. 2* (U.S. Naval School of Aviation Medicine, 1959).

7. Graybiel, A., Clark, B., MacCorquodale, K., and Hupp, D. I., 'Role of Vestibular Nystagmus in the Visual Perception of a Moving Target in the Dark,' *Amer. J. Psychol.*, 1946, 59, 259.

8. Gibson, J. J., *The Perception of the Visual World*, Chap. 7 (Houghton Mifflin, Boston, 1950).

9. Brown, J. F., 'The Visual Perception of Velocity,' *Psychol. Forsch.*, 1931, 14, 199.

10. ibid.

11. Teuber, H. L. and Bender, M. B., 'Alterations in Pattern Vision Following Trauma of Occipital Lobes in Man,' *J. Gen. Psychol.*, 1949, 40, 37.

12. This phenomenon was first investigated extensively by Wertheimer, M., 'Experimentelle Studien über das Sehen von Bewegung,' *Zschr. f. Psychol.*, 1912, 61, 161. Since then a large number of experiments has been carried out on the phenomenon which are discussed fully in Vernon, M. D., *A Further Study of Visual Perception*, Chap. VIII (Cambridge University Press, 1952).

13. Jones, E. E. and Bruner, J. S., 'Expectancy in Apparent Visual Movement,' *Brit. J. Psychol.*, 1954, 45, 157.

14. Brown, J. F., see note 9.

15. Gemelli, A., 'The Visual Perception of Movement,' *Amer. J. Psychol.*, 1958, 71, 291.

16. ibid.

17. Jones and Bruner, see note 13.

18. Comalli, P. E., 'Differential Effects of Directional Dynamics of Pictorial Objects on Real and Apparent Motion in Artists and Chemists,' *J. Psychol.*, 1960, 49, 99.

19. Teuber and Bender, see note 11.

20. Werner, H. and Thuma, B. D., 'A Deficiency in the Perception of Apparent Motion in Children with Brain Injury,' *Amer. J. Psychol.*, 1942, 55, 58.

21. Benussi, V., 'Versuche zur Bestimmung der Gestaltzeit,' *Ber. VI Kongress exp. Psychol.*, Göttingen, 1914.

22. Johansson, G., 'Studies on Motion After-Effects,' *Reports from the Psychological Laboratory*, No. 4 (University of Stockholm, 1954).

23. Wallach, H. and O'Connell, D. N., 'The Kinetic Depth Effect,' *J. Exper. Psychol.*, 1953, 45, 205; and Wallach, H., O'Connell, D. N., and Neissen, U., 'The Memory Effect of Visual Perception of Three-Dimensional Form,' *J. Exper. Psychol.*, 1953, 45, 360.

24. Langdon, J., 'Further Studies in the Perception of a Changing Shape,' *Quart. J. Exper. Psychol.*, 1953, 5, 89.

25. Gibson, J. J. and Gibson, E. J., 'Continuous Perspective Transformations and the Perception of Rigid Motion,' *J. Exper. Psychol.*, 1957, 54, 129; and Gibson, J. J., 'Optical Motions and Transformations as Stimuli for Visual Perception,' *Psychol. Rev.*, 1957, 64, 288.

26. Ames, A., 'Visual Perception and the Rotating Trapezoidal Window,' *Psychol. Monogs.*, 1951, 65, No. 7.

27. Allport, G. W. and Pettigrew, T. F., 'Cultural Influence on the Perception of Movement: the Trapezoidal Illusion among Zulus,' *J. Abn. Soc. Psychol.*, 1957, 55, 104.

28. Piaget, J., *Les Notions de mouvement et de vitesse chez l'enfant* (Presses Universitaires de France, Paris, 1946).

29. Piaget, J., *The Child's Construction of Reality* (Routledge & Kegan Paul, London, 1955).

30. Michotte, A., *La Perception de la causalité* (Publications Universitaires de Louvain, 1946).

31. Gemelli, A. and Cappellini, A., 'The Influence of the Subject's Attitude in Perception,' *Acta Psychol.*, 1958, 14, 12.

32. Olum, V., 'Developmental Differences in the Perception of Causality,' *Amer. J. Psychol.*, 1956, 69, 417.

33. Piaget, J. and Lambercier, M., 'La Causalité perceptive visuelle chez l'enfant et chez l'adulte,' *Arch. de Psychol.*, 1958, 36, 77.

34. Brenner, M. W., 'The Developmental Study of Apparent Movement,' *Quart. J. Exper. Psychol.*, 1957, 9, 169.

35. Michotte, A., see note 30.

36. Johansson, G., *Configurations in Event Perception* (Almqvist & Wiksells, Upsala, 1950).

CHAPTER 10: Attention and Perception.

1. Meisenheimer, J., 'Experimente im Peripheren Sehen von Gestalten,' *Arch. f. d. ges. Psychol.*, 1929, 67, 1.

2. Grindley, G. C., 'Psychological Factors in Peripheral Vision,' *Medical Res. Counc. Spec. Rep. Series*, 1931, No. 163.

3. Chapman, D. W., 'Relative Effects of Determinate and Indeterminate *Aufgaben*,' *Amer. J. Psychol.*, 1932, 44, 163.

4. Külpe, O., 'Versuche über Abstraktion,' *Ber. I Kongress exp. Psychol.*, Giessen, 1904.

5. Dallenbach, K. M., 'The "Range of Attention",' *Psychol. Bull.*, 1928, 25, 152.

6. Lawrence, D. H. and Laberge, D. L., 'Relationship Between Recognition Accuracy and Order of Reporting Stimulus Dimensions,' *J. Exper. Psychol.*, 1956, 51, 12.

7. Henneman, R. H., 'The Effect of Irrelevant Information upon Complex Visual Discrimination,' in *Form Discrimination as Related to Military Problems*, edited by Wulfeck, J. W. and Taylor, J. H. (National Academy of Science, Washington, D.C., 1957).

8. Wyatt, D. F. and Campbell, D. T., 'On the Liability of Stereotype or Hypothesis,' *J. Abn. Soc. Psychol.*, 1951, 46, 496.

9. Siipola, E., 'A Group Study of some Effects of Preparatory Sets,' *Psychol. Monogs.*, 1935, 46, No. 210.

10. Davis, D. R. and Sinha, D., 'The Influence of an Interpolated Experience upon Recognition,' *Quart. J. Exper. Psychol.*, 1950, 2, 132.

11. Kilpatrick, F. P., 'Two Processes in Perceptual Learning,' *J. Exper. Psychol.*, 1954, 47, 362.

12. Weiner, M., 'Perceptual Development in a Distorted Room,' *Psychol. Monogs.*, 1958, 70, No. 16.

13. Fox, C., 'A Study in Preperception,' *Brit. J. Psychol.*, 1924, 15, 1.

14. Christensen, J. M. and Crannell, C. W., 'The Effect of Selected Visual Training Procedures on the Visual-Form Field,' *U.S.A.F. W.A.D.C. Tech. Rep.*, 1955, 54–239.

15. Bruce, R. H. and Low, F. N., 'The Effect of Practice with Brief-Exposure Techniques upon Central and Peripheral Visual Acuity and a Search for a Brief Test of Peripheral Acuity,' *J. Exper. Psychol.*, 1951, 41, 275.

16. George, S. S., 'Attitude in Relation to the Psychophysical Judgment,' *Amer. J. Psychol.*, 1917, 28, 1.

17. Treisman, M. and Howarth, C. I., 'Changes in Threshold Level Produced by a Signal Preceding or Following the Threshold Stimulus,' *Quart. J. Exper. Psychol.*, 1959, 11, 129.

18. Baker, C. H., 'Attention to Visual Displays During a Vigilance Task. I. Biasing Attention,' *Brit. J. Psychol.*, 1958, 49, 279.

19. Enoch, J. M., 'Effect of the Size of a Complex Display upon Visual Search,' *J. Opt. Soc. Amer.*, 1959, 49, 280; Ford, A., et al., 'Analysis of Eye Movements During Free Search,' *J. Opt. Soc. Amer.*, 1959, 49, 287; Shackel, B., 'Eye Movements in a Simple Visual Task,' *Proc. XVIth Inter. Congr. Psychol.*, 1960 (not yet published).

20. Broadbent, D. E., *Perception and Communication*, Chap. 2 (Pergamon Press, London, 1958).

21. Mowbray, G. H., 'The Perception of Short Phrases Presented Simultaneously for Visual and Auditory Reception,' *Quart. J. Exper. Psychol.*, 1954, 6, 86.

22. Hylan, J. P., 'The Distribution of Attention,' *Psychol. Rev.*, 1903, 10, 373.

23. Humphrey, G., Dawe, P. G. M., and Mandell, B., 'New High Speed Electronic Tachistoscope,' *Nature*, 1955, 176, 231.

24. Smith, G. J. W. and Henriksson, M., 'The Effect on an Established

Percept of a Perceptual Process beyond Awareness.' *Acta Psychol.* 1955, 11, 346.

25. Kolers, P. A., 'Subliminal Stimulation in Problem-Solving,' *Amer. J. Psychol.*, 1957, 70, 437.

26. Mager, A., 'Neue Versuche zur Messung der Geschwindigheit der Aufmerksamkeitswanderung,' *Arch. f. d. ges. Psychol.*, 1925, 53, 391.

27. Poulton, E. C., 'Perceptual Anticipation and Reaction Time,' *Quart. J. Exper. Psychol.*, 1950, 2, 99.

28. Guilford, J. P., '"Fluctuations of Attention" with Weak Visual Stimuli,' *Amer. J. Psychol.*, 1927, 38, 534.

29. Dixon, N. F., 'Apparatus for Continuous Recording of the Visual Threshold by the Method of "Closed Loop Control",' *Quart. J. Exper. Psychol.*, 1958, 10, 62.

30. Pickford, R. W., 'Binocular Colour Combinations,' *Nature*, 1947, 159, 268.

31. Gellhorn, E., 'Über den Wettstreit im Nachbild,' *Arch. f. d. ges. Physiol.*, 1928, 218, 54.

32. Engel, E., 'The Role of Content in Binocular Resolution,' *Amer. J. Psychol.*, 1956, 69, 87.

33. Bagby, J. W., 'A Cross-Cultural Study of Perceptual Predominance in Binocular Rivalry,' *J. Abn. Soc. Psychol.*, 1957, 54, 331.

34. Pritchard, R. M., Heron, W., and Hebb, D. O., 'Visual Perception Approached by the Method of Stabilized Images,' *Canad. J. Psychol.*, 1960, 14, 67.

35. Berlyne, D. E., 'Conflict and Information-Theory Variables as Determinants of Human Perceptual Curiosity,' *J. Exper. Psychol.*, 1957, 53, 399; 'The Influence of Complexity and Novelty in Visual Figures on Orienting Responses,' *J. Exper. Psychol.*, 1958, 55, 289.

36. Mackworth, N. H., 'Researches on the Measurement of Human Performance,' *Medical Res. Counc. Spec. Rep. Series*, 1950, No. 268.

37. A fuller discussion of these and the following experimental findings is given in Broadbent, D. E., *Perception and Communication*, Chap. 6, see note 20.

38. Bartlett, F. C., 'Fatigue Following Highly Skilled Work,' *Proc. Roy. Soc. B*, 1943, 131, 247.

39. Bexton, W. H., Heron, W., and Scott, T. H., 'Effects of Decreased Variation in the Sensory Environment,' *Canad. J. Psychol.*, 1954, 8, 70; Heron, W., Doane, B. K., and Scott, T. H., 'Visual Disturbances after Prolonged Perceptual Isolation,' *Canad. J. Psychol.*, 1956, 10, 13.

40. Smith, S. and Lewty, W. 'Perceptual Isolation Using a Silent Room.' *Lancet*, 1959, ii, 342.

41. Leiderman, H., et al., 'Sensory Deprivation,' *A.M.A. Arch. Internal Medicine*, 1958, 101, 389.

42. Ditchburn, R. W., 'Physical Methods Applied to the Study of Visual Perception,' *Bull. Inst. Physics*, 1959, p. 121.

43. The original experiments were by Hochberg, J. E., Triebel, W., and Seamen, G., 'Color Adaptation, under Conditions of Homogeneous Visual Stimulation (*Ganzfeld*),' *J. Exper. Psychol.*, 1951, 41, 153. They have been repeated with similar results by D. M. Vowles, working in the Psychological Laboratory, University of Reading.

44. A whole series of experiments on these effects has been carried out by W. Cohen, some of which are summarized in 'Spatial and Temporal Characteristics of the *Ganzfeld*,' *Amer. J. Psychol.*, 1957, 70, 403.

45. Schaffer, H. R., 'Objective Observations of Personality Development in Early Infancy,' *Brit. J. Med. Psychol.*, 1958, 31, 174.

46. Perky, C. W., 'An Experimental Study of Imagination,' *Amer. J. Psychol.*, 1910, 21, 422.

47. Miller, J. G., 'Discrimination without Awareness,' *Amer. J. Psychol.*, 1939, 52, 562; Wilcott, R. C., 'Subliminal Stimulation *v.* Psychophysical Thresholds,' *Percept. Motor Skills*, 1957, 7, 29.

48. Goldstein, M. E., 'Subliminal Perception with Optical Illusions,' *J. Gen. Psychol.*, 1960, 62, 89.

49. Dixon, N. F., *The Effect of Subliminal Stimulation upon Cognitive and Other Processes* (Unpublished Ph.D. thesis, University of Reading).

50. Dixon, N. F., 'Apparent Changes in the Visual Threshold as a Function of Subliminal Stimulation,' *Quart. J. Exper. Psychol.*, 1958, 10, 211.

51. Edwards, A. E., 'Subliminal Tachistoscopic Perception as a Function of Threshold Method,' *J. Psychol.*, 1960, 50, 139.

52. The experimental work on the reticular formation is discussed fully in: Jasper, H. H., et al. (Editors), *Reticular Formation of the Brain* (Churchill, London, 1957); and Samuels, I., 'Reticular Mechanisms and Behavior,' *Psychol. Bull.*, 1959, 56, 1.

CHAPTER 11: The Relation to Perception of Motivation and Emotion.

1. Levine, R., Chein, I., and Murphy, G., 'The Relation of Intensity of a Need to the Amount of Perceptual Distortion,' *J. Psychol.*, 1942, 13, 283.

2. Lazarus, R. S., Yousem, H., and Arenberg, D., 'Hunger and Perception,' *J. Person.*, 1953, 21, 312.

3. Wispé, L. G. and Drambarean, N. C., 'Physiological Need, Word Frequency and Visual Duration Thresholds,' *J. Exper. Psychol.*, 1953, 46, 25.

4. Postman, L. and Crutchfield, R. S., 'The Interaction of Need, Set and Stimulus-Structure in a Cognitive Task,' *Amer. J. Psychol.*, 1952, 65, 196.

5. Eriksen, C. W., 'Some Implications for T.A.T. Interpretation Arising from Need and Perception Experiments,' *J. Person.*, 1951, 19, 282.

6. McClelland, D. C. and Liberman, A. M., 'The Effect of Need for Achievement on Recognition of Need-Related Words.' *J. Person.*, 1949, 18, 236.

7. Postman, L., Bruner, J. S., and McGinnies, E., 'Personal Values as Selective Factors in Perception,' *J. Abn. Soc. Psychol.*, 1948, 43, 142.

8. Solomon, R. L. and Howes, D. W., 'Word Frequency, Personal Values and Visual Duration Thresholds,' *Psychol. Rev.*, 1951, 58, 256.

9. The frequencies with which words occur in printed literature have been measured and are presented in Thorndike, E. L. and Lorge, I., *The Teachers' Word Book of 30,000 Words* (Bureau of Publications, New York, Teachers' College, Columbia University, 1952).

10. Postman, L. and Schneider, B. H., 'Personal Values, Visual Recognition and Recall,' *Psychol. Rev.*, 1951, 58, 271.

11. Seeleman, V., 'The Influence of Attitude upon the Remembering of Pictorial Material,' *Arch. Psychol.*, 1940, No. 258.

12. Secord, P. F., Bevan, W., and Katz, B., 'The Negro Stereotype and Perceptual Accentuation,' *J. Abn. Soc. Psychol.*, 1956, 53, 78.

13. Lindzey, G. and Rogolsky, S., 'Prejudice and Identification of Minority Group Membership,' *J. Abn. Soc. Psychol.*, 1950, 45, 37.

14. Pettigrew, T. F., Allport, G. W., and Barnett, E. O., 'Binocular Resolution and Perception of Race in South Africa,' *Brit. J. Psychol.*, 1958, 49, 265.

15. Marks, E. S., 'Skin Color Judgments of Negro College Students,' *J. Abn. Soc. Psychol.*, 1943, 38, 370.

16. Sherif, M., *The Psychology of Social Norms* (Harper, New York, 1936).

17. Luchins, A. S., 'Social Influences on Perception of Complex Drawings,' *J. Soc. Psychol.*, 1945, 21, 257.

18. Frenkel-Brunswik, E., 'Intolerance of Ambiguity as an Emotional and Perceptual Personality Variable,' *J. Person.*, 1949, 18, 108.

19. Bruner, J. S. and Goodman, C. C., 'Value and Need as Organizing Factors in Perception,' *J. Abn. Soc. Psychol.*, 1947, 42, 33.

20. See, for instance, Carter, L. F. and Schooler, K., 'Value, Need and Other Factors in Perception,' *Psychol. Rev.*, 1949, 56, 200; Bruner, J. S. and Rodrigues, J. S., 'Some Determinants of Apparent Size,' *J. Abn. Soc. Psychol.*, 1953, 48, 17; and Tajfel, H. and Cawasjee, S. D., 'Value and Accentuation of Judged Differences,' *J. Abn. Soc. Psychol.*, 1959, 59, 436. A fuller discussion of some of these experiments is given by Tajfel, H., 'Value and the Perceptual Judgment of Magnitude,' *Psychol. Rev.*, 1957, 64, 192.

21. Beams, H. L., 'Affectivity as a Factor in the Apparent Size of Pictured Food Objects,' *J. Exper. Psychol.*, 1954, 47, 197.

22. Gilchrist, J. C. and Nesberg, L. S., 'Need and Perceptual Change in Need-Related Objects,' *J. Exper. Psychol.*, 1952, 44, 369.

23. Lambert, W. W., Solomon, R. L., and Watson, P. D., 'Reinforcement and Extinction as Factors in Size Estimation,' *J. Exper. Psychol.*, 1949, 39, 637.

24. Proshansky, H. and Murphy, G., 'The Effects of Reward and Punishment on Perception,' *J. Psychol.*, 1942, 13, 295.

25. Tajfel, H., see note 20.

26. Schafer, R. and Murphy, G., 'The Role of Autism in a Visual Figure-Ground Relationship,' *J. Exper. Psychol.*, 1943, 32, 335.

27. See, for instance, Rock, I. and Fleck, F. S., 'A Re-examination of the Effect of Monetary Reward and Punishment on Figure-Ground Perception,' *J. Exper. Psychol.*, 1950, 40, 766; Jackson, D. N., 'A Further Examination of the Role of Autism in a Visual Figure-Ground Relationship,' *J. Psychol.*, 1954, 38, 339; Solley, C. M. and Sommer, R., 'Perceptual Autism in Children,' *J. Gen. Psychol.*, 1957, 56, 3; and Sommer, R., 'The Effects of Reward and Punishment During Perceptual Organization,' *J. Person.*, 1957, 25, 550.

28. Smith, K. R., Parker, G. B., and Robinson, G. A., 'An Exploratory Investigation of Autistic Perception,' *J. Abn. Soc. Psychol.*, 1951, 46, 324.

29. Verville, E., 'The Effect of Emotional and Motivational Sets on the Perception of Incomplete Pictures,' *J. Genet. Psychol.*, 1946, 69, 133.

30. Postman, L. and Bruner, J. S., 'Perception Under Stress,' *Psychol. Rev.*, 1948, 55, 314.

31. Smock, C. D., 'The Influence of Psychological Stress on the "Intolerance of Ambiguity",' *J. Abn. Soc. Psychol.*, 1955, 50, 177.

32. Spence, D. E., 'Success, Failure and Recognition Threshold,' *J. Person.*, 1957, 25, 712.

33. Postman, L. and Solomon, R. L., 'Perceptual Sensitivity to Completed and Incompleted Tasks,' *J. Person.*, 1950, 18, 347.

34. Eriksen, C. W. and Brown, C. T., 'An Experimental and Theoretical Analysis of Perceptual Defense,' *J. Abn. Soc. Psychol.*, 1956, 52, 224.

35. Postman, L. and Brown, D. R., 'The Perceptual Consequences of Success and Failure,' *J. Abn. Soc. Psychol.*, 1952, 47, 213.

36. Lysak, W., 'The Effects of Punishment Upon Syllable Recognition Thresholds,' *J. Exper. Psychol.*, 1954, 47, 343.

37. Reece, M. M., 'The Effect of Shock on Recognition Thresholds,' *J. Abn. Soc. Psychol.*, 1954, 49, 165.

38. Lazarus, R. S. and McCleary, R. A., 'Autonomic Discrimination Without Awareness,' *Psychol. Rev.*, 1951, 58, 113.

39. Murdock, B. B., 'Perceptual Defense and Threshold Measurements,' *J. Person.*, 1954, 22, 565.

40. Bruner, J. S. and Postman, L., 'Tension and Tension Release as Organizing Factors in Perception,' *J. Person.*, 1947, 15, 300.

41. Rosen, A. C., 'Change in Perceptual Threshold as a Protective Function of the Organism,' *J. Person.*, 1954, 23, 182.

42. Mangan, G. L., 'The Role of Punishment in Figure-Ground Reorganization,' *J. Exper. Psychol.*, 1959, 58, 369.

43. Jones, A., 'The Efficiency of Utilization of Visual Information and the Effects of Stress,' *J. Exper. Psychol.*, 1959, 58, 428.

44. Bruner, J. S. and Postman, L., 'Emotional Selectivity in Perception and Reaction,' *J. Person.*, 1947, 16, 69.

45. Bitterman, M. E. and Kniffin, C. W., 'Manifest Anxiety and "Perceptual Defense",' *J. Abn. Soc. Psychol.*, 1953, 48, 248; Postman, L., Bronson, W. C., and Gropper, G. L., 'Is There a Mechanism of Perceptual Defense?' *J. Abn. Soc. Psychol.*, 1953, 48, 215; Lacy, O. W., Lewinger, N., and Adamson, J. F., 'Foreknowledge as a Factor Affecting Perceptual Defense and Alertness,' *J. Exper. Psychol.*, 1953, 45, 169.

46. Beier, E. G. and Cowen, E. L., 'A Further Investigation of the Influence of "Threat-Expectancy" on Perception,' *J. Person.*, 1953, 22, 254.

47. Thorndike and Lorge, see note 9.

48. Cowen, E. L. and Beier, E. G., '"Threat Expectancy", Word Frequencies and Perceptual Prerecognition Hypotheses,' *J. Abn. Soc. Psychol.*, 1954, 49, 178.

49. Fulkerson, S. C., 'The Interaction of Frequency, Emotional Tone and Set in Visual Recognition,' *J. Exper. Psychol.*, 1957, 54, 188.

50. Gilchrist, J. C., Ludeman, J. F., and Lysak, W., 'Values as Determinants of Word-Recognition Thresholds,' *J. Abn. Soc. Psychol.*, 1954, 49, 423.

Notes and References

51. Newton, K. R., 'A Note on Visual Recognition Thresholds,' *J. Abn. Soc. Psychol.*, 1955, 51, 709.

52. Smock, C. D., 'The Relationship between Test Anxiety, "Threat-Expectancy" and Recognition Threshold for Words,' *J. Person.*, 1956, 25, 191.

53. Eriksen, C. W., 'Perceptual Defense as a Function of Unacceptable Needs,' *J. Abn. Soc. Psychol.*, 1951, 46, 557.

54. Lindner, H., 'Sexual Responsiveness to Perceptual Tests in a Group of Sexual Offenders,' *J. Person.*, 1953, 21, 364.

55. Rosenstock, I. M. 'Perceptual Aspects of Repression,' *J. Abn. Soc. Psychol.*, 1951, 46, 304.

56. Carpenter, B., Wiener, M., and Carpenter, J. T., 'Predictability of Perceptual Defense Behavior,' *J. Abn. Soc. Psychol.*, 1956, 52, 380.

57. McGinnies, E., 'Emotionality and Perceptual Defense,' *Psychol. Rev.*, 1949, 56, 244.

58. Aronfreed, J. M., Messick, S. A., and Diggory, J. C., 'Re-examining Emotionality and Perceptual Defense,' *J. Person.*, 1953, 21, 517.

59. Dixon, N. F., 'The Effect of Subliminal Stimulation Upon Autonomic and Verbal Behavior,' *J. Abn. Soc. Psychol.*, 1958, 57, 29.

CHAPTER 12: Perceptual 'Types' and their Relation to Personality.

1. Brunswik, E., *Perception and the Representative Design of Psychological Experiments* (University of California Press, 1956).

2. Benussi, V., 'Versuche zur Bestimmung der Gestaltzeit,' *Ber. VI Kongress exp. Psychologie*, Göttingen, 1914.

3. Gemelli, A. and Cappellini, A., 'The Influence of the Subject's Attitude in Perception,' *Acta Psychol.*, 1958, 14, 12.

4. Brunswik, E. (Ed.), 'Untersuchungen über Wahrnehmungsgegenstände,' *Arch. f. d. ges. Psychol.*, 1933, 88, 377; Brunswik, E., *Wahrnehmung und Gegenstandswelt* (Deuticke, Vienna, 1934).

5. Henneman, R. H., 'A Photometric Study of the Perception of Object Color,' *Arch. Psychol.*, 1935, No. 179.

6. Wohlwill, H. E., *Typische Verhaltenweisen im Wahrnehmen* (Schinkers, Hamburg, 1933).

7. Messmer, O., 'Zur Psychologie des Lesens bei Kindern und Erwachsenen,' *Arch. f. d. ges. Psychol.*, 1904, 2, 190.

8. Netschajeff, A., 'Zur Frage über die qualitative Wahrnehmungsform,' *Psychol. Stud.*, Ranschburg-Festschrift, 1929, p. 114.

9. Smith, F., 'An Experimental Investigation of Perception,' *Brit. J. Psychol.*, 1914, 6, 321.

10. Bartlett, F. C., *Remembering* (Cambridge University Press, 1932).

11. Jenkin, N., 'Two Types of Perceptual Experience,' *J. Clin. Psychol.*, 1956, 12, 44.

12. Singer, J. L., 'Personal and Environmental Determinants of Perception in a Size-Constancy Experiment,' *J. Exper. Psychol.*, 1952, 43, 420.

13. Jenkin, N., 'Size Constancy as a Function of Personal Adjustment and Disposition,' *J. Abn. Soc. Psychol.*, 1958, 57, 334.

14. Ardis, J. A. and Fraser, E., 'Personality and Perception: the Constancy Effect and Introversion,' *Brit. J. Psychol.*, 1957, 48, 48.

15. Klein, G. S., 'The Personal World Through Perception,' in *Perception: An Approach to Personality*, ed. by Blake, R. R. and Ramsey, G. V. (Ronald Press, New York, 1951).

16. Holzman, P. S. and Gardner, R. W., 'Levelling and Repression,' *J. Abn. Soc. Psychol.*, 1959, 59, 151.

17. Schlesinger, H. J., 'Cognitive Attitudes in Relation to Susceptibility to Interference,' *J. Person.*, 1954, 22, 354.

18. Bruner, J. S. and Tajfel, H., 'Cognitive Risk and Environmental Change,' *Bull. Brit. Psychol. Soc.*, 1960, No. 40, 2A.

19. Klein, G. S. and Schlesinger, H. J., 'Perceptual Attitudes toward Instability,' *J. Person.*, 1951, 19, 289.

20. Witkin, H. A., Lewis, H. B., Hertzman, M., Machover, K., Meissner, P. B., and Wapner, S., *Personality through Perception* (Harper, New York, 1954).

21. The literature on 'cognitive controls' is very extensive. The most detailed discussions are given in: Gardner, R. W., Holzman, P. S., Klein, G. S., Linton, H. B., and Spence, D. P., 'Cognitive control: a Study of Individual Consistencies in Cognitive Behavior,' *Psychol. Issues*, 1959, 1, No. 4; and Gardner, R. W., Jackson, D. N., and Messick, S. J., 'Personality Organization in Cognitive Controls,' *Psychol. Issues*, 1960, 2, No. 4.

22. Angyal, A. F., 'The Diagnosis of Neurotic Traits by means of a New Perceptual Test,' *J. Psychol.*, 1948, 25, 105.

23. Davis, D. R. and Cullen, J. H., 'Disorganization of Perception in Neurosis and Psychosis,' *Amer. J. Psychol.*, 1958, 71, 229.

24. Binder, A., 'Personality Variables and Recognition Response Level,' *J. Abn. Soc. Psychol.*, 1958, 57, 136.

25. Johansson, G., Dureman, I., and Sälde, H., 'Motion Perception and Personality,' *Acta Psychol.*, 1955, 11, 289.

26. Kaswan, J. W., 'Tachistoscopic Exposure Time and Spatial Proximity in the Organization of Visual Perception,' *Brit. J. Psychol.*, 1958, 49, 131.

27. Crookes, T. G., 'Size Constancy and Literalness in the Rorschach Test,' *Brit. J. Med. Psychol.*, 1957, 30, 99.

28. Rausch, H. L., 'Perceptual Constancy in Schizophrenia,' *J. Person.*, 1952, 21, 176.

29. Jenkin, N., see note 13.

30. Lyons, J., 'The Perception of Human Action,' *J. Gen. Psychol.*, 1956, 54, 45.

31. Thurstone, L. L., *A Factorial Study of Perception* (University of Chicago Press, 1944).

32. Vernon, M. D., 'Different Types of Perceptual Ability,' *Brit. J. Psychol.*, 1947, 38, 79.

33. Witkin, H. A., et al., see note 20.

34. Vernon, M. D., see note 32.

35. Thouless, R. H., 'Individual Differences in Phenomenal Regression,' *Brit. J. Psychol.*, 1932, 22, 216.

36. Smith, F., see note 9.

37. Thouless, R. H., see note 35.

38. Jenkin, N. and Feallock, S. A., 'Developmental and Intellectual Processes in Size-Distance Judgments,' *Amer. J. Psychol.*, 1960, 73, 268.

39. Carlson, V. R., 'Overestimation in Size Constancy Judgments,' *Amer. J. Psychol.*, 1960, 73, 199.

CHAPTER 13: Conclusion.

1. Bartlett, F. C., *Remembering* (Cambridge University Press, 1932).

2. Thurstone, L. L., *A Factorial Study of Perception* (University of Chicago Press, 1944).

INDEX

Index

*Some other Pelican books
on psychology are described
on the following
pages*

THE PSYCHOLOGY OF THINKING

Robert Thomson

A453

Ever since Aristotle defined man as a 'rational animal' psychologists have attempted to show how it is that men have a capacity, for thinking about themselves and their environment, which other animals have not managed to achieve. In recent years an increased interest has been shown by psychologists in the problem of describing and explaining the nature of thought. Indeed, one distinguished psychologist has said that the central problem for psychology today is the problem of thought. Not only does this book report some of the recent studies on thinking: it also attempts to evaluate the achievements and limitations of the work which has been carried out. It serves also as a general introduction to several branches of psychological inquiry: it discusses such varied topics as the intelligent behaviour of animals; the formation of a repertory of basic concepts by children; the direct experimental investigation of adult thought processes; the role of learning operations; and imaginative thinking in aesthetic and scientific work.

FREUD AND THE POST-FREUDIANS

J. A. C. Brown

A522

Freud and the Post-Freudians explains the main concepts of
Freudian psychology and goes on to review the theories of
Adler, Jung, Rank, and Stekel. Later developments in the
orthodox Freudian school are also discussed, as are those of the
American Neo-Freudians and Post-Freudians in England.

This is the first book published in Britain to bring together
all these psychological and sociological schools and criticize
them, both from the Freudian standpoint and that of the
scientific psychologists.

THINKING TO SOME PURPOSE

L. Susan Stebbing

A44

Despite the fact that we are 'better educated' than our fore-bears, there is little to show that we are either well trained or well practised in the art of Clear Thinking. Our powers of reasoning and discussion are less confident and reliable than than they ought to be, and the present insecurity of our civilization is, at least in part, attributable to our general ineptitude at weighing evidence and making up our minds.

Professor Stebbing wrote this Pelican as a manual of first-aid in Clear Thinking, and those who observe her shrewd advice will find themselves increasingly resistant to rumour, slipshod thinking, and hasty conclusions. She identifies and illustrates scores of booby-traps which lie in wait for the precipitate and illogical thinker, puts us on our guard against the slovenly misuse of language, and shows us how to use our minds and not our emotions in sorting out the facts. It will be a comfort to most readers to find that many of Professor Stebbing's most glaring examples of illogicality are quoted from sources which ought to know better.

THE PSYCHOLOGY OF SEX

Oswald Schwarz

A194

This book aims at giving a comprehensive and systematic description of the various forms of our sexual relationships in the course of life. As man's physical sexuality is the expression of a personal relationship, the psychological approach is the most adequate to the subject. Thus the book offers a psychology of not only sex but also of human relations as a whole.

As morality is the principle which governs and guards any human relationship, the main theme of the book is an analysis of the interaction of the physical sexual urge and the moral principle with the conclusion that nothing that is truly natural can be really immoral. Such a statement makes sense only if morality is properly defined and clearly distinguished from what one may call conventional taboos. The much-discussed 'problem of sex' then stands revealed as the result of confusion of the real or essential morality with time-honoured but outworn convention.

On this basis the author analyses the various forms of sexual activity: masturbation, homosexuality in youth, prostitution, 'affairs', and demonstrates that they are stages in a development which ultimately leads to marriage as the complete form of sexual relationship. A few case histories serve to illustrate the basic theory of this book and its application. The thesis that an 'essentially' moral sex life is the expression of the whole personality throws a light on, and provides a scientific basis for the discussion of, some social aspects of sex life, such as prostitution, birth control, and divorce.